Women in American Protestant Religion 1800–1930

A thirty-six volume reprint collection demonstrating the breadth and diversity of the roles played by women in American religion.

EDITED BY

Carolyn De Swarte Gifford
Coordinator of the Women's History Project
General Commission on Archives and History
United Methodist Church

CONSULTING EDITOR

Donald W. Dayton
Northern Baptist Theological Seminary

A Garland Series

The Power
of Faith

Joanna Bethune

Garland Publishing, Inc.
New York & London   1987

This facsimile has been made from a copy in the
University of Illinois Library.

For a complete list of the titles in this series,
see the final pages of this volume.

Library of Congress Cataloging-in-Publication Data

Bethune, Joanna.
   Power of faith.

   (Women in American Protestant religion, 1800-1930)
   Bibliography: p.
   1. Graham, Isabella, d. 1814.   2. Christian biography.
I. Title.   II. Series.
BRJ725.G77B48 1987   285'.131'0924 [B]   87-36129
ISBN 0-8240-0659-3

The volumes in this series are printed on
acid-free, 250-year-life paper.

Printed in the United States of America

THE

POWER OF FAITH,

EXEMPLIFIED

IN THE

LIFE AND WRITINGS

OF THE LATE

MRS. ISABELLA GRAHAM.

▲

NEW EDITION,

ENRICHED BY HER NARRATIVE OF HER HUSBAND'S DEATH, AND OTHER SELECT
CORRESPONDENCE.

The fear of the Lord is the instruction of wisdom; and before honor is humility.
The Lord will destroy the house of the proud; but he will establish the border of
the widow.—Prov. 15. 25, 33.

———————

PUBLISHED BY THE

AMERICAN TRACT SOCIETY,

150 NASSAU-STREET, NEW YORK.

CONTENTS.

~~~~~~~~~~~~~~~~~~~~~~~~~~~~~~~

CHAPTER I.

CHAPTER II.

CHAPTER III.

CHAPTER VIII.

CHAPTER IX.

CHAPTER X.

LIFE OF

MRS. ISABELLA GRAHAM.

~~~~~~~~~~~~~~~~~~~~~~

CHAPTER I.

Mankind take an interest in the history of those who, like themselves, have encountered the trials and discharged the duties of life. Too often, however, publicity is given to the lives of men splendid in acts of mighty mischief, in whom the secret exercises of the heart would not bear a scrutiny. The memoirs are comparatively few of those engaged in the humble and useful walks of active benevolence, where the breathings of the soul would display a character much to be admired, and more to be imitated.

As the celebrated Dr. Buchanan has observed, that if you were to ask certain persons, in christian countries, if they had any acquaintance with the *religious* world, they would say, " they had never heard there *was* such a world ;" so, whilst the external conduct of individuals is made the subject of much critical remark, the religion of the heart, the secret source of action, too frequently escapes unnoticed and unexplored.

It is only when the career of life is closed that the character is completely established. On this account, memoirs of the living are, in few instances, read with much interest; but when the soul has departed, and the body sleeps in dust, it may prove useful to survivors to examine the principles which led their departed friend to a life of honorable benevolence, and to a peaceful end.

Such considerations as these, and the urgent request of many respectable individuals, have induced the preparation of the following sketch of the life and writings of Mrs. ISABELLA GRAHAM, whose character was so esteemed, and whose memory is so venerated by all who knew her. The evident purity of motive which impelled her to activity in deeds of benevolence, at once commanded love and respect; which, in her case peculiarly, was unalloyed with any risings of jealousy, envy, or distrust.

Blessed with a spirit of philanthropy, with an ardent and generous mind, a sound judgment, and an excess of that sensibility which moulds the soul for friendship, a cultivated intellect and rich experience, her company was eagerly sought and highly valued by old and young. Though happily qualified to shine in the drawing-room, her time was seldom wasted there; for such a disposition of it would have been waste, contrasted with her usual employments. Her steps were not seen ascending the hill of ambition nor tracing the mazes of popular applause. Where the widow and the orphan wept, where the sick and the dying moaned, thither her footsteps hastened: and there, seen only by her heavenly Father, she administered to their temporal wants, breathed the voice of consolation on their ear, shed the tear of sympathy, exhibited the truths of the Gospel from the sacred volume, and poured out her soul for them in prayer to her Savior and her God.

In a few such deeds she rested not; nor was the story of them obtruded upon others, or recorded by herself The recollection of past exertions was lost in her zeal to accomplish greater purposes and greater good: her heart expanded with her experience, and her means were too limited, the active powers of her vigorous mind too feeble to fulfil the abounding desires of her soul in alleviating the miseries and increasing the comforts of the poor, the destitute, and afflicted. To learn the latent springs of such excellence is worthy of research: they may be all summed up in this, *The Religion of the Heart.*

The extracts from Mrs. Graham's letters and devotional exercises, which constitute so large a part of the following pages, will furnish the best development of her principles; and may, with the blessing of God, prove useful to those who read them. In all her writings will be manifested the power of *faith*, the efficiency of *grace;* and in them, as in her own uniform confession, Jesus will be magnified and self will be humbled. Her life was chiefly distinguished by her continual dependence on God, and his unceasing faithfulness and mercy towards her.

ISABELLA MARSHALL, afterwards Mrs. Graham, was born July 29, 1742, in the shire of Lanark, in Scotland. Her grandfather was one of the elders who quitted the established church with the Rev. Messrs. Ralph and Ebenezer Erskine. She was educated in the principles of the church of Scotland. Her father and mother were both pious: indeed her mother, whose maiden name was Janet Hamilton, appears, from her letters yet extant, to have possessed a mind of the same character as her daughter afterwards exhibited.

Isabella was trained to an active life, as well as favored with a superior education. Her grandfather, whose dying-bed she assiduously attended, bequeathed her a legacy of some hundred pounds. In the use to which she applied this money, the soundness of her judgment was thus early manifested. She requested it might be appropriated to the purpose of procuring a thorough *education*. When ten years of age, she was sent to a boarding-school taught by a lady of distinguished talents and piety. Often has Mrs. Graham repeated to her children the maxims of Mrs. Betty Morehead. With ardent and unwearied endeavors to attain mental endowments, and especially moral and religious knowledge, she attended the instructions of Mrs. Morehead for seven successive winters. How valuable is early instruction! With the blessing of God, it is probable that this instructress laid the foundation of the exertions and usefulness of her pupil in after-life. How wise and how gracious are the ways of the Lord! Knowing the path in which he was afterwards to lead Isabella Marshall, her God was pleased to provide her an education of a much higher kind than was usual in those days. Who would not trust that God, who alone can be *the guide of our youth ?*

Her father, John Marshall, farmed a paternal estate, called the Heads, near Hamilton. This estate he sold, and rented the estate of Elderslie, once the habitation of Sir William Wallace. There Isabella passed her childhood and her youth.

She had no definite recollection of the period at which her heart first *tasted that the Lord is gracious.* As long as she could remember she took delight in pouring out

her soul to God. In the woods of Elderslie she selected
a bush, to which she resorted in seasons of devotion.
Under this bush she believed she was enabled to devote
herself to God, through faith in her Redeemer, before
she had entered on her tenth year. To this favorite,
and, to her, sacred spot, she would repair, when exposed to temptation or perplexed with childish trou-
bles. From thence she caused her prayers to ascend,
and there she found peace and consolation.

Children cannot at too early a period seek the favor
of the God of heaven. How blessed to be reared and
fed by his hand, taught by his Spirit, and strengthened
by his grace!

The late Rev. Dr. Witherspoon, afterwards president
of Princeton college, was at this time one of the ministers of the town of Paisley. Isabella sat under his ministry, and at the age of seventeen publicly professed her
faith in Christ. In the year 1765 she was married to
Dr. John Graham, then a practising physician in Paisley, a gentleman of liberal education and of respectable
standing.

About a year after their marriage Dr. Graham, having
been appointed surgeon to the 60th or Royal American
regiment, was ordered to Canada, where that corps was
stationed. Mrs. Graham accompanied him, and a plan
was digested (with how limited a knowledge of the future will appear) for their permanent residence in America. Dr. Graham calculated on disposing of his commission, and purchasing a tract of land on the Mohawk
river, where his father-in-law, Mr. Marshall, was to follow him. The letter subjoined gives the interesting incidents of their voyage, and forms a pleasant introduc-

tion to the character of Mrs. Graham at this period of her life.

" QUEBEC, August 29, 1767.

" My DEAREST PARENTS,—This is the fifth letter I have written to you, although I know it is the first that can reach you. All the time I was at sea I kept a letter lying by me, in hope of getting it put on board some vessel bound for Britain; but I have met with many disappointments. We spoke several ships, but I never could get a letter put on board. At one time I was told the wind was too high, at another that the ship was at too great a distance, and so was put off till I began to understand a more substantial reason, viz. that it would cost the captain rather too much trouble.

" We have now, however, got safe here, after a tedious voyage of nine weeks, and I will give you a short account of what happened during that time.

" We sailed, as you know, from Greenock, June 10. For the first five or six days we had fine weather and fair winds, and got quite clear of land; after this, we had nearly six weeks of most tempestuous weather, and the wind, except for about two days, directly against us. The gentlemen after some time began to be very impatient; for my part I should not have cared although it had lasted twelve months. I had left all that was dear to me behind except one dear friend—that one was constantly with me—and although the rest of the company in the ship was very agreeable, yet I was the great object of his attention, and his invention was ever on the stretch to find amusement for me. It is not possible for me to say with what indulgent tenderness I was treated;

but though I love my husband even to extravagance, yet my dear friends whom I left behind have a large share of my heart. They dwell on my mind in the day-time ; and at night, when sleep lays the body aside and leaves the soul at liberty, she on the wings of imagination makes one skip over whole seas, and is immediately with those dear friends whose absence she so much lamented during the day, and in an imaginary body as truly enjoys you for the time as if really present with you.

" The gentlemen on board soon found reason to be thankful for the preservation of life, and got something very different to think of than fret at the contrary winds. A leak sprung in the ship, which alarmed them all so much that a consultation was held among them whether if any ship came near they should hail it and go on board wherever she was bound. I was perfectly unconcerned about the whole matter, not being aware of the danger, which was kept secret from me till we came on shore. I saw the men constantly pumping, but thought it was what they were obliged to do in every ship. After coming to land, on examining the ship, they found the leak to be so large that one might put his five fingers into it ; indeed, it seemed next to a miracle that she kept above water ; but every day of our lives may convince us what dependent creatures we are. While God's merciful providence protects us we are safe, though in the midst of apparent danger ; should he withdraw that protection but for a moment, inevitable evils surround us, even when we think ourselves in perfect safety.

" A proof of this we had in a most distressing event, which took place about six weeks after we left Green ock. The wind was in our favor, the day was fine, and we were all amusing ourselves on deck in various ways, when Captain Kerr, who was standing close by us, stumbling backwards fell overboard. He got above water before the ship passed him, and called to throw him a rope, but, alas! no rope was at hand, and before one was got the ship was out of his reach. Immediately they threw over a large hen-coop, but, poor man! he could not swim, so he soon disappeared. The boats were put out with great expedition, and in less than a quarter of an hour he was found. You may believe no means were left unemployed to restore animation; but, alas! the spirit had taken its final leave; it was no longer an inhabitant of earth, not the least signs of life appeared. The day after, being Sunday, his body was committed to the deep, from whence it had been rescued the day before. Dr. Graham read in public the Church of England burial service. Every one on board seemed much affected; I cannot tell you how much I was.

"About eight days after, we got to the Banks of Newfoundland; while there the fog was so dense we could not see forty yards in any direction, and the cold was excessive, notwithstanding the season of the year. There were a great many islands of ice floating on the water; I saw three within twenty yards of us, much larger than the ship. The captain said if the ship ran against any one of them she would be dashed to pieces. And here, again, my former observation holds good, for sure it could not be the art of man, either in the dark night or in the dense fog, which could protect the ship flying before the wind, through dangers so thick on every side of us. For several days and nights we saw neither sun nor stars, which distressed the captain much, for he knew not where we were, and apprehending we were near land, was afraid of running upon some rock; so we were obliged to cruise about till the atmosphere cleared.

" The sail up the river St. Lawrence is extremely pleasant. You know how fond I have ever been of wood and water. This country, in this respect, is quite to my taste, and could I only get half a dozen of those friends I could name settled down on either side of us, with five hundred pounds' worth of land to give to each, I should ask no more in this world.

" When we arrived the Doctor's friend Mr. Findley came on board, took us on shore, and brought us to his elegant mansion. He begged we would look on him as an old friend, feel perfectly at home, and remain with him as long as we could. Give my love to my dear boys;* you see them often, I have no doubt. Do, my dearest mamma, write me soon, and tell me all about them and yourself; and ever believe me, my dear parents, with the greatest affection, your

" Dutiful daughter,   I GRAHAM."

In a letter a month later, Mrs. Graham refers to the gay and fashionable circles to which they were introduced in Quebec, and mentions her visiting the beautiful Falls of Montmorency; but mourns over the low state of religion and the prevailing desecration of the Sabbath. She adds:

* Dr. Graham's two sons by a former marriage, who were left under the care of Mr. Davidson, Rector of the Grammar-school of Paisley.

"I have read *Doddridge's Rise and Progress*. I little knew what a treasure Mr. Ellis put into my hand when he gave me that book. I cannot say it is my daily companion, but I can with truth say, it is often so. Let my mind be in ever so giddy and thoughtless a frame, or ever so much busied in those amusements I am engaged in, it makes me serious, and gives my thoughts a different turn; there is scarce any situation the mind can be in but it will find something suitable there. I must not, however, make remarks on the particular contents of it; it would occupy more paper than I have to spare. I would have you purchase the book; I am sure you would like it; and when you have read it, it will be matter of great satisfaction to you that John and I have such a treasure in our possession. In it are contained every advice you could give us, and cautions against the temptations which, on account of youth, company and the country we are in, we are exposed to."

They were expecting to spend the winter in Quebec, but were ordered to *Montreal*, where Jessie, her eldest daughter, was born, and where Mrs. Graham received intelligence of the death of her infant son, who had been left with her mother in Scotland. Further orders were soon received for the Doctor to join the second battalion of his regiment at *Fort Niagara*, on Lake Ontario; Mrs. Graham followed him, and they continued here in garrison for four years, during which her second and third daughters, Joanna and Isabella, were added to her charge.

Under date of February 3, 1771, we find, from her own pen, the following description of her occupations and enjoyments, in a letter addressed to her beloved mother:

"My two Indian girls come on very well indeed. The eldest milked the cows all summer; she washes and irons all the clothes for the family, scrubs the floors, and does the most part of the kitchen work. The young one's charge is the children, and some other little turns when the infant is asleep. I teach them to read and to sew when they have any spare time. As for me, I find I have enough to do to superintend. You may be sure I help a little too now and then. I make and mend what is necessary for the family, for I must be tailor, mantua-maker, and milliner.

"In the forenoon the Doctor makes his rounds as usual. I generally trot about till two o'clock, dress the children, order dinner, dress myself, and twenty other things, which you know are necessary to be looked after by the mistress of a family. After dinner I sit down to my work, and we have always a book, which the Doctor reads when I can attend: when I cannot, he reads something else.

"As I am at present the only wife in the place, we have a regular tea-table, and now and then a little frugal supper; for the Doctor has come more into my way of thinking, and does not insist upon cutting a figure as much as some time ago. When alone, he reads and I work, as usual. He is seldom out, and never but when I am with him. We are easy in our circumstances, and want for nothing that is necessary; in short, my ever dear parents, my life is easy and pleasant. The Lord my God make it pious and useful.

"Could I place myself and family in the same circumstances, and every thing go on in the same manner, within a few miles of you, I should be happy for life; and were it not for this hope, which my heart is set upon, I could not be so, with all I have told you.

"We find the newspapers full of preparations for war; may the Lord dispose all hearts to peace, for I hate the sound, though it is the wish of the greatest number about me. There is no prospect of our leaving this place for a year yet. For my part I have only two reasons for wishing it. The first is, I should like to be in some christian society; the other, that I might do something towards getting home. To return to the gay world again I have no ambition. My family here, and my friends at home, engross all my attention; and when I see the one, and hear of the other being well, I am happy. Time never hangs heavy on my hand; I can always find employment, and amusement too, without the assistance of what go under the name of diversions.

"We have lately had several visits from a great family. The *Chief* of the Seneca nation having a daughter not well, brought her to the Doctor to see what could be done for her: he, his squaw or lady, and daughters breakfasted with us several times. I was kind, and made all the court to them I could, though we could not converse but by an interpreter. I made the daughters some little presents, and the Doctor would not be fee'd. Who knows but these little services may one day save our scalps. There have been several threatenings of an Indian war; thank God, it seems to be quite hushed again.

"War with civilized nations is nothing to war with Indians. They have no mercy, nor give any quarter to man, woman, or child; all meet the same fate, except where they take a liking to particular persons, those they adopt as their children, and use them as such.

"The Doctor joins in affectionate respects to my dear father, and you, the boys, and all our dear friends I am as much as ever, and will be to my latest breath, my dear mamma, your affectionate daughter,

"I. GRAHAM."

Mrs. Graham always considered the time she passed at Niagara as the happiest of her days, considered in a temporal view. The officers of the regiment were amiable men, attached to each other, and the ladies were united in the ties of friendship. The society there, secluded from the world, exempt from the collision of individual and separate interests, which often create so much discord in large communities, and studious to promote the happiness of each other, enjoyed that tranquillity and contentment which ever accompany a disinterested interchange of friendly offices. But this fort being detached from other settlements, the garrison were deprived of ordinances and the public means of grace, and the life of religion in the soul of Mrs. Graham sunk to a low ebb. A conscientious observance of the Sabbath, which throughout life she maintained, proved to her at Niagara as a remembrance and revival of devotional exercises. She wandered on those sacred days into the woods around Niagara, searched her Bible, communed with God and herself, and poured out her soul in prayer to her covenant Lord. Throughout the week, the attention of her friends, her domestic comfort and employments, and the amusements pursued in the garrison, she used to confess, occupied too much of her time and of her affections.

Here we behold a little society enjoying much comfort and happiness in each other, yet falling short of that pre-eminent duty and superior blessedness of glorifying, as they ought to have done, the God of heaven, who fed them by his bounty, and offered them a full and free salvation in the Gospel of his Son. No enjoyments nor possessions, however ample and acceptable, can crown the soul with peace and true felicity, unless accompanied with the fear and favor of Him who can speak pardon to the transgressor, and *shed abroad his love in the hearts* of his children: thus giving an earnest of spiritual and eternal blessedness along with temporal good.

The commencement of the revolutionary struggle in America rendered it necessary, in the estimation of the British government, to order to another and very diverse scene of action the sixtieth regiment, composed in a great measure of Americans.

Their destination was the *Island of Antigua ;* Dr. and Mrs. Graham, and their family, consisting of three infant daughters and two young Indian girls, sailed from Niagara to Oswego, and from thence, by a path through the woods, reached the Mohawk, which river they descended in batteaux to Schenectady. Here Dr. Graham left his family, and went to New-York to complete a negotiation he had entered into for disposing of his commission, to enable him to settle, as he originally intended, on a tract of land which it was in his power to purchase on the banks of the river they had just descended. The gentleman proposing to purchase his commission, not being able to perfect the arrangement in time, Dr. Graham found himself under the necessity of proceeding to Antigua with the regiment. Mrs. Graham, on learning this, hurried down with her family to accompany him, although he had left it optional with her to remain till he should have ascertained the nature of the climate, and the probability of his continuing in the West Indies.

At New-York they were treated with much kindness by the late Rev. Dr. John Rodgers, and others, especially by the family of Mr. Vanbrugh Livingston. With Mr. Livingston's daughter, the wife of Major Brown, of the sixtieth regiment, Mrs. Graham formed a very intimate friendship, which continued during the life of Mrs. Brown.

They embarked with the regiment, November 5, 1772, for Antigua.

CHAPTER II.

RESIDENCE AT ANTIGUA—DR. GRAHAM'S DEATH.

Within three weeks after their arrival at Antigua, six companies were ordered to the Island of St. Vincents to quell an insurrection of the Caribs. The Doctor accompanied them, and Mrs. Graham was called to the pain of separation under circumstances more trying than she had as yet experienced, as the war with savages might expose him to the most cruel death. In these circumstances she wrote him as follows:

"ANTIGUA, January 16, 1773.

"My dearest Doctor,—This goes by Mr. W——, who sails to-morrow; also a letter to Captain G———. Mr. M—— begs to be remembered to you: he has been foot and hand to me since you left. My dearest Doctor, suffer me to put you in remembrance of what you put in the end of your trunk the morning you left me,* and let it not lie idle. Read it as the voice of God to your soul. My dearest love, I have been greatly distressed for fear of your dear life; but the love I bear to your soul is as superior to that of your body, as the value of one surpasses the other; consequently my anxiety for its interest is proportioned. May Heaven preserve my dearest love—lead you, guide you, direct you, so can you never go wrong—protect and defend you, so shall you ever be safe, is the daily prayer of your affectionate wife,   I. GRAHAM.

"P. S. I am told that you have taken a number of prisoners. I know not if you have any right to entail slavery on these poor creatures. If any fall to your share, do set them at liberty."

On the 8th of June Mrs. Graham wrote to her mother, expressing her gratitude for her husband's safe return, and noticing some gratifying indications of the calm and peaceful state of his mind:

" You would be surprised to hear the Doctor preach. He says we ought to be thankful; we have hitherto

* Doddridge's Rise and Progress of Religion in the Soul.

been richly and bountifully provided for; we ought not to repine, nor doubt, seeing we have the same Providence to depend upon; that we ought not to set our hearts upon any thing in this world; being very short-sighted we cannot know what is proper for us. Having done for the best, when we are disappointed, we ought to rest satisfied that either what we wish is not for our good, or it will in some future dispensation of Providence be brought about another way and in a fitter time. Indeed, my dear mamma, in some things he is a better christian than I am. *May God make him so in every thing.*"

Thus was the Lord preparing his servant for what was so soon to follow, not his dismission from the regiment, which he so ardently desired, but from this world and its temptations and snares. Mrs. Graham's prayers were answered, but " by terrible things in righteousness."

She added a request that her mother would receive her eldest daughter, who, though at the early age of *five years*, she feared would receive injurious influences from the corrupt state of society around her, and accordingly, not long after, sent her to Scotland; but before her arrival her grandmother had been called to a better world. In reference to this event Mrs. Graham wrote to her bereaved father as follows:

" ANTIGUA, August 21, 1773.

" MY DEAREST PAPA,—The heart-rending tidings of my dear, my tender, my affectionate mother's death reached me yesterday. I am so distressed that I can scarcely write, and no wonder, for never was there such a mother! My loss is indeed great; but O! my dear, my afflicted father, how my heart bleeds for you. Father of mercies, support my aged parent, and enable him to place his hopes of happiness beyond this transitory world, and to follow the footsteps of the dear departed saint till he joins her in glory, never, never more to be separated.

"My dearest father, we may indeed mourn for ourselves; but she is happy—that is beyond all doubt. Her delight was with God while she was here; her closet was a Bethel; her Bible was her heart's treasure, and His people were her loved companions. She has now joined the innumerable company above, where she continues the same services without human frailty, and the enjoyment heightened beyond our highest conceptions.

"O then, my dear father, be comforted; let us now try to follow her; let her Savior now be ours, and then shall we be blest with like consolations.

"My dearest father, I cannot tell you how much I feel for you; my tears will not allow me, they flow so fast that I cannot write; what would I give to be with you! But these are vain words.

"The Doctor, however, fully expects that next summer will bring him leave to go home; then, I trust, we shall be in some fixed place of abode, and my dear papa, you will come and live with us. I shall feel it to be a privilege beyond what I can tell, to perform every service you stand in need of, soothe your pains and comfort you under the infirmities of old age.

"My dear, my worthy brother—how has that tender

letter, and the noble resolution he has taken, endeared him to me! It is certainly his indispensable duty to stay with you in your present solitary situation; such a dutiful, affectionate son must be a great comfort to you, and he will not lose his reward.

"I am anxious, my dearest father, to know the particulars of my mother's death? who attended her in her illness? was the nurse who was with her a good woman? was she sensible? did she expect death? and did she mention me, and leave me her blessing? my dear, dear father, tell me all.

"Farewell, my beloved father, may your God and Redeemer be your support and final portion, is the prayer of your affectionate daughter,   I. GRAHAM."

In her grief for the loss of her inestimable mother, Dr. Graham had said to her that "God might perhaps call her to a severer trial by taking her husband also," and the warning appeared prophetic; but her own words best describe the emotions of her bleeding heart.

To Miss Margaret Graham, Glasgow.

"MY DEAR SISTER,—Prepare yourself for a severe shock from an event that has robbed me of every earthly joy. Your amiable brother is no longer an inhabitant of this lower world. On the seventeenth of November he was seized with a putrid fever, which, on the twenty-second, numbered him with the dead, and left me a thing not to be envied by the most abject beggar that crawls from door to door. Expect not consolation from me: I neither can give nor take it.—But why say I so?—*Yes, I can.* He died as a christian, sensible to the last, and in full expectation of his approaching end. O, you knew not your brother's worth; you knew him not as a husband : he was not the same as when you knew him in his giddy years : he was to me all love, all affection, and partial to my every fault; prudent too in providing for his family. I had gained such an entire ascendancy over his heart as I would not have given for the crown of Britain.

"On Wednesday, at one o'clock, the seventeenth day of November, 1773, my dear Doctor was seized with a violent fever. I sent for his assistant, Dr. Bowie : he not being at home, Doctor Muir came, who prescribed an emetic in the evening, and his fever having greatly abated, it was accordingly given. In the morning Dr. Bowie thought him so well I did not ask for any other assistance. At ten o'clock his fever greatly increased, though not so violent as it had been the day before. He was advised to lose a little blood, which he did ; and towards evening it again abated.

"I found he was not quite satisfied with what had been done for him ; at the same time he would do nothing for himself. Thursday evening I begged Dr. Bowie to call in Dr. Warner's assistance, notwithstanding he assured me there was not one dangerous symptom. Friday morning they both attended, and both pronounced him in a fair way of recovery.

"About three o'clock Dr. Eird came, who seemed surprised the thing had not been done which Dr. Graham himself had been dissatisfied for the want of the day before. Soon after the medicine was sent; but, oh, my dear Doctor said it was then too late. In the evening they all again attended, and insisted there was no danger. Saturday morning he seemed very easy, and the physicians said he was in a fine way. The fever was gone; the decoction of bark prescribed; and they said he would be able to-morrow to take it in substance. I was not now the least apprehensive of danger, and was very earnest in prayer that the Lord would sancti fy his affliction, and not suffer it to go off without leaving a sensible effect on his mind. Nay, I even said in my heart, ' the rod is too soon removed, it will do him no good.' Oh, that fools will still persist to prescribe to infinite wisdom and goodness. I was soon severely punished.

"About eleven he took the hiccup. I did not like it, but little knew it was so dangerous a symptom as I afterwards understood. I sent for Dr. Bowie, who assured me that, though it was a disagreeable symptom with other attendants, in his case it was of no more consequence than if he or I were to take it. All that day it was so moderate that a mouthful of any liquid stopped it, though it always returned again: he often said it would be his death; but I imagined the pain it gave him extorted these words from him rather than a sense of danger, and was much pleased to hear him often pray that the Lord would give him patience and resignation to his blessed will, and still more to observe that he bore it with a patience beyond what was natural to him. He was of a quick temper, and being of a healthy constitution, was but little accustomed to pain; but, during the whole of his severe and trying affliction, I do not remember to have heard a murmuring word escape his lips; so that I cannot doubt but his prayers were heard, and the grace prayed for bestowed. In the evening the hiccup increased, and all that night it was very severe, so that he could not bear to be any way disturbed, nor could I possibly prevail upon him to take his medicine, from two in the morning until ten o'clock, when the physicians again attended and persuaded him to comply. This was Sunday. About mid-day Doctor Warner sent some old hock, with orders that he should take some in his drink, and now and then a little plain. When the wine was brought in and put on the table, he asked me what it was. I told him. He said, 'Yes, they are now come to the last shift.'

"Mr. Frank Gilbert, a good man, and, I believe, a real christian, having come to town to preach,—for he is a Methodist minister,—sent a note, kindly inquiring after him, and intimating, if it would be agreeable to him, he would visit him in the morning. He said, by all means, he should be very glad to see him. I said, 'My love, you know I have great faith in the prayers of God's people; suppose you should beg an interest in them this afternoon?' He answered, 'My dear, do you think they will forget me?' I said, 'I hope, my love, you are not ashamed to desire the prayers of the people of God; it is not now a time to mind the ridicule of the world.' He said, 'No, Bell, I care not a farthing for the whole world, and you may make it in my own request.'

"His disorder gained ground very fast that day, and I began to be much alarmed; yet still I thought it would not end in death, but though severe and dangerous, was sent in answer to my repeated, earnest prayers to awaken in him a real concern about his eternal interest, to set the world and its vanities in their true light, and bring about that entire change of heart which our blessed Lord styles the new birth, and without which, he says, we cannot enter the kingdom of heaven.

" It was now become very difficult for him to speak; but by the motion of his hands and eyes, which were continually lifted up when he had the smallest respite, I could easily see his thoughts were fixed on the importance of his situation; besides, many sentences and half sentences broke from his lips at different times, which left me without a doubt. 'Farewell,' said he, 'vain world; an idle world it is, nothing but shadows, and we keep chasing them as children do bubbles of water, till they break, and we find them nothing but air.'

" Observing this inward recollection, I seldom disturbed him. He was perfectly acquainted with the truth, and believed it. The doctrines of religion were often the subject of our conversation, and in every point of faith we entirely agreed: they only wanted to be felt and applied to the heart. I remained in silence to my dear husband, but not to my God: I was incessant in prayer, begging and beseeching that the Lord himself would carry on what he had so graciously begun; that he would every way suit himself to his necessities, and give conviction or consolation, as he saw needful; but when he spoke I endeavored to answer him from God's own word, as I was able or assisted. Once he exclaimed, 'Draw me, and I will run after thee;' at another time, 'Surely thou wilt not allow thy blessed Son to plead in vain for me, an obstinate sinner.' This was a degree of

faith and I endeavored to strengthen it. I said, 'My
love, you know the way to the Father, through Christ,
the only Mediator. You say right, he cannot plead in
vain; fly to him; cast yourself at his feet; trust in him;
hear his own invitation, 'Come unto me, all ye that are
weary and heavy laden, and I will give you rest;' 'whosoever cometh unto me I will in no wise cast out.' At
another time these words broke from his lips, 'Form
me, train me, prepare me for thyself.' Here was a
breathing after sanctification; might not the promise
be applied, 'I will create a clean heart, and renew a
right spirit within thee.'

"In the evening the physicians again attended, but
could hardly get a word from him. While they sat by
the bedside I went out to the gallery with Mrs. Grandidier; the apparent struggle she had to conceal her distress, the compassion and sympathy in her countenance struck me. I easily perceived she gave up hope,
and, I began to suspect, not from her own judgment
alone; she advised me to send away my children to a
friend's house, and to send for a person who was capable of assisting me, it being no longer proper for me to
be alone. Thus far I had not allowed any person to do
the least thing about him but myself, nor stirred from
his bed-side, except for a few minutes, to pour out my
soul into the bosom of my God. I hardly, if ever, prayed for his recovery, being willing the rod should remain till it effected the purpose for which it was sent,
and then I believed it would be removed—as if the
Lord was to follow exactly the rules prescribed by my
weak, foolish, ignorant heart.

"Hitherto I had suffered little, believing all to be the

answer to my prayers; but I had not seriously thought of parting with him. I was now truly alarmed, and determined to know, as far as appearances went, the worst. Accordingly I stopped Doctor Bowie on the gallery: 'Tell me, Doctor,' said I, ' what have I to expect? It is cruel to flatter me: if you give me some warning, and prepare me, I may, perhaps, be able to support it; but, if you suffer it to come upon me all at once, I shall certainly sink under the shock.' He was silent for some time, and then replied, 'I am really at a loss how to answer you.' I said, 'I will answer for you, there is no hope.' He said, 'God forbid—he is in great danger; but still there is hope; and, if you value his life, be calm.' I was composed. Strange composure; I neither cried nor complained; tears were denied a passage; I was fixed and dumb like a statue. Can I, or any one else, describe my situation, or what I felt at that moment? It was urged of what consequence it was that I should be composed, that I might be able to do my duty to him, as no one could supply my place to his satisfaction, and perhaps even now he might be in want of me. I returned to my post, which was, except when doing some necessary office about him, generally on my knees by his bed-side, partly that I might not lose the least whisper that came from his lips, and partly because it is my favorite posture for prayer, from which I could not cease, no not for one minute.

" There were different medicines prescribed for that night, some in case that others proved too strong for his stomach, others in case of the increase of the hiccup. I found my head confused and my memory incapable of retaining the variety of directions given; I

therefore accepted of the offer of a friend of his to sit
up with us that night, whom I begged to pay particular
attention to the directions, and to watch the proper
times the medicines were to be given. This he did with
great care, and my dear Doctor was very pliable in
taking them as they were offered. As for me, I was so
deeply engaged with the concerns of his soul, I was
unfit for any thing else.

"After Dr. Bowie let me know the danger he was in,
I sent a letter to Mr. Gilbert, begging he would not delay his visit till morning, as perhaps, by that time, he
might not be able to speak to him. Accordingly he
came; he asked him how he did; he answered, ' Very ill;'
he asked him the situation of his mind; he answered,
' Entirely resigned to the Divine will;' he asked him what
hopes he had; he said, ' his hope was in the mercy of
God, through Christ;' Mr. Gilbert said, ' You have no
dependence on any thing besides?' he said, ' No, no, I
have nothing else to depend upon.' Then the Doctor
desired him to pray, but at the same time to be short,
as he had but short intervals from the hiccup. After
prayer Mr. Gilbert told me it seemed difficult for him to
speak, and he did not think it would be prudent to say
more; that he would call again in the morning.

"Monday morning he was greatly weakened, having
had little rest all night from the severity of the hiccup.
At ten o'clock the physicians again attended; but I
could easily perceive they had but small hopes. My
Doctor asked Doctor Warner if he thought it would be
long before he would be at rest, who said his pulse was
still strong. He said, ' It is a hard thing to die!' Mrs.
Brannan came to spend the day with us, one of the

Methodist society, and Mr. McNab, whom my Doctor
desired to pray with him, which he did. All this day
he said little, but still continued in inward prayer, as
was visible by the motions of his hands and eyes: he
had many agonizing struggles, and often exclaimed,
'Lord Jesus, receive my spirit.' 'Blessed Jesus, come
and receive me to thyself—come—come—blessed Jesus,
come!' Once, after a long struggle, he exclaimed, 'Release me, O release me, and let me fly to the bosom of
my Father!' All this time I never parted from his bed-
side but a few minutes to give my soul a freer vent at the
throne of grace. I never prayed for life, but that he
might be washed, sanctified, and have all God's salvation completed in his soul, and be received into the
arms of his mercy. I also had been, and still was, very
importunate that God would give me some token, some
assurance that he would save his soul, and give him an
abundant entrance into the kingdom of his glory; and,
by all that I had heard, seen, and felt, I was now satisfied that the most merciful God had sealed his pardon
for Jesus' sake; and I found myself ready, dearly as I
loved him, to resign him into the hands of divine mercy; but still I breathed after some further manifestation.

"In the evening Dr. Galloway, an old acquaintance,
arrived from the island of Dominico, and hearing of his
friend's illness, came immediately to visit him. When
my Doctor heard his voice only whisper how he was,
he said, 'I hear Galloway's voice,' and stretched out his
hand; so fully had he his senses to the last. Upon his
feeling his pulse, he asked them if they thought he
would be long. Doctor Eird replied, 'You must not
talk of dying, but of living; you are stronger than when

I was here this morning, and I have seen many worse recover. Do, do be advised, take your medicine, and try for life.' These words brought a gleam of hope to my despairing soul, and what had been denied me for twenty-four hours, a flood of tears, and I was greatly relieved. I went out to the gallery and gave a free vent to my bursting heart. I now also begged the Lord for his life, and said in my heart, should he now be restored, how doubly blessed would he be, healed in soul and body. I returned to his bed-side and thus addressed my beloved: 'My dearest life, the doctors have still hopes, and we know nothing is impossible with God. Who knows what further service he may yet have for you in this world! or whether he may not give you to my prayers, and restore you to your Bell and family. God works by means; O be persuaded to take every thing prescribed, and pray to God for the blessing ; devote your future life to his service, and, for poor Bell's sake, offer up a petition for life.' He did not interrupt me, but answered, ' Disengage yourself, Bell, disengage yourself from me. I want to lift up my soul to God, and bless him for Jesus Christ.'

" Dr. Galloway was determined to stay with him all night, and see him take his medicine. Some time after, he had a severe attack of hiccup, and said to Dr. G., ' I hope you are now convinced?' He said, ' Of what?' My Doctor said, ' That dissolution is near.' A little after he said, ' Who died for all?' and again repeated, ' Who died for all?' I was forbid to speak to him as rest was so much wanted, so I answered, ' Christ, my love ; but give up your soul to God, and try to shut your weary eyes, and get a little rest for your body ;'—and so he

did, and got a little sleep. All that night he did every
thing he was desired, but would drink nothing but cold
water, which had been allowed him : the wine he would
not touch. His disorder increased so fast that Dr. Galloway, about five in the morning, said to me, 'I may go
home—I can be of no service, and I cannot stand it.' I
said, 'I suppose I need not disturb him any more with
medicine.' He said, 'No, you may give him what he
calls for.' Now, my God, all is over! I resign him up
to thee! Only one parting word ; something yet I require to assure my heart that thou wilt receive his soul.
Some time after he laid his hand upon Mrs. Brannan's
lap and made a sign to her ; afterwards he made a sign
to me, who was at the back of the bed, to come round.
Mrs. B. thought he wanted her to retire, which she
did. He looked after her. I said, 'My love, she thinks
you want to say something to me ; can you speak?' He
said, 'Join—pray,' which we did. He spoke no more
for some time, only 'Come, sweet Jesus,' and frequently, 'Receive my spirit.' These words were given for my
sake. I cried, 'I am satisfied, Lord, and I yield him up
to thee, with all my heart ; thou hast given me all my
asking. I will not be longer faithless, but believing.
Continue to support his departing soul, and let the enemy find nothing in him.'

The next attack of hiccup laid him back speechless,
and I believe senseless in the last parting work: he had
no further struggle, nor need of any person to support
him. I therefore again placed myself on my knees by
his bed-side, determined not to quit the posture till his
soul had entered its rest ; but nature was worn out, and
though I swallowed hartshorn and water in great quan-

tities, I was so overcome that I was obliged to lie down at the back of the bed to save me from fainting. Three hours did he continue in this last work of the heart. I watched his last, and delivered him up with a hearty prayer and a full assurance; but Oh, how earnestly I wished to go with him! I was, for the time, entirely insensible to my own loss; my soul pursued him into the invisible world, and for the time cordially rejoiced with the Spirit. I thought I saw the angel band ready to receive him, among whom stood my dear mother, the first to bid him welcome to the regions of bliss.

"I was then desired to leave the room, which I did, saying, 'My Doctor is gone. I have accompanied him to the gates of heaven: he is safely landed; that is now not him that lies there. You, nurse, will see it decently dressed; then I may again be permitted to take another parting kiss.' So, embracing the precious clay, I went into the parlor. Some friends came in to see me. My composure they could not account for: our sincere and tender regard for each other was too well known to allow them to impute it to indifference. My distress at parting with him, even for a couple of months, when he went to St. Vincents, and dejection of spirit the whole time till his return, left them as little room to impute it to want of sensibility: at last they imagined that I was stupified with grief and fatigue; but they little knew that at that hour I rejoiced; indeed I told them, but I suppose was not believed. I was asked if I had any thing particular to say respecting the funeral. I said, nothing—my charge is gone to rest; I would leave it to them. It was then proposed to bury next day at ten o'clock. I said that

was very early; they answered, by that time I would
be satisfied it was not too early.

"In the evening I returned to our bed-chamber to
take a last farewell of the dear remains. The countenance was so very pleasant I thought there was even
something heavenly, and could not help saying,'You
smile upon me, my love; surely the delightful prospect, opening on the parting soul, left that benign smile
on its companion, the body.' I thought I could have
stood and gazed for ever; but, for fear of relapsing into immoderate grief, I withdrew after a parting embrace, and with an intention not to ask for another, lest
a change in his countenance might shake my peace; for
oh, we are weak, and at certain times not subject to
reason. I went to bed purely to get alone, for I had
little expectation of sleep; but I was mistaken; nature
was fairly overcome with watching and fatigue. I
dropped asleep, and for a few hours forgot my woes;
but oh, the pangs I felt on my first awaking. I could
not for some time believe it true that I was indeed a widow, and that I had lost my heart's treasure—my all I
held dear on earth. It was long before day. I was in no
danger of closing my eyes again, for I was at that time
abandoned to despair, till recollection and the same
considerations which at first supported me brought me
a little to myself. I considered, I wept for one that
wept no more; that all my fears for his eternal happiness were now over, and he beyond the reach of being
lost; neither was he lost to me, but added to my heavenly treasure, more securely mine than ever. Those
snares and temptations arising from the corrupt cus-
toms of a degenerate age, which had so often caused my

fears, could never reach him there. The better, dearer half of myself was now secure beyond the possibility of falling, and waiting my arrival to complete his bliss. O happy hour, which shall also set my soul at liberty, and unite us, never to part more.

"In the morning I asked the nurse if there was any alteration; she said, no. I again returned to take another view, and was surprised to find his color and countenance unchanged. I began to be extremely uneasy at having consented to so early a burial. I returned again, and again; Oh, how I wished to have kept him for ever! Ten o'clock came; the company assembled; I became very uneasy; at last I discovered it to Dr. Bowie, begged he would only view him; how fresh the color; how every way like life! He assured me there was not the smallest doubt but that he was gone. I was not satisfied with this, but made them all inspect him. All agreed in the same thing, and I was obliged to yield, and the dear remains were ravished from my sight. What a night I passed the night after the funeral! I had ordered our own bed to be made up, and at the usual time retired; but in vain did I try to sleep; the moment my senses began to lose sensibility, I was in a kind of dream. Finding myself alone, I imagined he was out at supper, though he seldom was without me; now I thought I heard his foot on the stairs, and started up to listen if it were he, and to bid him welcome, when my roused senses told me what I could still hardly credit, that I had no husband to expect, and threw me into a fresh agony, which kept me awake till I had in some measure again reconciled myself to my solitary situation. But, having only slept a few hours since my dear Doctor was taken ill, I no sooner got my mind a little composed, than sleep again began to overpower my senses, when the same, or a similar imagination roused me.

" The morning came. When I was called down to breakfast, the sight of his empty seat distracted me. I returned to my room, though I thought it my duty to take some nourishment. I had it brought to me. Alas, I could no where turn my eyes but the sight was connected with this dear idea, and recalled past delights, never more to return. Our back windows looked into the garden, on which he had bestowed so much labor and pains, and which he was just bringing to perfection. Here we had spent many pleasant hours together, and indulged that freedom of conversation, the natural consequence of an unbounded confidence. The double arbor he had reared, and so contrived as to screen from both the south and the western sun, bid fair, in a short time, to screen us also from every eye. Hitherto we had been confined to morning hours, or afternoon, when it was shaded by the house ; but had often pleased ourselves with the hours we should spend in this cool retreat, even at noon-day, while, screened from the sun's scorching rays, we might enjoy the refreshing breeze through its leafy openings; but these delightful prospects were now for ever at an end!. I might, indeed, there take my seat ; but the tongue which every where charmed, was buried in deepest silence! The company, which rendered every scene pleasant, was gone, never to return: his sheep, his goats, nay, even the poultry, were often fed from his hand : every thing served to distract. As for my children, they were by kind friends kept for some time out of my sight ; for not only to view them fatherless distressed me, but their thoughtless mirth and play was altogether insupportable.

" I accepted an invitation from Mr. Gilbert's family to spend some time in the country with them; for though it was impossible for me to forget for one moment, yet, when these objects were removed from my sight, I was more able to turn my thoughts upward, to where my heart's treasure now is, and where I myself expect to be. We had two men-servants, and my two Indian girls ; one of the men I dismissed, the other I left to take care of the living creatures about the place. One of my girls I boarded where she would be in good company, and with my children and their maid I abandoned my solitary dwelling. I met with a very tender reception from that worthy family. My situation here was such as I both expected and wished, and attended with many outward circumstances which had the probability of making it supportable. I was allowed to be as much by myself as I chose. No one intruded on my privacy without my consent ; but one or other of the Mrs. Gilberts often visited me in my own room, and drew from my bursting heart all its griefs, sympathizing, soothing, and advising at the same time. They are both women of great piety, having for many years devoted their hearts, time, talents, and fortune to the service of God; and their two husbands likewise, whose business it has been to instruct the ignorant negroes without fee or reward. Had it not been for this family, I know not where the distraction of my mind might have ended."   *   *   *   *   *   *

Thus was Mrs. Graham, at the early age of thirty-one, left a widow in a land of strangers. Her husband, companion, protector, was gone: a man of superior mind, great taste, warm affection, and domestic habits. She was left with three daughters, the eldest of whom was not over five years of age, and expecting an increase of her infant charge. Of temporal property she possessed very little: she was at a distance from her father's house: the widow and the fatherless were in a foreign land. The change in her circumstances was as sudden as it was great.

That sympathizing heart, with which she was accustomed to receive and return the confidence of unbounded friendship, and thus, by reciprocal communion, to alleviate the trials and enrich the enjoyments of life, was chilled in death. All the pleasing plans, all the cherished prospects of future settlement in life were cut off in a moment. Whilst sinking into a softened indifference to the world, in the contemplation of her severe loss, she was, on the other hand, roused into exertion for the sustenance and support of her young family, whose earthly dependence was now necessarily upon her.

Not satisfied with the custom of the island, in burying so soon after life is extinct, her uneasiness became so great that her friends judged it prudent to have her husband's grave opened, to convince her that no symptoms of returning life had been exhibited there. The fidelity of her heart was now as strongly marked as her tenderness. She dressed herself in the habiliments of a widow, and determined never to lay them aside. This she strictly adhered to, and rejected every

overture afterwards made to her of again entering into
the married state. She breathed the feelings of her
heart in a little poem, in which she dedicated herself
to her God as a widow indeed.

On examining into the state of her husband's affairs,
she discovered that there remained not quite two hundred pounds sterling in his agent's hands.

These circumstances afforded an opportunity for the
display of the purity of Mrs. Graham's principles, and
her rigid adherence to the commandments of her God
in every situation.

It was proposed to her, and urged with much argument, to sell the two Indian girls, her late husband's
property; but no considerations of interest or necessity
could prevail upon her thus to dispose of immortal
beings, the work of her heavenly Father's hand. One
of these girls accompanied her to Scotland, where she
was married; and the other died in Antigua, leaving
an affectionate testimony to the kindness of her dear
master and mistress.

The surgeon's mate of the regiment was a young
man whom Dr. Graham had early taken under his patronage. The kindness of his patron had so far favored
him with a medical education that he was enabled to
succeed him as surgeon to the regiment.

Notwithstanding the slender finances of Mrs. Graham,
feeling for the situation of Dr. H——, she presented to
him her husband's medical library and his sword: a
rare instance of disinterested regard for the welfare of
another.

This was an effort towards observing the second table
of the law, in doing which she was actuated likewise

by that principle which flows from keeping the first table also. Nor was the friendship of Dr. and Mrs. Graham misplaced. The seeds of gratitude were sown in an upright heart. Dr. H——, from year to year, manifested his sense of obligation, by remitting to the widow such sums of money as he could afford. This was a reciprocity of kind offices, equally honorable to the benefactors and to them who received the benefit : an instance, alas ! too rarely met with in a selfish world.

It may here be remarked, in order to show how much temporal supplies are under the direction of a special providence, that Dr. H——'s remittances and friendly letters were occasionally received by Mrs. Graham until the year 1795 ; after this period her circumstances were so favorably altered as to render such aid unnecessary ; and from that time she heard no more from Dr. H——, neither could she learn what was his subsequent history.

It may be profitable here to look at Mrs. Graham, contrasted with those around her whose condition in the world was prosperous. Many persons then in Antigua were busy and successful in the accumulation of wealth, to the exclusion of every thought tending to holiness, to God, and to heaven. The portion which they desired they possessed. What then ? They are since gone to another world. The magic of the words, " my property," " an independent fortune," has been dispelled ; and that for which they toiled, and in which they gloried, has since passed into a hundred hands ; the illusion is vanished, and unless they made their peace with God through the blood of the cross, they left this world, and alas ! found no heaven before them. But amidst apparent affliction and outward distress, God was preparing the heart of this widow, by the discipline of his covenant, for future usefulness—to be a blessing, probably to thousands of her race, and to enter finally on that " rest which remaineth for the people of God."

Her temporal support was not, in her esteem, " an independent fortune," but a life of dependence on the care of her heavenly Father: she had more delight in suffering and doing his will than in all riches. " The secret of the Lord is with them that fear him, and he will show them his covenant." To those who walk with God, he will show the way in which they should go, and their experience will assure them that he directs their paths. " Bread shall be given them, and their water shall be sure." She passed through many trials of a temporal nature, but she was comforted of her God through them all; and at last was put in possession of an eternal treasure in heaven, " where neither moth nor rust doth corrupt, nor thieves break through and steal." May this contrast be solemnly examined, and the example of this child of God made a blessing to many!

In anticipation of her approaching trial, with which her own life might be suddenly terminated, Mrs. Graham *set her house in order*, and wrote the two following letters: one to her friend Mrs. Grandidier, to whom and her husband Capt. G. she committed the charge of her family and affairs; the other to her father in Scotland, commending her children to his protection. Her tender and affectionate appeals to each of them in respect to their own eternal welfare, are a beautiful specimen of that christian fidelity and love of the souls of men which so strongly characterized her future life.

"St. Johns, Antigua, 1774.

"My dear Mrs. G——, The long and steady friendship which has subsisted between us, in sickness and in
health, in prosperity and adversity, ever the same, without change or diminution, leaves me no room to doubt
that it will extend to my little family, and that you
will be as ready, to the utmost of your power, to be-
friend them, as you have been to the dear father already
gone, and your friend, who is, perhaps, about to follow.

"If it should please God to take me away in my approaching confinement, I leave you and Capt. G. full
power to dispose of every thing in this house, and belonging to me in this island, as you shall think most
for the advantage of my little family. You know my
extreme tenderness for their dear father made me unable to part with any of his clothes, but these can be of
no consequence to me when I shall again have joined
him for whose sake I kept them; you may therefore
dispose of them, and also of my own, if you think the
avails will be of more service to the children. But I
do not choose to leave any particular directions about
my trifling effects; you will consult with other friends,
and I am certain you will act for them to the best of
your judgment. It is a great relief to my mind that I
have such steady and tried friends to leave the charge
of them upon. Miss G— B. has promised to take J—,
and it is my desire that the others, and the infant yet
unborn, if it survive, be sent to my father, where I will
leave them to be disposed of and provided for by that
God who has fed me all my life, by their heavenly
Father, who has commanded me to leave my fatherless

children upon him, that he will preserve them alive, and whose promise I have, that he will never leave them nor forsake them.

"Mr. Reid will not be less kind to the offspring of his friend when they have lost, than when they were under a mother's protection. May the blessing of the widow and the fatherless follow him wherever he goes, and may God recompense him a thousandfold in blessings spiritual and temporal. Let Diana* be sent with my children; if there be an infant, you know a nurse must be found for it, whatever it cost. As for Susan,* I am at a loss what to do with her; my heart tells me I have no right to entail slavery upon her and her offspring; I know I shall be blamed, but I am about to be called to account by a higher power than any in this world for my conduct, and I dare not allow her to be sold. I therefore leave it to herself either to remain here, or if it be her desire, to accompany the children. I beg Mr. Reid will be kind enough to allow her a passage with the rest.

"And now, my dear friend, as the greatest happiness I can wish you, may that God whom I have chosen as my own portion, be yours also; may he, by his outward providence and by the inward operations of his Spirit on your heart, lead you to himself and convince you of the truth. But O! my dear friend, shut not your eyes and ears against conviction:—You are not satisfied that the Bible is indeed the word of God. Is it not worth inquiring into? What would you think of a man who had a large fortune, and the whole depending on proving some certain facts, and yet would not be at

* The two Indian girls.

the pains to inform himself? Are the interests of this
world of such importance, which, in a few fleeting years,
we must leave, and have done with for ever? and our
final state in the next, which is to fix us in happiness or
misery through the endless days of eternity, not worth
a thought? Think then, and seriously ask, 'What if it
be so? What if this be indeed the word of God given
by inspiration, for the rule of both our faith and manners, and by which we are to be judged? What if this
same God, who so kindly reveals his will to men, has
with it given the clearest evidences and strongest proofs
that it is his own word?' Think, I say, my dear friend,
if it should be so, what they deserve, who either reject
or neglect it without taking the trouble to inform themselves, or be convinced that it either is or is not of divine authority!

"How many great, learned, and wise men have sift-
ed these evidences with the greatest care, and the
deeper they entered into the search, the more clear
they appeared; even those whose lives are entirely contrary to it, and whose interest it is to wish it false, cannot deny. As to the various explanations of it—it is
every one's duty to read for himself, and although there
may be some parts of it too deep for every capacity,
and which may perhaps require a knowledge of the
history of the times to understand, yet the simple truths
of the Gospel, what we are to believe concerning God,
and what duties he requires of us, and what he forbids,
are equally plain and easy. If we can only once be
satisfied that it is indeed the word of God, set ourselves to study it with an unprejudiced mind, with a
sincere desire to know the truth and be led by it, with

earnest prayer, that the same Spirit which inspired the writers, would make it plain to our hearts and understandings, that God himself would teach us its true meaning, and save us from error, we shall, I venture to say, be taught all necessary knowledge, and be led in the way to eternal life, and not suffered to err; we have God's promise that it shall be so. 'If any man will do His will he shall know of the doctrine whether it be of God.'

"Forgive me, my dear friend; the subject appears to me so important that I know not how to have done. I love you with a true and sincere friendship: I love your soul, and am deeply interested in its eternal happiness. Once more I commit you to that God, who only can lead you to himself and to true happiness; and that you may know the truth of this from deep experience, to the eternal joy, peace and safety of your immortal soul, is the last prayer of your affectionate friend, who hopes to meet and rejoice with you in our Redeemer's kingdom.   ISABELLA GRAHAM.

Mrs. Graham to her Father.

" ANTIGUA, May, 1774.

"MY EVER-DEAR FATHER,—If this ever reach you, it will be when I have taken my final leave of this world, and received my portion for eternity in the next, when I hope I shall have gained the summit of my wishes, and be happy in the society of my dear husband and much-loved mother, in the kingdom of our Redeemer.

" My truly orphan children I have desired to be sent to you; though I see no visible way you have to provide for them, yet I am perfectly easy concerning them. I leave them upon that God who has fed me all my life, and whose tender care I have experienced in a thousand dangers; upon their, and my Heavenly Father, who has commanded me to leave my fatherless children upon him, and he will preserve them alive. The God of providence will prepare for them a home, and raise up friends, perhaps from a quarter neither you nor I could expect.

"My only concern and prayer to God for them is, that they may be early taught to love God and serve him; that they may fall into such hands as will carefully instruct them in the principles of morality and religion, and teach them the great, but too little thought of truth, that our chief business in life is to prepare for death. As to the polite parts of education, I look upon them as of no consequence; they may be as good christians, perhaps better, without than with them; the perfection of their nature no way depends upon them. I am equally indifferent what station of life they may occupy, whether they swim in affluence or earn their daily bread, if they only act their part properly, and obtain the approbation of their God, in that station wherein he, in his infinite wisdom, sees fit to place them.

"Remember to give my love to all my dear children. I reckon all that sprung from my dear Doctor mine; and though I did not suffer a mother's pangs for them, Heaven knows how equally I love them with those who cost me dearer. Tell them I leave them a mother's blessing, and my last prayers, if it please God to continue my senses, shall be for their best interests.

"And now, my dear father, suffer one parting word, though from one no way entitled to advise: this is the

third loud call for you to be also ready ; according to
the course of nature you must very shortly follow ;
you can have very little more to do in this world, and
therefore the smallest share of your attention is due to
it. The young, the gay, the giddy and thoughtless
hold it a wise maxim to forget their departed friends
as soon as possible ; this may be worldly, but it cannot
be heavenly wisdom. To be fully and entirely resigned
to the will of God in all things is certainly the charac-
teristic of a christian ; but this is perfectly consistent
with the most tender remembrance. That resignation
(but indeed it deserves not the name) which consists
in forgetfulness, in banishing thought and drowning
reflection in worldly cares and amusements, can be no
grateful offering to Him who has commanded us to have
our loins girt and our lamps trimmed, and to be always
ready, for in such an hour as we think not ' the Son of
man cometh.' How often are we commanded to watch,
to set our affections on things above,—to be dead to
the world,—to lay up treasure for ourselves in heaven.
These injunctions are inconsistent with forgetfulness ;
and if it be our duty to meditate on death and eternity,
nothing more naturally leads our minds to that subject
than the recollection of departed friends, who, if pious,
are not lost, but only gone a little while before, taken
from our earthly and added to our heavenly treasure.

" Believe me, my dear father, to a mind abstracted
from the world and devoted to God, death, though solemn, has nothing dreadful in it ; on the contrary, to a
mind rightly disposed it is rather a desirable object.
Just conceptions of God, and converse with him, will
very soon change the aspect of the king of terrors to a

welcome messenger, who comes to set open the gates of immortality, and to usher us into the kingdom of our heavenly Father. And now may our most gracious God grant you, through your few remaining days, his direction and consolation; may he bestow upon you that peace which the world can neither give nor take away; and when the appointed time of your change shall come, may the comforts of his Holy Spirit so cheer and refresh your soul, that you may be able, without a doubt or a fear, to resign it into the hands of your Redeemer.

"Give my love to Hugh. The sentiments expressed in his letters bespeak him a worthy brother, and deserving of my highest esteem. I would have written to him, but I have still some directions to commit to writing concerning my little family, and my hour is at hand; but tell him I will remember him in my last prayers. I charge him not to banish the idea of his worthy and now glorified mother, lest with that he also forget her precepts; but prepare to meet us who are gone before; and Oh! that our meeting may be with joy on both sides. It is hard for youth, in the present age, to follow our christian pattern. Every real christian, every Bible christian, must lay his account with being branded with the name of enthusiast; but tell him to remember that the opinion of the world cannot alter the nature of holiness nor the maxims of Christ. Let him read, think, and judge for himself with an unprejudiced mind; with a hearty desire to know and be led by the truth; to be taught of God, and conformed to his will in all things, and I venture to promise he will not be suffered to err. But let him avoid disputes about religion, they are seldom productive of any good; let him fortify his mind against banter and ridicule, it is no small degree of persecution. Yet, if he be determined to follow his Lord, he must expect to meet with it, and I know from experience it is hard to bear. I have found the safest way is to receive it in silence; for those who are disposed to ridicule the appearance of religion in another, are not in a fit disposition to be convinced by any argument, at least at that time, and few can dispute without heat, which is a transgression against the virtue of meekness, and very apt to lessen our love to the person who opposes us. We lose the spirit of brotherly love in hotheaded zeal; which perhaps deserves a harder name, but conceals itself under that appearance, and it is no small victory gained over ourselves if we are able to love, wish well to and be ready to serve those whose sentiments differ from ours.

"I leave you and yours, and mine, upon the Fountain of all goodness, and may the peace of God, which passeth all understanding, keep your hearts and minds in the knowledge and love of God, and of his Son Jesus Christ our Lord; and the blessing of God Almighty, the Father, Son and Holy Ghost, be amongst you, and remain with you always. Amen.

"Your ever dutiful and affectionate daughter,

"ISABELLA GRAHAM."

It pleased God to preserve the life of Mrs. Graham, and to make her the grateful mother of a son, whom she called after the name of his father, and endeavored, in humble trust, to consecrate to the Author of his being.

Having now no object to induce her to stay longer at

Antigua, she disposed of her slender property, and placing her money in the hands of Major Brown, requested him to take a passage for herself and family, and to lay in their sea-stores. After seeing a railing placed around the grave of her beloved husband, that his remains might not be disturbed until mingled with their kindred dust, she bade adieu to her kind friends, and with a sorrowful heart turned her face towards her native land.

CHAPTER III.

RETURN TO SCOTLAND—SCHOOL IN EDINBURGH.

No ship offering at this time from Antigua for Scotland, Mrs. Graham embarked with her family in one bound to Belfast, Ireland. Major Brown and his brother-officers saw her safely out to sea; and he gave her a letter to a gentleman in Belfast, containing, as he said, a bill for the balance of the money she had deposited with him. After a stormy and trying voyage she arrived in safety at her destined port. The correspondent in Ireland of Major Brown delivered her a letter from that officer expressive of esteem and affection, and stating that as a proof of respect for the memory of their deceased friend, he and his brother-officers had taken the liberty of defraying the expenses of her voyage.

Consequently the bill he had given was for the full amount of her original deposit ; and thus, like the brethren of Joseph, *she found all her money in the sack's mouth*. Being a stranger in Ireland, without a friend to look out for a proper vessel in which to embark for Scotland, she and her children went passengers in a packet; on board of which, as she afterwards learned, there was not even a compass. A storm arose and they were tossed to and fro for nine hours in imminent danger. The rudder and the mast were carried away; every-thing on deck thrown overboard; and at length the vessel struck in the night upon a rock, on the coast of Ayr, in Scotland. The greatest confusion pervaded the passengers and crew. Amongst a number of young students, going to the University at Edinburgh, some were swearing, some praying, and all were in despair. The widow only remained composed. With her babe in her arms she hushed her weeping family, and told them that in a few minutes they should all go to join their father in a better world. The passengers wrote their names in their pocket-books, that their bodies might be recognized and reported for the information of their friends One young man came into the cabin, asking, "Is there any peace here?" He was surprised to find a female so tranquil; a short conversation soon evinced that religion was the source of comfort and hope to them both in this perilous hour. He engaged in prayer and then read the 107th Psalm. Whilst repeating these words, " he maketh the storm a calm, so that the waves thereof are still," the vessel swung off the rock by the rising of the tide. She had been dashing against it for an hour and a half, the sea making a breach over her, so that the hold was now nearly filled with water. Towards morning the storm subsided, and the vessel floated until she rested on a sand-bank. Assistance was afforded from the shore, and the shipwrecked company took shelter in a small inn, where the men seemed anxious to drown the remembrance of danger in a bowl of punch. How faithful a monitor is conscience! This voice is listened to in extreme peril; but, oh, infatuated man! how anxious art thou to stifle the warnings of wisdom in the hour of prosperity! Thousands of our race, no doubt, delay their preparation for eternity, until, by sudden death, they have scarcely a moment left to perform this solemn work.

Mrs. Graham retired to a private room, to offer up thanksgiving to God for his goodness, and to commend herself and her orphans to his future care.

A gentleman from Ayr, hearing of the shipwreck, came down to offer assistance; and in him Mrs. Graham was happy to recognise an old friend. This gentleman paid her and her family much attention, carrying them to his own house and treating them with kindness and hospitality.

In a day or two after this she reached Cartside, and entered her father's dwelling; not the large ancient mansion in which she had left him, but a thatched cottage, consisting of three apartments. Possessed of a too easy temper and unsuspecting disposition, Mr. Marshall had been induced to become security for some of his friends whose failure in business had reduced him to poverty. He now acted as factor of a gentleman's estate in this neighborhood, of whose father he had been the intimate friend, with a salary of twenty pounds sterling per annum and the use of a small farm.

In a short time, however, his health failed, and he was

deprived of this scanty pittance, being incapable, as the proprietor was pleased to think, of fulfilling the duties of factor.

Alive to every call of duty, Mrs. Graham now considered her father as added, with her children, to the number of dependents on her industry. She proved indeed a good daughter; faithful, affectionate, and dutiful, she supported her father through his declining years; and he died at her house, Feb. 13, 1783, aged 75, during her residence in Edinburgh, surrounded by his daughter and her children, who tenderly watched him during his last illness.

Having resided two years at Cartside, she removed to Paisley in 1778, where she taught a small school. The slender profits of such an establishment, with a widow's pension of sixteen pounds sterling, were the means of subsistence for herself and her family. When she first returned to Cartside a few religious friends called to welcome her home. The gay and wealthy part of her former acquaintances, who, like the butterfly, spread their silken wings only to bask in the warmth of a summer sun, found not their way to the lonely cottage of an afflicted widow. Her worth, though in after-life rendered splendid by its own fruits, was at this time hidden, excepting to those whose reflection and wisdom had taught them to discern it more in the faith and submission of the soul, than in the selfish and extravagant exhibitions of that wealth bestowed by the bounty of Providence, but expended too often for the purposes of vanity and dissipation.

In such circumstances, the christian character of Mrs. Graham was strongly marked. Sensible that her heavenly Father saw it good, at this time, to depress her outward condition, full of filial tenderness, and like a real child of God resigned to whatever should appear to be his will, her conduct conformed to his dispensations. With a cheerful heart, and in the hope of faith, she set herself to walk down into the valley of humiliation, "leaning upon Jesus," as the beloved of her soul. "I delight to do thy will, Oh my God, yea, thy law is within my heart," was the spontaneous effusion of her genuine faith. She received, with affection, the scriptural admonition, "Humble yourselves therefore under the mighty hand of God, that he may exalt you in due time, casting all your care upon him, for he careth for you."

She laid aside her children's fine frocks, and clothed them in homespun. At Cartside she sold the butter she made, and her children were fed on the milk. It was her wish to eat her own bread, however coarse, and "to owe no person any thing but love." At Paisley, for a season, her breakfast and supper was porridge, and her dinner potatoes and salt. Peace with God and a contented mind supplied the lack of earthly prosperity, and she adverted to this her humble fare, to comfort the hearts of suffering sisters, with whom she corresponded at a later period of life, when in comfortable circumstances.

Meantime the Lord was not unmindful of his believing child; but was preparing the minds of her friends for introducing her to a more enlarged sphere of usefulness.

Her pious and attached friend, Mrs. Major Brown, had accompanied her husband to Scotland, and they now resided on their estate in Ayrshire. Mr. Peter

Reid, a kind friend when in Antigua, was now a merchant in London. This gentleman advised her to invest the little money she had brought home, (and which she had still preserved,) in muslins; which she could work into finer articles of dress, and he would ship them in a vessel of his own, freight free, to be sold in the West Indies. His object was partly to increase her little capital, and partly to divert her mind from meditating so deeply on the loss of her lamented husband. The plan so kindly proposed was soon adopted; the muslin dresses were shipped; but she soon afterwards learned that the ship was captured by the French. This was a severe loss, and more deeply felt, as it was received at the time when her father was deprived of his office.

Mrs. Brown, after consulting with the Rev. Mr. Randall of Glasgow, the Rev. Mr. Ellis of Paisley, Lady Glenorchy and Mrs. Walker of Edinburgh, proposed to Mrs. Graham to take charge of a boarding-school in that metropolis.

The friends of religion were of opinion that such an establishment, under the direction of one possessing the qualifications of Mrs. Graham, would be of singular benefit to young ladies destined for important stations in society. Her liberal education, her acquaintance with life, and her humble yet ardent piety, were considered peculiarly calculated to qualify her for so important a trust.

Another friend had suggested to Mrs. Graham the propriety of opening a boarding-house in Edinburgh, which he thought could, through his influence, be easily filled by students.

She saw obstacles to both; a boarding-house did not

appear suitable, as her daughters would not be so likely to have the same advantages of education as from a boarding-school; and to engage as an instructress of youth on so large a scale, with so many competitors, appeared for her an arduous undertaking.

In this perplexity, as in former trials, she fled to her unerring counsellor, the Lord, her covenant God. She set apart a day for fasting and prayer. She spread her case before the Lord, earnestly beseeching him to make his word "a light to her feet and a lamp to her path;" and "to lead her in the way in which she should go;" especially that she might be directed to choose the path in which she could best promote his glory and the highest interests of herself and her children. On searching the Scriptures her mind fastened on these words, in John 21 : 15, "Simon, son of Jonas, lovest thou me more than these? He saith unto him, Yea, Lord; thou knowest that I love thee. He saith unto him, Feed my lambs."

Never, perhaps, was this commandment applied with more filial confidence, or accompanied with a richer blessing since the days of the Apostle, than in the present instance.

Her determination was accordingly made. She resolved to undertake the education of youth, trusting that her Lord would make her an humble instrument of training some for his service on earth, and his praises in heaven. Here was exhibited an instance of simple yet powerful faith in a believer surrounded by temporal perplexities, and of condescension and mercy on the part of a compassionate God. Light unseen by mortal eyes descended on her path.

How weak, perhaps enthusiastic, would this have appeared to the busy crowd, blind to the special providence exercised by the God of Heaven towards all his creatures. She felt the pressure of her affliction; but, like the Psalmist, *gave herself unto prayer :*

> " Prayer ardent opens heav'n, lets down a stream
> Of glory on the consecrated hour
> Of man in audience with the Deity."

Though her faith was strong, yet her mind was under such agitation, from her total want of funds to carry her plan into effect, and from other conflicting exercises, as to throw her into a nervous fever, which kept her confined to her bed for some weeks. On her recovery, she felt it her duty to *go forward*, trusting that He, who had directed her path, would provide the means that were necessary to enable her to walk in it: she sold her heavy furniture, packed up all her remaining effects, and prepared to set out from Paisley for Edinburgh, on a Monday, in the year 1779.

On the Saturday previous she sat by her fire musing and wondering in what manner the Lord would appear for her at this time, when a letter was brought to her from Mr. Peter Reid, enclosing a sum of money which he had recovered from the underwriters, on account of Mrs. Graham's muslins captured on their passage to the West Indies. Mrs. Graham had considered them as totally lost, but her friend had taken the precaution to have them insured.

With this supply she was enabled to accomplish her object, and arrived in Edinburgh with her family. Her friend Mrs. Brown met her there, and stayed with her a few days, to comfort and patronise her in her new undertaking. Mrs. Brown was her warm and constant friend until her death, which occurred at Paisley in 1782, when she was attending the communion. She bequeathed her daughter Mary to Mrs. Graham's care. But in 1785 the daughter followed the mother, being cut off by a fever in the twelfth year of her age.

It may be proper here to introduce the name of Mr. George Anderson, a merchant in Glasgow, who had been an early and particular friend of Dr. Graham. He kindly offered his friendly services, and the use of his purse, to promote the welfare of the bereaved family of his friend. Mrs. Graham occasionally drew upon both. The money she borrowed she had the satisfaction of repaying with interest. A correspondence was carried on between them after Mrs. Graham's removal to America, until the death of Mr. Anderson, in 1802.

During her residence in Edinburgh she was honored with the friendship and counsel of many persons of distinction and piety. The viscountess Glenorchy; lady Ross Baillie; lady Jane Belches; Mrs. Walter Scott, (mother of the poet;) Mrs. Dr. Davidson; and Mrs. Baillie Walker, were amongst her warm personal friends. The Rev. Dr. Erskine, and Dr. Davidson, (formerly the Rev. Mr. Randall of Glasgow,) and many respectable clergymen, were also her friends. She and her family attended on the ministry of Dr. Davidson, an able, evangelical, useful pastor.

Her school soon became respectable in numbers and character. Her early and superior education now proved of essential service to her. She was indefatigable in her attention to the instruction of her pupils. While she was faithful in giving them those accomplishments which were to qualify them for acting a distinguished part in this world, she was also zealous in directing their attention to that Gospel by which they were instructed to obtain an inheritance in that to come. She felt a high responsibility and took a deep interest in their temporal and spiritual welfare. As "a mother in Israel," she wished to train them up in the ways of the Lord.

She prayed with them morning and evening; and on the Sabbath, which she was careful to devote to its proper use, she took great pains to imbue their minds with the truths of religion. Nor did she labor in vain. Although she was often heard to lament of how little use she had been compared with her opportunities of doing good, yet when her children, Mr. and Mrs. B. visited Scotland in 1801, they heard of many individuals, then pious and exemplary, who dated their first religious impressions from those seasons of early instruction which they enjoyed under Mrs. Graham while in Edinburgh.

Mrs. Graham's manner in the management of youth was peculiarly happy. Whilst she kept them diligent in their studies, and strictly obedient to the laws she had established, she was endeared to them by her tenderness; and the young ladies instructed in her school retained for her in after-life a degree of filial affection which was expressed on many affecting occasions This was afterwards remarkably the case with her pupils in America. Her little republic was completely governed by a system of equitable laws. On every alleged offence, a court martial, as they termed it, was held, and the accused tried by her peers. There were no arbitrary punishments, no sallies of capricious passion. The laws were promulgated, and obedience was indispensable ; the sentences of the courts martial were always approved, and had a salutary effect. In short, there was a combination of authority, decision and tenderness in Mrs. Graham's government that rendered its subjects industrious, intelligent, circumspect and happy. She enjoyed their happiness ; and in cases of sickness, she watched over them with unremitting solicitude and care, sparing no expense to promote their restoration to health.

A strong trait in her character was distinctly marked by her educating the daughters of pious ministers at half price. This was setting an example worthy of imitation. It was a conduct conformable to scriptural precept. Said Paul, "If we have sown unto you spiritual things, is it a great thing if we shall reap your carnal things? Do ye not know that they which minister about holy things live of the things of the temple? Even so hath the Lord ordained that they which preach the Gospel should live by the Gospel."

Always conscientious in obeying the commandments of her God, she observed them in this matter, giving, in her proportion, at least the widow's mite.

By another plan (for she was ingenious in contrivances to do good) she greatly assisted those in slender circumstances, especially such as were of the household of faith. Believing that the use of sums of ten, fifteen, or twenty pounds in hand would be serviceable by way of capital to persons in a moderate business, she was in the habit of making such advances, and taking back the value in articles they had for sale. She charged no interest, being amply repaid in the luxury of her own feelings, when she beheld the benefit it produced to her humble friends. The board of her pupils being paid in advance, she was enabled to adopt this plan with more facility. Were her spirit more prevalent in the world, what good might be done! The heart would be expanded, reciprocal confidence and affection cherished; and instead of beholding worms of the dust fighting for particles of yellow sand, we should behold a company of affectionate brethren, leaning upon and assisting each other through the wilderness of this world. "Look not every man on his own things," said Paul, "but every man also on the things of others. Bear ye one another's burdens, and so fulfil the law of Christ."

On the subject of promoting the external accomplishments of her scholars, it became a question how far Mrs. Graham was to countenance them in their attendance on public balls—to what length it was proper for her to go so as to meet the received opinions of the world in these concerns. She consulted with her pious friends, and wrote to *Lady Glenorchy* on the subject. Her ladyship's letter in reply is so excellent that the serious reader will be gratified with its insertion.

"BARNTON, December 27, 1781.

"DEAR MADAM,—I received your letter last week, and also one some time ago from Mrs. Walker, in which she desired me to send you my sentiments upon the alteration you had made, and still thought of making, upon your plan.

"I have since endeavored to consider, with all the attention of which I am *at present* capable, the arguments that may be brought on both sides of the question; and with regard to the first point—the *practisings*, I will frankly own that, could you send your young ladies to one where *girls only* are admitted, I should more readily yield my opinion of the matter to those christians who have advised you to it. But, as I learn that it is a promiscuous dance of boys and girls, I must in conscience say that I look upon such a meeting to be as pernicious in its effects upon the minds of young people, as balls and public assemblies on persons of riper years. When you mentioned the subject to me first, I thought it had been a practising of girls *only*, else I should then have given you my sentiments fully upon that head.

" As to the *reading of plays*, or any part of them, to your young people, I must own, it does not appear to me to be expedient: it may be productive of bad consequences, and the *good* arising from it is, at most, uncertain. It is, no doubt, very desirable to enlarge young people's minds and improve their taste as well as their persons; but such is the state of things in this world, that to attain this to the degree wished for by every person of refined taste, some things must be sacrificed of much greater value—for example, a girl cannot acquire the smart, polished air of a person of fashion, without imbibing too much of the spirit of the world. *Vanity* and *emulation* must be awakened and cultivated in the heart, before she will apply herself with diligence to outward accomplishments; nor can her mind and taste be much improved in *polite* literature without losing its relish for simple truth. I grant you, there are a few christians in the world who have acquired the outward accomplishments of it, and have, by grace, been enabled to turn these to good account; who, like the Israelites, having spoiled the Egyptians, have made use of *their* jewels in adorning the tabernacle: but this can never serve as an argument on your side of the question. If the Lord sees fit to manifest his power and grace by plucking a brand from the burning, this is no reason why children should be initiated into the ways of sin and folly, in hopes that some time or other He will bring them out. We are never to do evil that good may come: and this brings the question to a short issue.

"Do you think it lawful for christians to attend public places, or to spend their time in reading plays? Do you think these things tend, either immediately or remotely, to promote the glory of God? If you do not, I cannot see how you, *as a christian*, can have any hand in introducing young ladies to the one or in giving them a taste for the other.

"This, dear madam, is *my* view of the matter: but I do not wish *you* to walk by *my* light. I believe all the children of God are *taught by him*, and ought to follow the dictates of their own consciences: I therefore pretend not *to advise* you, but shall endeavor to *pray* that the great *unerring* Counsellor may give you divine wisdom to be your teacher, to lead you into all truth, and to keep you from every thing inconsistent with his holy will.

"I have met with so many interruptions since I began this letter, that I fear that it is hardly intelligible. I shall be sorry if I have said any thing that gives you uneasiness; your spirits seem low, and your business does not succeed so well as could be wished: perhaps

I ought rather to have employed my pen in the way of consolation and encouragement, than by throwing in fresh matter of perplexity. Sure I am, I do not *mean* to add affliction to the afflicted; but rather have been impelled, from a regard to truth, to write my real sentiments, as you desired. Your friend and humble servant,
W. GLENORCHY."

In after-life, Mrs. Graham was of opinion that she and her scholars had gone too far in conformity with the opinions and manners of the world. A reference to this deviation from what she considered a close christian walk in life, will be frequently found in her subsequent exercises.

Lady Glenorchy being in a delicate state of health, made frequent use of Mrs. Graham as her almoner to the poor. On one of these visits Mrs. Graham called on a poor woman with a present of a new gown. "I am obliged to you and her ladyship for your kindness," said the poor woman rich in faith; "but I maun gang to the right airth first; ye wad na hae come, gin ye had na been sent; the Lord hath left me lately wi' but ae goon for week day and Sabbath, but now he has sent you wi' a Sabbath-day's goon." Meaning, in plain English, that her thankfulness was first due to the God of providence, who had put it into the hearts of his children to supply the wants of this poor disciple.

Mrs. Graham used to repeat with pleasure an anecdote of her friends Mr. and Mrs. Douglas. Mr. Douglas was a tallow-chandler, and furnished candles for lady Glenorchy's chapel. The excise-tax was very high on making those articles, and many persons of the trade

were accustomed to defraud the revenue by one stratagem or another. Religious principle would not permit
Mr. Douglas to do so. Mrs. Graham one evening was
remarking how handsomely the chapel was lighted.
" Ay, Mrs. Graham," said Mrs. Douglas, " and it is all
pure—the light is all pure, it burns bright." It would be
well if christians of every trade and profession were to
act in like manner; that the merchant should have no
hand in unlawfully secreting property, or encouraging
perjury to accumulate gains; that the man of great
wealth should have neither usury nor the shedding of
blood by privateering to corrode his treasures; that all
should observe a just weight and a just measure in their
dealings, as in the presence of God. Let every christian
seek after the consolation of Mrs. Douglas, that the
light which refreshes him may be pure.

It being stated as matter of regret, that poor people
when sick suffered greatly, although while in health
their daily labor supported them, Mrs. Graham suggested the idea of every poor person in the neighborhood laying aside *one penny a week* to form a fund for
relieving the contributors when in sickness. Mr. Douglas undertook the formation of such an institution. It
went for a long time under the name of " The Penny
Society." It afterwards received a more liberal patronage, has now a handsome capital, and is called " *The
Society for the Relief of the Destitute Sick.*"

In July, 1786, Mrs. Graham attended the dying bed
of her friend and patroness, Lady Glenorchy: this lady
had shown her friendship in a variety of ways during
her valuable life; she had one of Mrs. Graham's daughters for some time in her family, condescended herself

to instruct her, and sent her for a year to a French boarding-school in Rotterdam. She defrayed all her expenses while there, and furnished her with a liberal supply of pocket money, that she might not see distress without the power of relieving it. So much does a person's conduct in maturer years depend upon the habits of early life, that it is wise to accustom young people to feel for and to contribute in their degree to the relief of the afflicted and the needy.

Lady Glenorchy was a character in whom was eminently displayed the power of religion. Descended from an ancient family, married to the eldest son of the Earl of Broadalbaine, beautiful and accomplished, she was received into the first circles of society. With her husband she made the tour of Europe, visiting the several courts on that continent. Yet all these things she "counted but loss for the excellency of the knowledge of Christ Jesus her Lord." She became a widow while yet in the bloom of youth. She devoted herself to the service of the Lord, and was made singularly useful. She kept a regular account of her income, and of the different objects to which it was applied. She built and supported several chapels in England, and erected one in Edinburgh, in which pious ministers of different denominations should be admitted to preach.

She also built a manufactory for the employment of the poor, where the education of children was strictly attended to: even the porters' lodges on each side of her gate were occupied as schools for the neighboring poor. Her pleasure-grounds were thrown open for the accommodation of the numbers who usually come from a distance to attend a communion season in Scotland.

In a year of scarcity the same grounds were planted with potatoes for the supply of the poor. She distributed with great judgment various sums of money in aid of families who were poor, yet deserving. She never encouraged idleness or pride, and often remarked that it was better to assist people to do well in the sphere which Providence had assigned them, than to attempt to raise them beyond it. There was so much wisdom in the active application of her charities, as to render them both efficient and extensive. She seldom was seen in these works of beneficence; her object was to do good: the gratitude of those on whom she bestowed benefits was no part of her motive, or even of her calculation. What she did she did unto God, and in obedience to his commands: her faith and hope were in God.

She contributed largely to the public institutions established at Edinburgh in her day. Of one or two of the most useful she was the first to suggest the idea, always accompanying her recommendation with a handsome donation to encourage the work.

The venerable Society for the Promotion of Christian Knowledge and Piety shared largely her patronage; and, at her death, she bequeathed them five thousand pounds.

She indulged the hope of seeing a union of exertion, amongst all christian denominations, for sending the Gospel to the heathen. How delighted would she have been with the Missionary Societies of London and elsewhere, had her life been spared to behold their extensive operations!

She sold her estate of Barnton that she might apply the money to a more disinterested object than her personal accommodation, and that her fortune might be expended with her life. "I recollect here," said Saurin in one of his sermons, " an epitaph said to be engraven on the tomb of Atolus of Rheims : *He exported his fortune before him into heaven by his charities—he is gone thither to enjoy it.*"

This might be truly said of Lady Glenorchy. In her manner she discovered great dignity of character tempered with the meekness and benevolence of the Gospel. Her family was arranged with much economy, and a strict regard to moral and religious habits. She usually supported some promising and pious young minister as her chaplain, which served him as an introduction to respectability in the church. With very few exceptions, all those who entered her family as servants were in process of time brought under religious impressions. So far it pleased the Lord to honor her pious endeavors to render her family one of the dwellings of the God of Jacob.

Mrs. Graham had the honor of attending the death-bed, and of closing the eyes of this distinguished child of God. It had been Lady Glenorchy's express desire that Mrs. Graham should be sent for if within twenty miles of her when such attendance should be necessary.

The following letter to a daughter, two months later, gives us another illustration of the self-denial and anxiety for the salvation of the soul, with which Mrs. Graham personally ministered to the needy and the suffering, and how skilfully she improved these scenes for the benefit of others.

"EDINBURGH, September, 1786.

"MY DEAR DAUGHTER,—Such a scene as I have been witness to!—poor M. B——— is gone to her last abode—her state is fixed for ever. I attended her sickbed for eight successive days and nights, except perhaps for an hour that I lay down in the same room. I held by life to the very last, because I feared she was not in a fit state to die.

"She took every medicine that was prescribed for her, which I administered with my own hand; but the time appointed to end her mortal state had arrived, and go she must. She lived four days after the physicians had lost all hope, and I think I never witnessed greater distress. I watched every word with anxious care to find if any breath of prayer was to be heard; but, alas! I had no such satisfaction. As she was insensible after the first few days, it was not to be expected she could either think or pray.

"Oh! why will sinners resist the grace of God and spend the precious time given to seek and find it in thoughtless folly? What can they do, on such a bed of distress, who have no God? Time misspent and gone—opportunities unimproved and gone—calls resisted never to be repeated—death hunting the soul through every avenue of life—a dreadful, unknown, unthought of eternity at hand—an awful Judge, and no Advocate secured to plead. A time was when a kind Savior was expostulating with them, 'Why will you die?' 'Hear, and your soul shall live;'—'Ask and you shall receive;'—'Seek and you shall find;'—'Knock and it shall be opened unto you;'—'Look unto me, all ye ends of the earth, and be ye saved;'—'Let the wicked for-take his way, and the unrighteous man his thoughts, and let him return unto the Lord, and he will have mercy upon him, and to our God, for he will abundantly pardon;'—'Ho! every one that thirsteth, come ye to the waters.'—(Blessings purchased by Christ: pardon of sin, reconciliation with God, new heart and spirit, all that is necessary for time and eternity.) 'He that hath no money,' (no merit, no good about him, no claim upon any account whatever,) 'Come, buy and eat, without money and without price;'—'Why spend ye your money, (time, talents, affections, desires,) for that which is not bread, (and cannot satisfy;) incline your ear and come unto me; hear, and your soul shall live, and I will make with you an everlasting covenant. Now is the accepted time, now is the day of salvation; to-day, if ye will hear his voice, harden not your heart.'

"Such is the language of the dear Redeemer to sinners every day, in his written word, from the pulpit, and in the dispensations of his providence; but oh! the madness of sinners who will not think, who will not attend, will not apply to this Savior, whose sole errand into this world was to seek and to save sinners, yea, the very chief; but they will not put their souls into his hands nor give him any service. A time will come, and we are forewarned of it, when this same inviting Savior will say: 'Because I have called and ye refused, stretched out my hand and no man regarded, I also will laugh at your calamity, and will mock when your fear cometh.'

"Improve this dispensation, my dear child, beg of the Lord to search you and try you, and see that your hopes be well grounded.   Your affectionate mother,

I. GRAHAM."

The following to her beloved friend Mrs. Walker, shows the impressions made on the mind of Mrs. Graham by visiting *the place of her nativity and the scene of her struggles with this world's adversity*, when the hand of God was heavy upon her.

"EDINBURGH, September, 1787.

"MY DEAR MADAM,—I have been on a jaunt for nearly three weeks; my school mostly dismissed, the remainder I left with Miss S——. Goodness and mercy have followed me, and the Lord has taken care of my house also in my absence. Yours was put into my hand on my return, and brought fresh cause of thankfulness; your observation, that we were mutually feeding on the same allowance, continues to hold. I too have been considering the works and doings of the Lord, and many of them have been renewed in my memory by the scenes I have passed through.

"I visited the seat of my juvenile years with my dear and only brother. There I recollected the days of my vanity, and the Lord's patience and long-suffering; my repenting, my returning, his pardoning, his blessing; my backslidings, his stripes and chastisements, his restoring and recovering, yea, many and many times. There, too, I found my old acquaintances no more; most of them had finished their course under the sun; some I could still clasp in the arms of faith, as united to the glorious Head, and now singing the song of Moses and the Lamb. From the idea of others, I was obliged to turn away and say, 'The Judge of all the earth shall do right.'

"I recollected a lowly cottage, where lived a pious father, mother, two daughters, and a son; where the voice of prayer seldom ceased, the voice of complaint was seldom heard;—not one stone remained upon another; only the bushes which surrounded it, and the ruins of a little garden, the seat of secret communion of each with their God in turn; for one little earth-floored place was all their house-convenience, and in the winter's storm their little cow-house, built under the same humble roof, was their secret temple. I found three had gone to glory: of the other two I could learn no tidings; but I shall see them one day in very different mansions. I saw others spreading like a green bay tree, adding field to field, and dwelling alone, servants and dependants excepted.

"I saw my father's cottage, in the day when the Lord pressed him down, and the place where my dear glorified mother poured out many prayers for me and mine; my own retirement too, after the vanity I had seen of human life, and when tired and sick of it, I sought to end my days in solitude, saying, ' it is enough; here let thy servant depart in peace, and let my children be reared in obscurity.' Then I returned to the town where my husband had practised as a physician, where I had been respected and tasted largely of life's comfort. I saw the house we had lived in, and many tender scenes passed; to this same town I had returned a widow, helpless and poor, neglected and forgotten. I saw the house where I had taught my little school, and earned my porridge, potatoes, and salt; when I found myself totally neglected by some who once thought themselves honored by my acquaintance; while others, once shining in affluence, were now reduced to humble dwellings.

" The Lord has been saying, ' Know and consider all the way by which I have led thee, to prove thee, and try thee, to show thee what was in thine heart, that he might do thee good in thy latter end.' He is now saying, ' Whatsoever thy hand findeth to do, do it with thy might ;'—' Occupy till I come.' Oh, for a thankful heart, a loving, a zealous heart, a meek and humble heart ! Oh, for diligence and steadiness in the path of duty, a due sense of our own weakness and inability, of the Lord's power and all-sufficiency, and firm faith in the same ! Give my love to ——, she is the Lord's: her Heavenly Father mingles her cup ; not one unnecessary bitter drop shall be put into it ; bid her trust in the Lord ; the time, the set time for deliverance shall come. I can witness, with many thousands on earth, and an innumerable company in heaven, that he is the best of masters. I have suffered much, yet not one word of all that he has said has failed. I expect to suffer more ; but whatever bitter draughts may yet await me, I would not give one drop of my Heavenly Father's mixing for oceans of what the world styles felicity.   I. GRAHAM."

Under another date she adds :

" When we trace the tenderness of our Daysman's conduct through the whole of his tabernacling here below, and add to this the many gracious words which he spake, and to these again what were spoken by the disciples by his authority, can we refuse to cast all our burdens on Him, and to trust Him with ourselves and them ? You know how sweet it is, in the time of tumultuous distress, when the spirit is overwhelmed, when God's mercy seems clean gone for ever, and his promise to fail, how sweet to get even a lean upon the Savior; but when he, as he does at times, takes the soul out of itself, and away from forebodings, reasonings and suppositions, to his own divine attributes, and gives it a believing view of its interest in them all, in his wisdom as unerring, his power as almighty, his goodness as boundless, his faithfulness unchanging; when we add to these his humanity, and consider that our High Priest was in all points tempted as we are, yet without sin, and that he has a feeling for our infirmities;—when we find him listening to every petition—a widowed mother for her son—the centurion for his servant—weeping with two sisters over a brother's grave—embracing and blessing the little children whom mothers, like you and me, pressed through the crowd, in spite of the reprehensions of disciples, to present to him—accepting the effusions of Magdalene's penitent heart with tender consolation; oh, how near does this bring the Divinity to us, and how sweetly may we confide in such tenderness! Oh, my friend, He rests in his love! Let us rest in our confidence. All shall be well."

When Dr. Witherspoon visited Scotland in the year 1785 he had frequent conversations with Mrs. Graham on the subject of her removal to America: She gave him at this time some reason to calculate on her going thither as soon as her children should have completed the course of education she had proposed for them. She had entertained a strong partiality for America ever since her former residence there, and had indulged a secret expectation of returning. It was her opinion, and that of many pious people, that America was the country where the Church of Christ would pre-eminently flourish. She was therefore desirous to leave her offspring there.

After some correspondence with Dr. Witherspoon, and consultation with pious friends, her plan received the approbation of the latter; and having had an invitation from many respectable characters in the city of New-York, with assurances of patronage and support, she arranged her affairs for quitting Edinburgh. The Algerines being then at war with the United States, her friends insisted on her chartering a small British vessel to carry herself and family to the port of New-York. This increased her expenses; but Providence, in faithfulness and mercy, sent her at this time a remittance from Dr. Henderson, the young friend of Dr. Graham, who succeeded him as surgeon of the regiment; and a legacy of two hundred pounds bequeathed her by Lady Glenorchy, as a mark of her regard, was now of great use to her.

Thus in the month of July, 1789, Mrs. Graham once more prepared *to go into a land which the Lord seemed to tell her of.*

The two following extracts from her private journal indicate the state of her mind and heart previous to leaving Edinburgh.

" EDINBURGH, March, 1789.

" *Leave thy fatherless children, I will preserve them alive; and let thy widows trust in me ;*" Jer. 49 : 11 ; the Lord's promise, which he made to me in the days of my widowhood, and which I have made the subject of my prayers from day to day, taking the words in a spiritual sense. The Lord has done wonders for me and mine since the day I was left a widow with three orphans, and the fourth not born, in a strange land, without money, at a distance from friends; or rather without friends. Hitherto he has supplied all my wants, and laid to hand every necessary and many comforts; supporting character and credit, making a way for me through the wilderness, pointing out my path, and settling the bounds of my habitation.

" For all these blessings I desire to be grateful to the God of providence, whose is the earth and the fulness thereof; but these I cannot take as the substance of the promise; neither have they been the chief matter of my prayers. The salvation and the life I have wrestled for is that which Christ died to purchase, and lives to bestow—even spiritual life, and salvation from sin. My God knows I have held fast this view of the words, seeking first the kingdom of God for my children, leaving temporals to be given or withheld, as may best suit with the conversion and sanctification of their souls. I have not asked for them health, beauty, riches, honor, or temporal life; God knows what share of these consists with their better interests; let him give or withhold accordingly. One thing I have asked of the Lord, one thing only, and will persist in asking, trust in him for, and for which I think I have his promise—even the life of their and my soul. 1 Thess. 5 : 23, is my petition for me and mine; verse 24, my anchor of hope, preceded by Jeremiah 49 : 11."

" EDINBURGH, March 17, 1789.

" This day from the head of his own table did the Lord, by his servant Mr. R——, proclaim his name the I AM, and called on me to write under what I would, for time and eternity. My soul rejoices that God is, and that he is what he is; nothing less than himself can content me, nothing more do I desire.

" This great I AM is my portion—what can I ask beside? He hath opened my eyes to see his excellency; he hath determined my will, to choose him for my portion. He hath arranged and set in order a rich testament sealed by the blood of his own Son, containing every blessing for time and for eternity. All my heart's desire is there promised, and faith given to believe there shall be a full performance. What have I to say then, but Amen, do as thou hast said? Father, glorify thy name. Thou hast said, ' then will I sprinkle clean water upon you, and ye shall be clean; from all your filthiness and from all your idols will I cleanse you. A new heart also will I give you, and a new spirit will I put within you; and I will take away the stony heart out of your flesh, and I will give you a heart of flesh; and I will put my Spirit within you, and cause you to walk in my statutes, and ye shall keep my judgments and do them. And ye shall dwell in the land that I gave to your fathers; and ye shall be my people, and I will be your God.' Amen; Lord, do as thou hast said. Behold, I take hold of thy covenant for myself and for my children. It is well ordered in all things, and it is sure. My heart accords to every part of it. Wilt thou guide us by thy counsel while we live, and afterwards receive us to thy glory? Amen and Amen—do as thou hast said.

" If we forsake thy laws, and go astray; if we depart from thee and break thy commandments, wilt thou visit our faults with rods, and our sins with chastisements. Blessed promise, Amen, Lord, do as thou hast said: seeing thy loving-kindness is secured to us, and thou wilt not cast us off from being thy people, nor alter that which thou hast spoken; wilt thou keep us as the apple of thine eye? wilt thou cover us with the shadow of thy wing? Art thou my Husband? art thou the Father of my fatherless children? wilt thou be the stay of these orphans, and their and my shield in a strange land? wilt thou perfect what concerns us? wilt thou care for us? wilt thou *never leave us, never forsake us?* in the valley of the shadow of death shall thy rod and staff support us? What can thy servant say but Amen, do as thou hast said!"

CHAPTER IV.

SCHOOL IN NEW-YORK—DEATH OF HER PASTOR DR. JOHN MASON—LAST NEWS OF HER SON.

Mrs. Graham, after a pleasant though tedious voyage, landed in New-York on the 8th day of September, 1789, where she and her family were received with the greatest cordiality and confidence. The late Rev. Dr. Rodgers and Rev. Dr. John Mason were especially kind to her. She came eminently prepared to instruct her pupils in all the higher branches of female education; and the

4*

favorable change effected by her exertions was soon visible in the minds, manners, and accomplishments of the young ladies committed to her care. She opened her school on the 5th of October, 1789, with five scholars, and before the end of the same month the number increased to fifty. She not only imparted knowledge to her pupils, but also, by her conversation and example, prepared their minds to receive it in such a manner as to apply it to practical advantage. While she taught them to regard external accomplishments as ornaments to the female character, she was careful to recommend the practice of virtue as the highest accomplishment of all, and to inculcate the principles of religion as the only solid foundation for morality and virtue. The annual examinations of her scholars were always well attended, and gave great satisfaction. General Washington while at New-York honored her with his patronage. The venerable and amiable Bishop of the Episcopal Church in the state of New-York, then the Rev. Dr. Benjamin Moore, was never once absent from those examinations. She was sensible of his friendship, and always spoke of him in terms of great esteem and respect.

She united in communion with the church under the pastoral care of the Rev. Dr. Mason. This excellent man was her faithful friend and wise counsellor. Under his ministry her two daughters, Joanna and Isabella, joined the church in the year 1791. Her eldest daughter Jessie, who had made a profession of religion in Scotland, was married in July, 1790, to Mr. Hay Stevenson, merchant of New-York, and she became a member of the church under the care of Dr. Rodgers, where her husband attended.

In the year 1791 her son, who had been left in Scotland to complete his education, paid his mother a visit. Mrs. Graham, considering herself as inadequate to the proper management of a son, had at an early period of his life sent him to the care of a friend, who had promised to pay due attention to his morals and education. The boy had a warm affectionate heart, but possessed, at the same time, a bold and fearless spirit. Such a disposition, under proper management, might have been formed into a noble character; but he was neglected, and left in a great measure to himself by his first preceptor.

For two years of his life he was under the care of Mr. Murray, teacher of an academy at Abercorn. He was a man truly qualified for his station. He instructed his pupils with zeal; led even their amusements; and to an exemplary piety added the faithful counsel of a friend. He loved, and was therefore beloved. Under his superintendence John Graham improved rapidly, and gained the affections of his teacher and companions. Happy for him had he continued in such a suitable situation. He was removed to Edinburgh to receive a more classical education. Being left there by his mother and sisters, the impetuosity of his temper and a propensity for a sea-faring life induced his friends to place him as an apprentice in the merchant-service. He was shipwrecked on the coast of Holland, and Mr. Gibson, of Rotterdam, a friend of Mrs. Graham, took him to his house, and enabled him to come to the United States. He remained at New-York for some months. His mother deemed it his duty to return to Scotland to complete his time of service. He evidently inclined to the profession of a sailor; she therefore fitted him out handsomely, and he embarked for Greenock in the same ship with Mr. John M. Mason, the only son of Dr. John Mason, who went to attend the theological lectures at the Divinity Hall in Edinburgh.

The following extract shows the anguish of Mrs. Graham's mind in parting with her son, and how she cast him upon the covenant mercy of her God, placing a blank, as to temporal things, in her Lord's hand, but holding on with a fervent faith and hope to the promise of spiritual life.

"NEW-YORK, May 20, 1791.

"This day my only son left me in bitter wringings of heart: he is again launched on the ocean, God's ocean. The Lord saved him from shipwreck, brought him to my home, and allowed me once more to indulge the yearning of my heart over him. Short has been the time he has been with me, and ill have I improved it: he is gone from my sight, and my heart bursts with tumultuous grief. Lord, have mercy on the widow's son—' the only son of his mother, and she a widow!'

"I ask nothing in all this world for him: I repeat my petition—save his soul alive; give him salvation from sin. It is not the danger of the seas that distresses me; it is not the hardships he must undergo; it is not the dread of never seeing him more in this world: it is because I cannot discern the fulfilment of the promise in him. I discern not the new birth nor its fruits, but every symptom of captivity to Satan, the world, and self-will. This, O this is what distresses me: and in connection with this, his being shut out from ordinances, at a distance from Christians; and shut up with those who forget God, profane his name, and break his Sabbaths.

"O Lord, many wonders hast thou shown me; thy ways of dealing with me and mine have not been common; add this wonder to the rest: call, convert, regenerate, and establish a sailor in the faith. Lord, all things are possible with thee: glorify thy Son, and extend his kingdom by sea and land; take the prey from the strong. I roll him over upon thee. Many friends try to comfort me; miserable comforters are they all. Thou art the God of consolation; only confirm to me thy gracious word, on which thou causedst me to hope in the day when thou saidst to me, 'Leave thy fatherless children, I will preserve them alive.' Only let this life be a spiritual life, and I put a blank in thy hand as to all temporal things. 'I wait for thy salvation.' Amen."

Three months afterwards she learned that a press-gang had boarded the ship in which her son was, and although he was saved from their grasp by a stratagem of the passengers, yet all his effects were taken away from him. In the following reflections on this event, the anxious mother shows that she would not withdraw the blank she had put into her Redeemer's hands.

"NEW-YORK, August 18, 1791.

"Thus far the Lord hath tried me, and kept me to my choice. This night I have tidings, through a letter to Dr. M. that my son has been seized by the press-gang. Through God's help he escaped; but all his assortment of necessaries that his sisters and I made

up with so much care, labor, and expense, they have
carried off, and he is once more left naked. Satan
and a corrupt heart unite in tempting me to complain.
Dare I utter a word or harbor a murmuring thought?
Would I withdraw the blank I have put into the Redeemer's hand? Has he not hitherto done all things
well? Have not my own afflictions been my greatest
blessings? Have not I asked for my children their
mother's portion? Has not God chiefly made use of
afflictions as means of hedging me in, and shutting me
up to my choice of this portion, as well as showing me
that He is a sufficient portion without any other?
When matters have been at the worst with me as to
this world, my triumphs in God have been highest, and
prospects for eternity brightest.

"Has the Lord given me in some measure victory
over the world? Do its honors, riches, and gaudy
splendor appear to me empty and vain, and not worth
an anxious thought? Does provision of food and raiment by the way through this wilderness seem all that
is necessary? and is it my wish, as well as form of
prayer, that the Lord may give that in kind and degree
which he sees fittest for me? And shall I covet that
for my child which I despise for myself? Alas! Lord,
it is because he feeds not on better things, and sometimes I fear he has no better portion. Still, still foolish.
Was it when I was full, or when in want, that I returned
to my heavenly Father? Do I desire, have I asked and
persisted in asking for my children, salvation from
sin and self? Do I anxiously wish them to reach and
to surpass my present measure of submission and resignation to thy will—to enjoy God in all things, and no-

thing without him ? And shall I, dare I complain when I see the Lord making use of the same means which first brought me to myself, and recovered me also from numberless backslidings since I first tasted the blessedness of his chosen ?

"Lord, I renew my blank. I afresh roll them all over upon thee. I will try to look on, in the faith that all things shall work together for good to their souls, and that I shall yet see the day, or if I see it not, that it will come, when they shall bow at thy footstool, sink into the open arms of thy mercy in Christ, melted down in holy, humble, acquiescing, cordial submission to thy severest dealings with them ; when thou shalt put a new song into their mouths, and they shall sing as I do now, 'It hath been very good for me that I have been afflicted.' 'I wait for thy salvation.' Amen."

Again we mark her trust in God in the more common events of life, and her gratitude in the reception of blessings from his hand.

"NEW-YORK, September, 1791.

"Many have been my burdens of late ; strangers laid upon me to provide for, even when I thought I had not sufficient to give to all their due and provide for my own family. But what is that to me ; the Lord increases business, lays more largely to hand, bears me and my burdens, provides for me and strangers. Lord, it is al. well : give when thou wilt, and call for it again when and for what purpose thou wilt ; it is thine own. I am thine, and all that thou givest me is thine ; the world calls it mine, but I call it thine. If it be thy will, lead me in a plain path, or if thou lead me by a way which I know not, hold up my goings, so shall I be in peace and safety still. Amen."

" This day did the Lord's sent servant, in a solemn manner, take us all to witness, and call in the witness of angels, that we had once more avouched ourselves to be the Lord's, and that once more Christ and his salvation had been offered to all within the walls. This same day, for the second time, have my two daughters sat down at the Redeemer's table among his professing people, and, I have reason to think, given their hearty assent to his covenant.

" Glory! glory! glory! to the hearer of prayer. I have cast my fatherless children on the Lord, and he has begun to make good my confidence. *One thing*, one only thing have I asked for them, leaving every thing else to be bestowed or withheld as consisting with that : I seek for my four children and myself, first of all, *the kingdom of God.*

" My God from day to day adds many other comforts, and strengthens my hopes by promising appearances, that *the grain of mustard seed* is sown in the hearts of my three daughters. They have joined themselves to the people of God, and I have reason to think the Lord has ratified their surrender of themselves to him ; he has made them willing for the time, and he will hedge them in to the choice they have made.

" Saturday, September, 1791, the Lord made me a grandmother, assisted my poor weakly girl, and gave a son to her and my arms. ' There was joy that a man child was born into the world,' and according to thy word ' she remembered no more the anguish.'

" Thanks be to God for this salvation ; but, Lord, this is but a small thing with thee. Look, O look on this twig from a guilty stock; poor, helpless, feeble creature, it can do nothing for its body, and still less for its soul. O God of *the spirits of all flesh*, give it a plunge in *the blood of Jesus*—cleanse, O cleanse him from original sin, and now, even now, in thy own sovereign and mysterious way, sow *the grain of mustard seed* in his soul."

In the spring of 1792 Mrs. Graham and her family were called to a severe trial by the translation of their beloved pastor, Dr. Mason, to a better world. A few months before his decease, whilst preaching to his peo ple, his recollection failed, his sermon was gone from his mind, and he sat down in his pulpit unable to proceed. After a short pause he arose and addressed his people in a pious and affectionate strain; he considered this event as a call from his heavenly Master to expect a speedy dismission from the earth, and solemnly admonished them also to be prepared for the will of God. His people, who loved him, were affected to tears. An illness soon followed, which terminated in the death of the body. He departed on the night when Mrs. Graham took her turn of watching with him, and she closed his eyes, which she always accounted a privilege and honor bestowed upon her by her Divine Master. But this tender and affecting scene is best described in a letter which she wrote to her sympathizing friend Mrs. Walker, of Edinburgh.

" New-York, April, 1792, Sabbath noon.

" My dear Madam,—It is not my custom to take my
pen on this day even to write to a christian friend,
having occasion for the whole time with my family or
in secret with my God; but I cannot go to dinner, I
cannot eat, I cannot talk to my girls; my heart must
bleed afresh on the same altar upon which it has often
been pierced. O, madam, my dear Dr. Mason goes, and
leaves me here alone: in all probability his course is
nearly finished, and his crown awaits him. Five physicians now attend him closely. I have seen him often,
and he says, ' All is well, all will be well.' Of the physicians he said, ' Yes, yes, it is very well—they are useful men in God's hand—they may be instrumental in
patching up the tabernacle a little. If it be raised to
usefulness I am content; if not to usefulness, I do not
desire it. I feel no concern about the issue of this; the
will of the Lord be done.'

" I say Amen; but, Oh, I feel alone. I should need
large communications from his Master to fill up this
blank. I cannot write for weeping; now my face is so
swelled I cannot go to church. I called at his house
this morning, found the doctors in the parlor, and
learned from them the worst. The bell was ringing for
church. I stifled as much as possible my grief; would
fain have come home to give it vent, but durst not be
absent from the house of God. I heard a stranger in
Doctor Rodger's church; our doors are closed; his
text was,—' *Henceforth I call you not servants but
friends*'—he ran the parallel between human friendship and that subsisting between Christ and his disciples. I ought to be comforted, nay, I am comforted.

"The Bible lies open before me; it is full of consolation; but all is in prospect. I look at God, what he is in himself, what he is to his people *now*, and what he will be to *eternity;* the consolations of hope are mine; but, for the present, I feel like the sparrow on the house-top, or like a pelican in the wilderness; and when I think on my years and the robustness of my constitution, and that I may have a long journey before me, I am not able to look at it. At the same time, when I consider my children, who, having lost their pastor, who bore them on his heart to the throne of grace, have double need of a mother, I dare not indulge a wish, far less put up a petition for release. Oh, that I could get under the influence of that spirit which I have witnessed in my dear pastor,—that entire confidence in God,—that perfect resignation to his will,—that complacency in all he has done, is doing, or will do,—that rest in God, of which he seems to be put in possession even now, while his breast is laboring and heaving like a broken bellows, and he cannot fetch one full breath. Oh, what cannot God effect!

"*Sunday Evening.*—I have again seen my dear pastor, and discern the clay dissolving fast. The words of dying saints are precious, and his are few. He thus accosted me: "I am just waiting the will of God; for the present I seem a useless blank in his hand; I can say very little; be not too anxious for my life, but transfer your care to the church; my life or death is but a trifle; if the Lord have any use for me, it is easy for him to raise me up still; and if he do, it will be agreeable to observe his hand distinct from men; if he should not, you will all be cared for; leave all to him

and seek his glory." He could say no more, nor will I
to-night, but address myself to our Lord on his behalf,
yours, my own, and our dear concerns.

"Several days have elapsed since I last wrote; our
dear Doctor still lives, often recruits, and again is reduced; but man can do no more; my last page, before
the vessel sails, shall be of him.

"As to myself and family, we are as the Lord would
have it with us, and, I make no doubt, as we need. Business very full; a house full of boarders, and about
sixty scholars. I begin to feel the effects of fatigue or
age, I know not which. The almond-tree flourishes;
those that look out at the windows begin to be darkened; but the keepers of the house stand firm, and all the
wheels and springs discharge their office, though more
heavily; there is no judging of my days by present appearances. Well, let me once more return to my rest
—*God;* commit my way to him, who shall bring to pass
what is best, and in the end shall complete my happiness.

" *April* 23, *Monday.*—It is finished. My dear Minister's bitter draught is over. On Thursday, the 19th of
this month, a quarter before ten o'clock A. M. the Lord
received his spirit and laid his weary flesh to rest. He
had a sore conflict with the king of terrors, who seemed
allowed to revel through every part of his mortal frame:
his legs were mortified to his knees; he had not been
able to lie down for four weeks, and died in his chair.
Like his Master, he groaned, but never complained:
he had a draught of his Master's cup, but the bitter ingredient, *desertion,* made no part of it. I had the honor
to close his dear eyes, and to shut those dear lips from

whence so many precious truths have proceeded, and to mix with the ministering spirits who attended to hail the released. This honor I had desired, but did not reckon myself worthy, and hardly hoped for it; but the Lord saw the wish, though never formed into a petition, and indulged me. I bless him for it. And now farewell, human friendships, let me gird up the loins of my mind, and run with patience the little further, looking unto Jesus, and following also him, my pastor, 'who, through faith and patience, now inherits the promises.'

"This is a great work finished. Dr. Mason was 'a city set on a hill.' He was with the army during all the war after the evacuation of New-York; had great influence over the soldiers; preached the Gospel of peace uniformly, but never meddled with politics, though he was fully capable. In every situation the Lord supported him in uniformity and consistency of character, and carried him through without a single spot or stain. Glory to God in the highest for this repeated proof of his faithfulness. 'Mark the perfect man, and behold the upright, for the end of that man is peace.'   I. GRAHAM."

Great was the grief of Dr. Mason's congregation on his removal. In him, to great learning were united meekness, prudence, diligence, and knowledge of the world, and an affectionate superintendance of the interests, spiritual and temporal, of his flock. He so arranged his avocations and studies in regard to time, that he had always a few hours in the afternoon to devote to visiting the families of his congregation. So regular was the order he observed, that Mrs. Graham and her family knew when to calculate on seeing him, and always expected him with the anticipation of profit and pleasure. Once every week they were sure of seeing him, if in health. His visits were short, his conversation serious, awakening, instructive, and affectionate. He inquired about their temporal affairs, and in cases of difficulty gave them his best advice. His counsels were salutary; his knowledge of the world and his discrimination of character rendered him well qualified to advise. In one of his visits to Mrs. Graham she mentioned to him the want of good servants as one of her trials. "Mrs. Graham," said he, "have you ever prayed to the Lord to provide good servants for you? Nothing which interests our comfort is too minute for the care of our Heavenly Father."

To one of her daughters, who felt a strong inclination to profess her faith in Christ by joining the communion of his church, but yet was afraid that her heart was not sufficiently engaged for the service of God, Dr. Mason proposed the following question: "If," said he, "the world, with all its wealth, pleasures, and power, were placed in one scale, and Christ alone in the other, which would your heart freely choose as a portion?" On her replying there would be no hesitation as to her choice of Christ, he gave her encouragement to profess her faith, although it might not at present amount to the full assurance of hope.

He was indeed a faithful shepherd of his flock, and his people mourned for him as for an affectionate father. It is much to be desired that his example were more followed by Christian pastors. To preach with eloquence and acceptance is a talent of great value in a minister of the Gospel; this makes him respected, and his congregation admire him, because, for one reason, they are proud of him; but to gain their affections, to make a congregation the children of an aged pastor, or the friends and brethren of a younger one, let the minister visit the families of his people; this will seal on their hearts the regard which their understandings had already dictated.

Very few ministers have been more remarkable for a strict attention to this duty, than the late Dr. John Mason and his venerable and attached friend Dr. Rodgers. When the former died, the latter exclaimed, "I feel as if I had lost a right arm!"

The congregation, bereaved of their pastor, wrote immediately to his son, the late Rev. Dr. John Mitchell Mason, to hasten his return from Edinburgh to New-York; and after preaching to them with great acceptance for several months, he was ordained and installed pastor of the church in April, 1792. Mrs. Graham entertained for him the most affectionate attachment, and this attachment was reciprocal.

At this date we find some of Mrs. Graham's delightful devotional exercises.

"New-York, 1793.

"Blessed Lord, thou hast, to the praise of thy grace, given me the heritage of them that fear thy name; thou hast prepared my heart to pray and inclined thy ear to hear; thou hast drawn me into thy fold, and hast fed me in thy green pastures. I rejoice in Israel's Shepherd; not one of his flock shall be lost. Often have I wandered from his presence and sought pasture among the swine, but my Shepherd has ever drawn or driven me back. He has a rod and I have felt it; but I bless the hand and kiss the rod.

"Oh, how wonderful to look back and see 'all the way by which he has led me, to prove me, to try me, to show me what was in my heart, that he might do me good at my latter end.' Amen, my God, I leave myself in thy hands. I should lose myself; but thou wilt keep me from foes without and foes within. What then have I to care for? My Shepherd careth for all; he slumbers not nor sleeps, and he will perfect what concerns me; of this I am as sure as that I now write it.

"The law of thy mouth is better unto me than gold and silver. O how I love thy law, it is my meditation all the day. Thou, through thy commandments, (or the whole of thy truth,) hast made me wiser than my teachers. The law of God makes the simple wise. How sweet are thy words unto my taste, yea, sweeter than honey to my mouth. Through thy precepts I get understanding, therefore I hate every false way. 'Thy word is a lamp unto my feet, and a light unto my path.' How safe, how happy are they who are taught by the word of God! 'Blessed art thou, Simon Barjona, for flesh and blood hath not taught thee this, but my Father who is in heaven.'

"O my children! enrich your minds with a full acquaintance with the word of God! lay it up in your memories, when you can do nothing more; be assured, if ever you are made wise unto salvation, it must be by this word; if ever you are taught of God, he will teach you by the words contained in the Bible. 'Search the Scriptures, for they are they which testify of me;' search the Scriptures, for in them are contained the words of eternal life. 'Be followers of them who, through faith and patience, now inherit the promises.'

"Holy David went forward, heavenward, improving in the knowledge of God, of himself, and of God's plan of salvation for ruined sinners, by studying the word, the works, and the providences of God, but chiefly the word of God; praying for, watching for the influences of God's Spirit on his judgment and thinking powers: it was by this that he became wiser than his teachers. He was a king, and had the cares of the nation to occupy his mind; he was a man of war, and had that art to study. But, O the privilege of the christian! he goes through every part, even of his earthly way, leaning upon God. David could say, even of war, 'The Lord teaches my hands to war, and my fingers to fight.' 'The Lord subdues the people under me.' In temporals and in spirituals, he is my shield, my strength, my buckler, my strong tower. 'I shall not fear what man can do unto me.' 'In Judah's land God is well known; there he brake the spear, the bow, and the battle.' He ascribes all to God. We hear nothing of his own wisdom, his disciplined armies, his order of battle and warlike powers, though attention to all these was his duty, and not neglected by him. He devoted all his natural talents to God; he exercised them diligently, but still he knew and acted under the influence of that knowledge, that 'unless the Lord build the house, the builders lose their pains; unless the Lord keep the city, the watchmen watch in vain.' He, as well as worldly men, chose the means best adapted to the end proposed. Let natural men assert, and let it be admitted, that David knew better how to use a sling and a stone, than mail, helmet, and sword; therefore he chose them. But follow David until he meets the hostile foe. Do we hear a word of his art as a slinger, as a marksman? though we may suppose he was expert at both. 'Thou comest to me with a sword, a spear, and a shield; but I come in the name of the Lord of hosts, the God of the armies of Israel whom thou hast defied; and this assembly shall know that the Lord saveth not with sword and spear, (these are not essential,) for the battle is the Lord's, and he will give you into our hands.'

"How comfortably might christians go through life did they walk with God in their daily business and occupations, carefully observing the leadings of providence, cautiously avoiding either running before or lagging behind; but in all things making their requests known to God; at all times committing their way to him, being careful about nothing, but to use with diligence the means of grace, and also the means of acquiring the good things of life, leaving the issues of both to God, in the full assurance that what is good the Lord will give. 'Trust in the Lord, and do good; so shalt thou dwell in the land, and verily thou shalt be fed.' In spirituals and in temporals, 'the hand of the diligent maketh rich.' Be 'not slothful in business, fervent in spirit, serving the Lord.'

"Lord, teach me thy law graciously, in all its perfection, its extent, order, beauty and harmony, and grant me all the assistance provided to enable a lost, depraved, corrupted child of Adam, to set out in thy good ways, to go forward, and to finish in the same course; and all the consolation, joy, and peace which thou hast provided

to be enjoyed in a measure even here, and to be perfected in the world to come. Amen."

" *Hosea*, 14. ' O Israel, return unto the Lord, for thou
hast fallen by thine iniquity.' Yes, fallen, O how fallen
from God the only good, the fountain of happiness!
Lost his image, which was the glory of man in para-
dise! Lost that sweet complacency and delight in his
perfections and attributes which innocence enjoyed!
Lost rectitude of reason and judgment! No longer can
we judge of excellence, no longer love what God loves.
Our wills no longer straight with his will, but crooked,
opposing God, and choosing evil instead of good. ' Oh
Israel! thou hast destroyed thyself, but in me is thy
help.' Amen, says my soul, in thee is my help."

" NEW-YORK, October 3, 1793.

" *Isaiah*, 44 : 5. ' One shall say, I am the Lord's, and
another shall call himself by the name of Jacob; and
another shall subscribe with his hand unto the Lord, and
surname himself by the name of Israel.'

" I, as one, subscribe to the truth of all that God has
said: I, as one, subscribe my assent to all he has done.
I set my Amen to his well-ordered covenant, well ordered
in all things and sure. And this is the covenant, even
Christ, the sum and substance, for he hath given him to
be a covenant of the people. The whole and every part
of it is God's covenant. To me it must be a testament,
the New Testament in Christ's blood. To me it must
be a covenant of gifts and promises. I can be no party,
having nothing to give; nothing with which to covenant. He hath said, ' Thou hast destroyed thyself, but
in me is thy help.' Amen. Be my help, my deliverer!

" 'Look unto me, all ye ends of the earth, and be saved; for I am God, and there is none else.' I do look unto thee alone for salvation. Thou art God; there is none else: besides thee there is no Savior.

" 'I will pour water on the thirsty, and floods on the parched ground. I will pour my Spirit upon thy seed, and my blessing upon thy offspring.' Amen. I yield my soul into thy hand, dry and parched, to receive thy showers of reviving, quickening, fructifying grace."

Writing about this date to her beloved friend Mrs. O——, of Edinburgh, Mrs. Graham, for the encouragement of her friend, gives her, in confidence, the following record of her own christian experience:

" It is now, I think, thirty-five years since I simply, but solemnly, accepted of the Lord's Christ, as God's gift to a lost world. I rolled my condemned, perishing, corrupted soul upon this Jesus, exhibited in the Gospel as a Savior from sin. My views then were dark compared with what they now are: but this I remember, that at the time I felt heart-satisfying trust in the mercy of God, as the purchase of Christ; and for a time rejoiced with joy scarce supportable, singing almost continually the 103d Psalm.

" I took a view of the promises of God, and wrote out many of them, and called them mine; and among the foremost was that in Psalm 89 : 30–33; and well has the Lord kept me to it, and made it good: for, my dear friend, never was there a more unsteady, unwatchful christian; never did the children of Israel's conduct in the wilderness depict any christian's heart and con-

duct in the Gospel-times better than mine; and just so
has the Lord dealt with me. When he slew me, then I
trusted in him; when he gave me carnal ease and comfort, I forgot my Rock and rebelled. Often did I stumble
too from legality, instead of looking at my own weak
ness and impotence, and trusting wholly in my Redeemer's strength. I was wroth with myself, wondered
at myself, and thought it impossible I could be as I had
been. I made strong resolutions, yea, vows, and became
a slave in means to hedge in this wandering, worldly,
vain, flighty heart; but, alas! a few months found me
where I was, with scarce a thought of God from morning to night; prayer huddled over in words that had no
effect on my heart; and the fear of hell the chief re-
straint from sin or spur to duty. Then, in general, the
Lord had some affliction for me, which laid me afresh
at his feet, and made me take a fresh grasp of Christ,
and a fresh view of his covenant: then again I felt safety, joy, peace and happiness.

"Thus, by line upon line, by precept upon precept, ay,
and by stripe upon stripe, he taught me that I could not
walk a moment alone. This is now my fixed faith; and
in proportion as I keep it in sight, I walk safely; but I
still forget, and still stumble and still fall; but I am lifted up and taught lesson after lesson; and I shall stumble and shall fall while sin is in me; but the last stumble shall come, and the last stripe shall be laid on, and
the last lesson taught, and that which concerns me shall
be perfected. O! then shall I look back, and see 'all
the way by which he has led me, to prove me and try
me, and show me what was in my heart, that he might
do me good in my latter end.'

"I am often, even in this valley of darkness and ignorance, allowed this retrospective view; and am led to say not one word of all that he promised has failed. 'Hitherto the Lord hath helped, he hath been the guide of my youth, and even unto hoar hairs will he lead me;' and when he calls me to pass through the valley of the shadow of death, I shall even then fear no evil, for his rod and staff shall support me; and I shall enter into the presence of my Redeemer, white and clean drest in his most perfect righteousness; angels and saints shall know me in this glorious robe; my Redeemer will acknowledge me as his ransomed, and I shall be for ever with the Lord."

To Mr. A. D., Edinburgh.

"NEW-YORK, 1793.

"I have just been reading over my dear friend's precious letters, and am refreshed anew by the same truths and uniform experience of every christian; which all amounts to this, that the Lord is the portion of his people, and that whom he loves, he loves to the end. My soul melts with tenderness when I recollect my fellow-travellers in the wilderness; those dear associates with whom I have so often taken sweet counsel; who so often comforted me with the same comforts with which they themselves were comforted. I am also led to recollect some who have finished their warfare; some whose trials were sharp and long; but who, through the same grace in which we trust, were steadfast to the end; and now inherit a crown of life—the reward of grace, not of debt.

"I rejoice to hear that your children are promising; I

think it is the greatest comfort a parent can enjoy in this world. I have a large share of it in my three daughters; but my prodigal is not come to himself; he still feeds on husks, nor thinks of the plenty in his Father's house. I had great hopes last winter; I heard he had been very ill in consequence of very severe treatment from his captain. The Lord has been emptying him from vessel to vessel, and I have been waiting the issue; but mine eyes almost fail. I have great hopes that God's time of mercy will come. I am also satisfied that it will be the best time; but still I cry, O how long! My dear friends, I think I would recommend it to you to *keep your children about you.* No other had ever the influence over him that I had; and I regret that I did not bring him with me.

"Our young Timothy, J. M. is a perfect champion for the Gospel of Jesus; the Lord has well girded him and largely endowed him; he walks closely with God, and speaks and preaches like a christian of long experience: he was ordained about two months ago in his father's church, and a few weeks after married a lady of eminent piety, and preached all the day, both the Sabbath before and after: no levity, no novelty appeared in word or gesture, which is not always the case with the best at such times. There is probably no church in New-York whose discipline is as strict, nor one which has so many communicants. He is reckoned a man of great talents and an orator; and many of even the idle and careless go to hear him.

"A few Sabbaths ago he preached from these words, 'I am determined to know nothing among you, save Jesus Christ, and him crucified.' After proving that all the

Scriptures, from the beginning of Genesis to the end of Revelation, pointed to Christ and his great work of redemption; and, asserting that that sermon could not be called the Gospel of which he was not the subject, he spoke home to his audience, and told them that this, through the aid of Divine Grace, was his firm purpose, to dwell on redeeming love. He was sure no subject would be welcome to any christian, where Christ was not to be found; nor would any such subject ever convert a sinner; and therefore, if any were about to take their place there, expecting to hear any new or strange thing, let them not disappoint themselves. Oh! for a thankful heart! the Lord has indeed done wonders for me and mine; and blessed be his name for this mercy also, that in a remarkable manner, by a strange concurrence of circumstances, he hedged me in to become a member of this congregation, where I am led and fed with the same truths which nourished my soul in Zion's gates, at Edinburgh; and I am helped to sing the Lord's song in a foreign land. Often have I been tempted to hang my harp upon the willow, 'when Zion I thought on;' but this was, and sometimes still is my sin and ingratitude; for I ought to build houses, and plant vineyards, and seek the good of the land; for he has a small vineyard here, which he waters and cultivates, and I ought to labor therein, and do whatsoever my hand findeth to do with diligence, and say, 'the earth is the Lord's and the fulness thereof; heaven is his throne, the earth his footstool,' and he fills all things and all places.

"What aileth thee, Hagar?' O what a God of mercy is our God! Often has he hailed me in some such lan guage: 'What aileth thee?' why is thy countenance sad? am I not better to thee than ten friends? Then has he turned my heart to him, made me feel myself close to him; he has suffered me to lean on his bosom, hang on his arm and lisp out, *Abba*. At such blest moments I have thought the whole earth but one point, and from that to heaven but one step, and the time between but as one moment; and my company here sufficient to satisfy me by the way. At such blest moments I felt perfect, full, entire satisfaction with all that God is, all that he does; and could trust him fully with all my concerns, spiritual, temporal, and eternal. But, alas! by and by, like a peevish child, I began to fret, wish this, wish that; grieve for this, grieve for that; fear this, fear that; stagger, stumble, fall. O what a God of patience and long-suffering! And O how rich that well-ordered covenant, that provides suitable grace for all these unsteady seasons! It is my greatest consolation that the Lord knows it all. There are times when I cannot see him, but every moment he sees me. I should fall off and leave him, but he holds me fast and never leaves me. O blessed plan, where God secures us in safety, even from ourselves! We have not only destroyed ourselves, and he has been our help; but we are ever destroying ourselves, and still he renews this help.

"Well, what shall we say? Father, glorify thy name, and let us lie in thy hand as clay in the potter's, till thou finish thy workmanship, and fit us vessels of mercy, to be filled with happiness, when thou shalt have done thy good pleasure in us, and by us, in this world, through the grace that is in Christ Jesus, who loved us, and gave himself for us; to whom be glory, honor and praise in the church below, and in the general assembly above, now and ever. Amen.

"My love, my heart's love, to my dear Mrs. D ——. I am ever your affectionate friend in the bonds of the Gospel,   ISABELLA GRAHAM."

Early in 1793 Mrs. Graham heard from a worthy clergyman at Greenock, who, at her request, paid attention to her son, that he had been very ill of a fever, and subsequently subject to epileptic fits. In one of these he had fallen from the mast-head, and was rendered unfit for service for many months. The gentleman to whom he was apprenticed permitted him to leave. In these circumstances Mrs. Graham addressed to him the following letter:

"MY LONG-LOST BUT STILL-DEAR SON,—If this ever reach you, hearken to the voice of your mother, your only parent, and to the voice of God by her. Oh, my son, you have had a long race in the service of Satan: he has kept you in bondage and made you his drudge. You are far advanced in the broad way that leads to destruction—to that place of endless torment prepared for the devil and his angels, to which Satan is dragging you. He has even been seeking the destruction of your body, that he might have you secure.

"Oh, my son, think. Has he proved a good master? What have you found in his service? and has he not disappointed all your gayest hopes, and fed you with husks? Have you, my son, been happy? Are you not obliged to drive away your own reflections? I know you are. Dare you, my son, sit down and think over all the past, all the present, and look forward to the future with any degree of comfort? My son, you cannot Hear then the word of the Lord; that Lord, that merciful Lord, who has seen you in all your rebellion, heard every profane oath you may have uttered, seen your rioting among the sons of Belial; yet what is his voice to you? Oh, my son, it is not, Bind him hand and foot and cast him into the lake that burns with fire and brimstone; where there is weeping, and wailing, and gnashing of teeth, where the worm dieth not, and the fire is not quenched. No, my son, the door of mercy is still open to you; the Lord calls, 'O sinner, thou hast destroyed thyself, but in me is thy help.' 'Only repent, so iniquity shall not prove your ruin.' 'Hearken unto me, ye stout-hearted, that are far from righteousness: I bring near my righteousness; it shall not be far off, and my salvation shall not tarry.' 'Hear, and your soul shall live.' 'Believe in the Lord Jesus Christ and thou shalt be saved'—saved from hell; saved from Satan and his snare; saved from the force of corruption in your heart.

"I do not call upon you, my poor corrupt boy, to turn from sin and work righteousness in your own strength; this you can no more do than the Ethiopian can change his skin; but I do call upon you to receive the whole of God's salvation, and power to resist sin is a principal part of it. In God's word it is said, that the Lord gave Christ to be a covenant to the people: we have to covenant with him on our part; we are all poor, lost, miserable creatures, I as well as you, by nature; but the Lord Christ is God's gift to sinners. All the other promises are made to those who have received and accepted of this gift; but Christ himself is God's gift to sinners—to the chief of sinners—*to you, John Graham, by name*—and the Bible says, to as many as receive him, to them gives he power to become the sons of God. God gave Christ to become the price in our hand; we take this gift, and offer back, as the price of our redemption, his atoning sacrifice, his all-perfect righteousness; and on this ground we are entitled, by his own plan, which he prepared from first to last, to plead for the full accomplishment of all the promises in the Bible: for the pardon of sin; yea, for an entire new nature.

"Oh, my son, open your Bible, go to your knees, look out words there fit for your case; present them humbly before God, turn all the promises you find there, all the offers, all the calls, all the commands, all the threatenings into prayer, for you of yourself can do nothing, and ask that God, for Christ's sake, may pour out on you the spirit of prayer. I know not how to have done, yet I well know, unless the Lord soften your poor obdurate heart, it will still remain hard. Oh, my son, be willing to put it in his hand, to receive his salvation, and give yourself up to his guiding. I beg you will read with care the 15th chapter of the gospel of Luke. The Lord spoke these parables to show how very willing he is to receive returning sinners. Your mother and all your sisters are willing to follow his example; return to us, my son. We will watch over you, we will pray over you, and we will try, by every endearing method, to restore you not only to health but to comfort. Your sisters wish you to come; all your friends are willing to receive you; we will not upbraid you.

"Do, my dear, leave Greenock; come out to us by any way you can find, I will pay your passage here; or if you can get to any port in America, you can write me from that, and I will get you forwarded here; and, after you are here, if you still wish to follow the sea, we can get you a berth in some trading vessel from this. All your friends here send best wishes. And now, my son, I commend you to the Lord. Oh, that he may bless this to you.

"Your affectionate mother,   I. GRAHAM."

The last intelligence that Mrs. Graham received of her unfortunate son was in a letter from himself, dated Demarara, 1794, in which he states that he had sailed from Amsterdam in a Dutch vessel; was taken by the French, and re-taken by the English; had arrived at Demarara in the ship *Hope;* and should he not soon hear from his mother, would return to Europe with a fleet which was shortly to sail under convoy. Mrs. Graham notices this event as follows:

"NEW-YORK, February 20, 1794.

"This day I have a letter from my poor wanderer. It is more than a year since I heard of him. Accept of my thanks, good and gracious Lord. I feared his cup had been full, and he called out of the world with all his sins on his own head; for I have no tidings of his turning from his sinful courses, or fleeing from the wrath to come, by taking hold of the hope set before him.

"I bless thee, O I bless thee, for thy sparing mercy, thy long-suffering, thy patience, thy forbearance. Yea, even to him, thou hast been more than all this. Thou hast been his preserver, his provider; thou hast watched over him in many imminent dangers, in the great deeps, in burning and in frozen climes.

" Thou hast followed him with thy preserving mercy and temporal bounty. He is still in the land of the living, and among those who are called to look unto thee and live. Still thou feedest my hopes of better things for him. Thou sufferest my prayers to lie on the table of thy covenant. I will trust, I will hope, I will believe, that in an accepted time thou wilt hear me, and in a day of thy power thou wilt bow his stubborn will, and lay him an humble suppliant at thy feet. O, I trust thou wilt bring this poor prodigal to himself, and turn his steps towards his Father's house. See how he feeds with the swine upon husks, and even these not his own. O turn his thoughts to his ' Father's house, where there is bread enough, and to spare.'

" ' Lord, remember thy gracious word, on which thou hast caused me to hope,' and which has ever been my comfort in the time of my affliction, and in my straits my only relief.

" He is again launched into thy great ocean. Lord, he is far from every friend and from every means of grace, and for any thing I know, far from thee by wicked works—under thy curse and hateful in thy sight; but thou, God, seest him. Means are not necessary, if thou willest to work without. Thou canst find an avenue to his heart at once. Dead as he is, vile as he is, guilty as he is, far from help of man, and in the most unlikely situation to receive the help of God, yet I know all these hinderances, all these mountains shall melt as wax at thy presence.

" Lord, I believe, thou knowest I believe, that if thou but speak the word, this dead soul shall live; this vile, this guilty soul shall be cleansed, shall be renewed, and my son be changed to a humble, thankful, genuine child of God, through the cleansing blood of atonement, through the imputation of the Redeemer's righteousness and the implantation of thy Spirit. I can do nothing for him, but thou canst do all this. I wait for it, Lord, I wait for thy salvation. Lord, let there be 'joy in heaven over this one sinner repenting.' I roll him on thee. I trust in thy sovereign, free, unmerited mercy in Christ. Amen."

All inquiries instituted by kind friends respecting this son proved fruitless; and as a vessel named the *Hope* was some months after reported as having been taken by the French, it is perhaps probable that he died in a French prison.

Thus again had his afflicted mother to exercise faith and submission, not without hope toward God that the great Redeemer had taken care of, and would finally save this prodigal son. She had known a case in her father's family which excited their solicitude and encouraged her hope. Her younger brother, Archibald Marshall, a lad of high temper, though possessed of an affectionate heart, had gone to sea, and was not heard of at all for several years. A pious woman, who kept a boarding-house in Paisley, found one of her boarders one day reading Doddridge's Rise and Progress of Religion in the Soul, with Archibald Marshall's name written on the blank leaf. On inquiry, the stranger told her that he got that book from a young man on his death-bed as a token of regard. That young man was Archibald Marshall—he was an exemplary christian; "and I have reason," added he, "to bless God that he ever was my messmate." The woman who heard this account, transmitted it to Mr. Marshall's family, who were known to her. Mrs. Graham had no such consolatory account afforded to her; but under much yearning of heart she left this concern, as well as every other, to the disposal of that God "who doeth all things well."

Again she sings of mercy in a sweet meditation.

"NEW-YORK, October 1, 1794.

"'Return unto thy rest, O my soul, for the Lord hath dealt bountifully with thee.'

"Blessed be the Lord, for he hath showed me his marvellous loving-kindness in a strong city—Christ, the city of refuge.

"Thou hast given me my heart's desire, and hast not withholden the request of my lips. 'One thing have I desired of the Lord,' and through life sought after for myself and the children whom thou hast given me; 'that all the days of our lives we might dwell in the house of the Lord,' behold his beauty, and inquire in his holy temple; that in the time of trouble he would hide us in his pavilion, in the secret of his tabernacle, and set our feet upon a rock.

"O thou incarnate God! Thou blessed temple not made with hands! Thou blessed pavilion, in which thy people hide in the time of trouble, and are safe! Thou Rock of Ages, on which we build our hopes for time and eternity, and defy the assaults of sin, Satan, and the world! Thou Jehovah-Jesus art all these to thy people. Thou broughtest them 'from a fearful pit and from the miry clay; thou settest their feet upon this spiritual rock, and establishest their goings; thou puttest a new song in their mouths, even praise unto their God.' Many have seen it and sung it; many now see and sing it; many shall see and sing it, and trust in the Lord. They find in thee all that is expressive of life; all that is expressive of safety; all that is expressive of comfort; all that is expressive of happiness.

" ' O how many are thy wonderful works which thou hast done! and thy thoughts which are to us-ward! they cannot be reckoned up in order unto thee: if I would declare and speak of them, they are more than can be numbered.' Thou, thy blessed self, art the sum and substance of every good to man. All this I know; all this have I at different times experienced; and yet my heart is heavy, my spirits depressed. There is no cause, O no! Thy very afflictive providences have met my wishes, and been so many answers to my prayers.

" Thou Husband of the widow, thou Father of the fatherless! O how fully, how manifestly hast thou fulfilled these relations to thy worthless servant! Thou, in my early widowhood, didst call me to *leave my fatherless children on thee*, annexing the promise that *thou wouldst preserve them alive.*

" Thou didst put it into my heart to plead the promise in a spiritual sense; to ask, to hope, to wait for the new birth, the life which Christ died to purchase, and lives to bestow.

" In three of these fatherless I have seen thy work. Long did the grain of mustard-seed lie buried among the weeds of worldly-mindedness; long were my hopes and fears alternate; but now the blessed discipline of the covenant has been exercised; I have witnessed it, I have felt it—suffered the rod with them and for them, but waited for the fruits in hope; and glory to thee, dear Husband and Father, I have not waited in vain. Thou hast written *vanity*, and opened our eyes to read vanity written on every earthly enjoyment, except so far as thou art enjoyed in them. Thou hast enabled not only thine aged servant, but her children, to put a blank into thy hand, and to say, ' Choose thou for us.' We take hold of thy covenant, and choose it for our portion. Is not this, O Lord, the full amount of my desires? Thou wilt finish the work in thy own time, and by means of thy appointing. Amen. Lord, do as thou hast said."

CHAPTER V.

DEATH OF HER DAUGHTER—FIRST MISSIONARY SOCIETY IN NEW-YORK.

In July, 1795, Mrs. Graham's second daughter, Joanna, was married to Mr. Divie Bethune, merchant in New-York. In the following month her eldest daughter, Mrs. Stevenson, was seized with a fatal illness. Possessing a most amiable disposition and genuine piety, she viewed the approach of death with the composure of a christian and the intrepidity of faith.

She had been in delicate health for some years, and now a complication of disorders denied all hope of re-

covery. She sung a hymn of triumph until the struggles of death interrupted her. Mrs. Graham displayed
great firmness of mind during the last trying scene, and
when the spirit of her daughter fled, the mother raised
her hands, and looking towards heaven, exclaimed, '*I
wish you joy, my darling.*' She then washed her face,
took some refreshment, and retired to rest.

Such was her joy of faith at the full salvation of her
child; but when *the loss of her company* was felt, the
tenderness of a mother's heart afterwards gave vent to
feelings of affectionate sorrow: nature will feel, even
when faith triumphs. In her devout meditations before
God, Mrs. Graham improves this event as follows:

" October 4, 1795.

"Why, O why is my spirit still depressed? Why
these sobs? Father, forgive. 'Jesus wept.' I weep,
but acquiesce. This day two months the Lord delivered my Jessie, *his Jessie,* from a body of sin and
death, finished the good work he had begun, perfected
what concerned her, trimmed her lamp, and carried
her triumphing through *the valley of the shadow of death.*
She overcame through the blood of the Lamb.

"I rejoiced in the Lord's work, and was thankful
that the one, the only thing I had asked for her, was
now completed. I saw her delivered from much corruption within, from strong and peculiar temptation
without. I had seen her often staggering, sometimes
falling under the rod; I had heard her earnestly wish
for deliverance from sin, and when death approached
she was more than satisfied; said she had been a great
sinner, but she had a great Savior; praised him and

thanked him for all his dealings with her; for hedging her in, for chastising her; and even prayed that sin and corruption might be destroyed if the body should be dissolved to effect it. The Lord fulfilled her desire, and, I may add, mine. He lifted upon her the light of his countenance; revived her languid graces; increased her faith and hope; loosed her from earthly concerns, and made her rejoice in the stability of his covenant, and to sing, 'All is well, all is well; good is the will of the Lord.' I did rejoice, I do rejoice; but, O Lord, thou knowest my frame; she was my pleasant companion, my affectionate child: my soul feels a want. O fill it up with more of thy presence; give yet more communications of thyself.

" We are yet one in Christ our head—united in him: and though she shall not return unto me, I shall go to her, and then our communion will be more full, more delightful, as it will be perfectly free from sin. Christ shall be our bond of union, and we shall be fully under the influence of it.

" Let me then gird up the loins of my mind, and set forward to serve my day and generation, to finish my course. The Lord will perfect what concerns me; and when it shall please him, he will unclothe me, break down these prison-walls, and admit me into the happy society of his redeemed and glorified members: then ' shall he wipe away all tears from my eyes,' and I shall taste the joys which are at his right hand, and be satisfied for evermore."

Mrs. Graham made it a rule to appropriate *a tenth* part of her earnings to be expended for pious and charitable purposes. She had taken a lease of two lots of ground on Greenwich-street from the corporation of Trinity Church, with a view of building a house on them for her own accommodation; the building, however, she never commenced. By a sale which her son, Mr. Bethune, made of the lease in 1795 for her, she got an advance of one thousand pounds. So large a profit was new to her. "Quick, quick," said she, "let me appropriate the tenth before my heart grows hard." What fidelity in duty! what distrust of herself! Fifty pounds of this money she sent to Mr. Mason in aid of the funds he was collecting for the establishment of a Theological Seminary. Her own version of this matter we have in a letter to her familiar friend Mrs. Walker, of Edinburgh:

"1795.

"MY DEAR MRS. W——, My last informed you that we had been made to taste of the Lord's visitation, (the yellow-fever,) but in great mercy had been spared in the midst of much apparent danger. I have now in my house a girl who lost both father and mother, and many whole families were cut off; my house was emptied; my school broken up; we confined to town, and heavy duty laid upon us at the same time. I trembled again for fear of debt; but *the Lord brought meal out of the eater.*

"Three years ago, when tried by having one house taken over my head, another bought, and obliged to move three times in as many years, some speculating genius brought me under the influence of the madness of the times, and persuaded me I might build without money. It is quite common here to build by contract. I could not purchase ground, but I leased two lots of

church land, got a plan made out, and worried myself
for six months, trying to hatch chickens without eggs.
I had asked the Lord to build me a house, to give suc
cess to the means, still keeping in view covenant provision, " what is good the Lord will give." After many
disappointments I said, Well! I have asked—I am refused—it is not good—the Lord will not give it: he will
provide, but in his own way, not mine.

" Of course I had to pay ground-rent, which in three
years amounted to two hundred and twenty dollars. I
think I hear you say, I never could have believed that
Mrs. Graham could be guilty of such folly—nor I; but
seeing and hearing of many such things, I fancied myself very clever. Last year a basin was formed, and
wharves around it opposite to the said lots; the epidemic
raging on the other side of the city brought all the vessels that came in round to them, and great expectations
were formed for this new basin; houses and stores
sprung up like mushrooms, and Mr. B—— sold my lease
for one thousand pounds. Lo! and behold, part of it is
already spent. All my provision through this wilderness has been so strongly marked by peculiar providences, my mind seems habituated to a sense of certainty. I feel my position of earthly good safer and
better in my Lord's hand than in my own."

In the ensuing year we find the following outbreath-
ings of her rich christian experience:

" January 3, 1796.

"Philippians, 4 : 4–7. 'Rejoice in the Lord alway, and
again I say, rejoice. Let your moderation be known
unto all men. The Lord is at hand.

" ' Be careful for nothing ; but in every thing by prayer and supplication, with thanksgiving, let your requests be made known unto God. And the peace of God, which passeth all understanding, shall keep your hearts and minds, through Christ Jesus.'

"Christ Jesus!—What does not this name comprehend! He is mine, and all is mine. I do rejoice in the Lord, yea, more or less, I rejoice always. This heart of mine is sensible to every human affliction ; my tears flow often and fast : I weep for myself, and still more for others : but in these very moments of heart-wringing bitterness there is a secret joy that Jesus is near ; that he sees, knows and pities. He is Jehovah as well as Jesus, and could have prevented the affliction under which I groan ; but for my good, and the good of those near and dear to me, he suffered it, or prepared it. The good of his people is connected with his glory ; they cannot be separated : therefore, Father, glorify thy name ; I rejoice, and will rejoice. The Lord can remove, and will remove the affliction the moment it has answered the gracious purpose for which it was sent. I would not wish it one moment sooner. While it lies heavy, he is my Almighty Friend, my rest, my staff of support.

" ' In time of trouble he shall hide me in his pavilion ; in the secret of his tabernacle shall he hide me ; he shall set me up upon a rock.' Psalm 27 : 5.

" ' The Lord is my strength and my shield ; my heart trusted in him, and I am helped, therefore my heart greatly rejoiceth ; with my song I will praise him,' and in his strength and by his grace, let my ' moderation be known unto all men'. My *Lord is at hand ;* at hand to support, at hand to overrule, at hand to deliver. Therefore I rejoice always.

"Blessed be God for the heart-easing, heart-soothing privilege of *casting all my cares upon him,* and for the blessed assurance that *he careth for me* and mine: that he allows, invites, yea, commands me to be careful for nothing, but in all things, by prayer and supplication, with thanksgiving, to let my requests be made known unto him, who is man, and touched with the feeling of our infirmities (Jesus wept,) and God, the Almighty God, to support, overrule, deliver. Therefore my heart rejoiceth always."

"May 16, 1796.

"Psalm 89 : 30. 'If his children forsake my law, and walk not in my judgments, if they break my statutes and keep not my commandments, then will I visit their transgression with the rod, and their iniquity with stripes: nevertheless, my loving-kindness will I not utterly take from him, nor suffer my faithfulness to fail; my covenant will I not break, nor alter the thing that is gone out of my lips.' Amen. Blessed promise! Oh, it is *a well ordered covenant, and it is sure.* Of all the provisions of the covenant, this has been to my soul among the most comfortable. Thanks be to God for the discipline of the covenant; often has it been administered: thou knowest, and I know in part, how necessarily, although I shall not know nor understand all, until that blessed rod shall have perfected its correction, and shall never more be lifted up.

"Many ups and downs has thy servant experienced in this vale of tears; many tears have watered these now aged cheeks; in a variety of ways hast thou stricken, and at times stripe has followed stripe, but mercy and love accompanied every one of them. I bless thee; Oh, I praise thee, that I have seldom received a stripe but I had with it a token of love. Sin was embittered, a Savior endeared, and grace given *to kiss the rod,* and cleave to him *that had appointed it.* And now I can read in legible characters, where in many instances thy check met my wandering steps, stopt me short of huge precipices, and preserved me from destroying even my worldly comfort. In some instances (I thank thee they have not been many) thou hast been pleased to let me alone, to let me pursue my own way, ways so wise in my own eyes that I have either not sought counsel at all, or sought it as Balaam did, with my heart set on my own will.

"In some cases thou hast let me *eat of the fruit of my own doings,* and let me weary myself in my own way, until I found it not only *vanity and vexation of spirit,* but sometimes a labyrinth from which I could find no escape: then did I cry unto the Lord; then did I remember my backslidings; then did I seek unto the cleansing fountain and to the appointed Mediator, the maker up of the breach: then did I experience afresh the Lord's power to save.

"In how many instances has he given a sudden turn to providences which have been made means of my deliverance; not only so, but brought good out of my evil, so that I have been made to wonder, and to say, 'Surely this is the finger of God.'

"I destroy myself, but in thee is my help found. O let these wanderings end: fix it deep on my mind, that in the Lord only have I wisdom as well as strength: that 'it is not in man that walketh to direct his steps.' When shall I learn to live simply on Christ, by the light of his pure ùnerring word, and the Spirit coinciding; and have done with these carnal reasonings, the wisdom of men! 'Search me, O Lord, and know my heart; try me, and know my thoughts, and see if there be any wicked way in me, and lead me in the way everlasting. Amen.' "

"May 28, 1796.

"This is the *anniversary of my dear Jessie's birth*, no more to call us together here; but I yet remember it as a day in which our God was merciful to me, and made me the mother of an heir of salvation. I bless, I praise my covenant God, who enabled me to dedicate her to him before she was born, and to ask only *one thing* for her as for myself, even an interest in his great salvation, leaving it to him to order the means, time and manner as of her natural birth and ripening age, so of her spiritual birth and ripening for glory; he accepted the charge, and he has finished the work, to his own glory, to her eternal happiness, and my joy and comfort. I have witnessed remaining corruption fighting hard against her, and bringing her again and again into captivity 'to the law of sin and death warring against her.' I have seen the rod of God lie heavy upon her, according to the tenor of the covenant, when she forsook 'his laws and went astray:' when she walked not in his judgments, but wandered from his way, *he visited her faults with rods and her sins with chastise ments, but his loving-kindness he never took from her*, (though he often hid it,) nor altered the word which he

had spoken, *that he would never leave her, never forsake
her;* that in due time he would *deliver her from all her
enemies.* I perceived her desires to be delivered from
the world and the body, and taken home to the bosom
of her God, since that appeared at times the only way
she could be delivered from sin. I heard her lament
her unfruitfulness, her unsteadiness: I heard her exclaim, ' Oh, what a sinner! what a great sinner!' and,
' Oh, what a Savior! Oh the goodness of God in hedging me in, and saving me from myself; *his covenant
stands* fast, it is established, it is sure.' I witnessed a
God pardoning sin, yet taking vengeance on inventions.
I witnessed the sinner, after being sixteen years in the
school of Christ, (taught by his ministers, and most ef-
fectually by his rod,) taking shelter in ' the city of refuge,' in the atonement of God's providing, and in ' a
surety righteousness,' and finishing her struggles with,
' All is well!' My heart echoed, and does echo, and will
to all eternity, ' All is well!' Glory to God; sing, not
unto her, not unto me, not unto any creature, but ' to
God be the glory,' that she is now delivered from ' a
body of sin and death, and made meet to be a partaker
with the saints in light.' HALLELUJAH.

" June, 1796

" Psalm 122. ' I was glad when they said unto me,
Let us go into the house of the Lord.'

" ' The house of the Lord—whither the tribes go up,
the tribes of the Lord unto the testimony of Israel, to
give thanks unto the name of the Lord,' to seek his
face, to learn his will, to taste his love, to behold his
glory, to enjoy God as their own God and reconciled
Father.

"Lord! let my heart be warmed more towards thy house; I have sought and found thee in thy sanctuary, read thy providences, and been taught thy will; I have tasted thy love and beheld thy glory; I have enjoyed thy presence as my own reconciled Father in Christ Jesus; I have been satisfied with thy goodness, as with marrow and fatness; and yet how cold and languid at times, how little desire to return, how small my expectations, how wandering my imagination! How do I sit before thee as thy people, and my heart with the fool's eyes at the ends of the earth! Lord, I should blush and be ashamed were a fellow-mortal to see my heart at times. I may hide my eyes from viewing vanity, but the evil lies within. O Lord, thou knowest the cause. After all I have heard, seen, tasted and handled of the word of life, I am still of myself an empty vessel, unable to speak a good word or think a good thought. Great are thy tender mercies, O Lord. 'Quicken me according to thy word; turn thou away my eyes from beholding vanity, and quicken me in thy way: then shall I run in the way of thy commandments when thou hast enlarged my heart.'

"The house of God—the owner, the builder and maker is God, and it is his peculiar treasure. Christ is the foundation and *chief corner-stone*, and his house are we, built upon him, cemented together, a spiritual building; the foundation cannot fail, the corner-stone can never give way; neither can we fall to pieces or be separated from him.

"The house of God—'Jerusalem, Zion, the rest of God, where he delights to dwell,' where he will for ever stay; the house of God, the Church, yea, the body of Christ: Christ the head, his people the Church, his members whose life is in him, and derived from him; and because he lives we shall live also. Lord, enlarge my understanding to comprehend more and more ' of the height and depth, length and breadth of the love of Christ, which passeth all understanding.' Open my eyes to behold wondrous things in thy law and Gospel. I am as yet but a babe: Glory to God that I am what I am, a babe in Christ. I shall be nourished with life and strength from my divine Head; educated and nurtured by the blessings of the new covenant. I shall arrive at the perfection of stature appointed, *and stand in my lot at the latter day.* Amen."

" August 4, 1796.

"A day to be remembered."

" Rose at four, not to mourn—no, but to repeat my grateful thanks to my covenant God for the work he finished this day last year, in delivering my weak, feeble, tossed and tried Jessie from *a body of sin and death*, and giving her ' the victory through Jesus Christ, who loved her and gave himself for her.' To thee she was dedicated ere she saw the light; to thee a thousand times I repeated the dedication, begging that thou mightest bring her within *the bond of thy covenant;* this was the sum and substance of all my askings for her. I witnessed the time of her second birth, saw the tears of conviction and remorse. I witnessed thy loosing her bonds, and tuning her heart and tongue to praise redeeming love. I witnessed the teaching of thy Spirit, and the enlightening of her eyes, and the taste thou gavest her of thy salvation; I thought her *mountain stood strong*, and she would not be easily *moved;* but who can tell the deceitfulness of the human heart? Too soon did we all *turn aside like a deceitful bow*, forsook *the fountain of living waters, and hewed out broken cisterns that could hold no water.* Glory to God for the discipline of the covenant, that he did not cast us off, but chastened and corrected He repeated the discipline stripe upon stripe: I stood by and saw it, and though my heart melted at times, I said, ' She is in her Father's hand, let him do his pleasure.'

" I too was unfaithful to her, thou knowest, and often entered into the same vanity of mind, which stifled the love of God in our hearts, instead of guarding her and warning her; still, still the Shepherd of Israel followed after both, and with the precious rod restored both, time after time, till it pleased thee to finish her warfare, and deliver her from both body and sin. Lord, I thank thee for all the circumstances, for the privilege of attending her in her warfare, for the cheerfulness of her spirits, for the rich support we all experienced, for the view we all had of thy faithfulness and fatherly dealing, and for her last words, "All is well." O yes! every thing thou doest is well, and this was peculiarly well. I resigned her to thee with joy and thankfulness, and I still acquiesce. Her thou hast taken, me thou hast left, to be yet exercised with further discipline. It is well—*thy will be done.* O help me to profit by every pang! Let sin be mortified and my soul be purified; enlarge my heart to run the ways of thy commandments. Now may *I lay aside every weight*, and that vanity of mind which *doth so easily beset me*, and hath been the secret spring of much backsliding both to myself and to my children. Lord, destroy it. O let me now live to God, closely and consistently; down with my will, with self in every form! O purify my motives, and let my whole heart, soul, body, substance and influence in the world be devoted to thee! Empty me of every thing that is my own, and let 'Christ live in me the hope of glory,' and let the glory of thy workmanship in my soul redound to thee, and thee alone! Amen."

"August 13, 1796.

"Colossians, 2 : 6. 'As ye have received Christ Jesus the Lord, so walk ye in him, rooted and built up in him, and established in the faith, as ye have been taught, abounding therein with thanksgiving.'

" O Lord, this is what I pant after! I would fain have done with wandering. Lord, thou knowest, for the work is thine. I have received the Lord Jesus as thy gift to a lost world, as thy gift to me an individual of that world, as having made peace by the blood of the cross. I account it a faithful saying, worthy of all acceptation, that 'Christ came into the world to save sinners, of whom I am chief.' I have received thee as the Lord my righteousness, crediting thy own word, that 'Christ is the end of the law for righteousness,' and that 'there is no condemnation to them that are in Christ Jesus.' I have received thee as 'the covenant given of the people.' In all the relations by which thou art held out to me in this Bible, so far as I know or understand, I have received thee. I have no hope in myself, no trust in myself, nor any views of communication from God of any kind, but through the one 'mediator between God and man, the man Christ Jesus.'

"O my God, what is my life, what is my happiness but a continual receiving! Thou art 'the bread of life' that must keep alive the living principle in my soul. In thee 'dwelleth all the fulness of the Godhead bodily.' Thy people are complete in thee; thou art their head they are thy body, and by joints and bands have nou rishment ministered to them, and are knit together, and increase with the increase of God.

" This, oh this is what my soul pants after, closer and more intimate union and communion. I would be trans formed into thine image; I would be thy temple; I would have thee live in me, walk in me, make me one with thee; I would be delivered from self-will, self-wisdom, self-seeking; I would be delivered from that philosophy and vain deceit which spoils souls and leads them off from their head : then, and not till then, shall I cease to wander, shall 'run and not be weary, walk and not faint.' Then shall 'I run in the way of thy commandments,' and no longer turn aside to crooked ways. Then shall I eat and drink, work and recreate, all to thy glory. Lord, send thy Spirit into my heart, that he may continually ' take of the things of Christ and show them unto me ;' that I may grow and be no longer a babe, but arrive at the ' fulness of stature in Christ Jesus,' and more steadily, and more purely, and more zealously, and, O! more humbly live to God, and glorify him in the world. Amen."

The following extracts of letters to her friend Mrs. Walker, show how ardently *the true missionary spirit* burned in the heart of Mrs. Graham, and how efficiently it was exemplified, not only in her pecuniary donations but her active and self-denying efforts to diffuse information and enlist others in so worthy a cause. The efforts alluded to in the first extract evidently gave rise to the event recorded in the second, *the formation of the first Missionary Society in New-York.* It is delightful also to notice her attachment to christians of other denominations, and the gratitude with which she remembered kindness received by herself when Providence had cast her lot on what was truly missionary ground.

" Do you remember how much I used to say about our dear Methodist Society in Antigua? and the three holy, harmless, zealous Moravian brethren? and how the preachers gave each other the right hand of fellowship, forgetting their differences, in that land of open hostilities, on the kingdom of their common Lord. Thither the Lord brought me from a land of entire barrenness, where, as far as I know, a Gospel sermon was never preached. Here I was brought into great affliction, and to pass through the severest trial that I ever experienced before or since.

" The Lord brought me into this fold, a poor straggling lamb, who had for five years herded among the goats; and little difference was there between them and me, except that my soul longed after green pastures and rejoiced to hear the shepherd's voice, and when I heard it I knew it, though from one who did not belong to my original fold; these good people nourished me with tenderness, bore with patience my carnality. When my dear husband was taken ill they wrestled for him in prayer; Mr. Gilbert was every day with him; the Lord heard and gave a joyful parting; yes, joyful, never did I experience such joy; then they sympathized with and soothed the widowed heart, fed her with promises, and in a measure established her; thus they wrought with

God in calling in one, and restoring another; never, never shall I forget the labors of love of that dear little society.

"How many such stragglers as I may be wandering in both East and West Indies, and may be restored by these precious missionaries. I owe them, of my labors, more than others. I send you a bill for *fifty pounds*. I have received eighteen copies of the Missionary Magazine, as far as No. 9. I have got subscribers for them all, who will continue; pay these, and send me what more numbers have been published by the return of the Edinburgh packet, also eighteen complete sets from the beginning. I hope to be successful in disposing of them also. I suppose the sermons go to the same fund; send me a hundred sermons, I will see to get them disposed of; send them single, not bound, and of the best; perhaps they may pave the way for more to follow; every little helps; drops make up the ocean. We cannot yet produce any thing; we are gathering intelligence, and endeavoring to collect money; but I grudge that what we can spare should be idle in the meantime; the cause is one; pay the magazines at once, and the sermons if you have enough of my money. I hope to remit again in September. I have a great wish to have a finger in your pie in some way; if I must not subscribe past our own society, I may sell books for yours. Ever, my dear friend, yours,   I. GRAHAM."

To the same.

"1796-7.

"I thank my friend for her letter. I rejoice with you, and bless the widow's God. He has indeed been so to us, to the full amount of the promise. I have now much

to sing of, little to complain of; my dear girls and Mr
B—— go forward steadily, having laid aside the weights
of amusements and gayety, and seem determined to follow the Lord fully through good and through evil report. Bless the Lord, O my soul, and forget not all his
benefits. We have a full school, and a very comfortable
set of girls. The Lord has delivered from all heavy
burthens.

"Last week a considerable number of ministers and
lay christians met for the third time, and *established a
Society for sending missionaries among the Indians, and
also among the poor scattered settlers on the frontiers.*
A sermon was preached in the evening in one of the
Dutch churches, 'The liberal deviseth liberal things,'
&c. after which an address was read by the Secre-
tary, (our dear Mr. Mason,) which, when printed, I will
send you.

"The society is to keep up a correspondence with
your and the other societies. If they can effect any
thing themselves, apart here in America, well; if not,
they will throw their subscriptions into the common
funds and get help from you. This view is very pleasant to us. There is great need of itinerant preachers
in our back settlements; they are scattered, and no
churches of any kind; even in some thick settled countries they will not pay a minister. These are 'the high
ways and hedges;' O that the Lord may compel them
to come in.   I. GRAHAM."

We next find Mrs. Graham administering consolation
and imparting instruction to a lady residing near Boston, (Mrs. C——.) With this lady Mrs. Graham formed

an acquaintance in New-York shortly after her arrival in America. She was then a gay young widow; but having a strong and cultivated mind, was delighted with Mrs. Graham and family; and a friendship was formed between them, which ceased only with their lives.

As a proof of her friendship, Mrs. C—— wished to introduce her young female friends into gay fashionable society This Mrs. Graham opposed; and while she stated her reasons she endeavored to persuade her young friend to come out from the world and cast in her lot with the people of God.

" A word spoken in due season, how good it is." This was verified in the case of Mrs. C——, who, like her friend, was destined to enter the heavenly kingdom "through much tribulation." She afterwards entered the marriage state, and became a second time a widow while her children were still young; and though not destitute, her income was considerably reduced; which circumstances may throw light on parts of Mrs. Graham's letters. Unhappily there was no evangelical minister near her place of residence, which, with the want of early religious training, may account for so much darkness as to her spiritual state. Mrs. Graham often visited her, and it pleased God in due time to scatter the darkness. Mrs. C—— for many years fully enjoyed the consolations of religion. She trained up her children according to the maxims of her friend, and had the happiness of seeing them following in her steps. One (Mrs. J. W.) she saw depart in peace; and her own dying-bed was soothed by the prayers and attentions of her son, an esteemed and highly useful clergyman in one of our populous cities. As Mrs. C—— adopted the signature of *Pilgrim*, the letters to her inserted in the former editions of this memoir, are noticed as addressed to P——.

To Mrs. C., a Lady near Boston.

"February 10, 1797.

"MY EVER-DEAR FRIEND,—The desire of writing you a long letter has occasioned too much delay on my part. One thing I can assure you of, you have been much on my mind, and the subject of all our prayers.

"Tears of joy ran down my cheeks when J—— told me the state of your mind, and I thank our good and gracious God for opening your eyes to see *the vanity of this world, the corruption of your own heart, your need of atoning blood*, and of a better righteousness than your own. Hail, my sister in Jesus! flesh and blood hath not taught you this, but your Father who is in heaven; the work is his, evidently his; and being begun, he will carry it on, and finish it too. Commit your soul then into his hand; he ' came not to call the righteous, but *sinners* to repentance ;' his errand to our world was to seek and to save the *lost.* Trusting in his mercy, through Christ, your soul is as safe as his word is true; for none perish that trust in him.

"'Trust in the Lord with all thy heart, and lean not to thine own understanding ;' be not discouraged because of deadness, darkness, wandering, want of love, want of spirituality, want of any kind. Who told you of these evils and wants? the Sun of righteousness shining into your soul has shown you many of the evils there—but the half you know not yet. The more you learn of the holiness and purity of the Divine nature and the spirituality of his law, the more you will be dissatisfied with every thing yours. Even a holy apostle said, ' In me, that is, in my flesh (or natural mind) dwelleth no good thing. The flesh lusteth against the Spirit, and the Spirit against the flesh; so that the things that I would, I do not; and the things that I would not, those I do. Yet it is not I, (not my new nature,) but sin that dwelleth in me; for to will is present with me, but how to perform that which is good I find not.'

" If this was the case with the apostle, who sealed his testimony with his life, is it strange that you and I should have hearts full of all abominable things? These realities are cause of deep humility before God, but none of despair or doubt. All are alike guilty and vile, the whole head is sick, and the whole heart unsound; therefore we need a whole Christ to atone for our sin, to cover our naked souls with his imputed righteousness, and to be surety for us; to sanctify us by his Spirit, and prepare us for the purchased inheritance. O try to rest in him: believe it, you are complete in him; give over, my dear friend, poring and diving into your own heart and frames, and try to trust in an almighty Savior to save you from foes without and foes within. Read Romaine's Walk and Life of Faith: he himself attained to a high degree of holiness by getting out of himself, and trusting, resting, believing from day to day, for grace, for every duty, as it occurred. The promise runs, ' as thy day so shall thy strength be.'

" I cannot at this distance, and knowing nothing of characters, offer you any advice with respect to outward means; but if you know any truly pious, spiritual minister, I should think it your duty to lay open your mind to him. You may find in books matter as good as any man living can speak; but it is the Lord's appointed way, and he often honors his servants, his ministers, by making them messengers of peace and comfort to his children. 'Are any sick, let them call for the elders of the church, and let them pray over them.' See how the christians of old associated with one another! I am now doubly yours, &c.   I. G."

"April 14, 1797.

"Eternity seems very near. I have often thought so without any visible cause. Well, it will come; a few more rolling years, months, weeks or days will assuredly land me on Canaan's happy shore. Then shall I know and enjoy what ear hath not heard, eye seen, nor heart conceived, even the blessedness that is at God's right hand. I have desired, though I know not that I have asked, to glorify God on my death-bed, and to leave my testimony at the threshold of eternity, that not one word of all that my God has promised has failed. He has been—O what has he not been! In all my trials, all my afflictions, all my temptations, all my wanderings, all my backslidings, he has been all that the well-ordered covenant has said. Let this Bible tell what God in Christ, by his Spirit and his providence, has been to me; and let the same Bible say what he will be to me 'when flesh and heart fails;' yea, when 'the place that now knows me shall know me no more.' Perhaps when the messenger does come I shall not know him, but depart in silence. Well, as the Lord wills, he knows best how to glorify himself. Jesus shall trim my lamp and perfect his image on my soul, sensible or insensible. I shall enter into his presence, washed in his blood, clothed in his righteousness, and my sanctification perfected. I shall ' see him as he is,' and be like him.

" Mourn not, my children, but rejoice; ' gird up the loins of your mind' and set forward on your heavenly journey through this wilderness. So far as I have followed Christ, so far follow my example; still living on Christ, depending on him for all that is promised in the well-ordered covenant. O stumble not into the world except when duty calls; at best it is a deadly weight, a great hinderance to spiritual-mindedness, and in as far as it gets a footing in your heart, it will not only mar your progress but your comfort. Lord, feed my children constantly with ' thy flesh and thy blood,' that they may never hunger nor thirst for this world, but grow in the divine life, and in the joy and comfort of the Holy Ghost. Amen."

" *October* 20, 1797.

" How condescending is our covenant God! All we have or enjoy is from his hand; he gave us our being; our lives, although forfeited a thousand times, have been preserved. *Our bread has been given us, and our water sure;* and not only these necessaries, but many comforts and good temporal things have fallen to our lot; *thou hast furnished our table*—hast provided medicines and cordials when sick. Lord, I thank thee for all these mercies, but above all, that we can call thee our reconciled Father: that we have them not as the world have them, who are far from thee, and have no portion among thy children, nor interest in thy well-ordered covenant; but that we have them as thy redeemed, as part of covenant provision, and with a covenant blessing, and among the *all things* that work together for our good. Lord, enable us to be rich in good works. How condescending, that thou accept-est a part of thine own as free-will offerings, and hast an-nexed promised blessings to those *who consider the poor;* hast said, 'he who giveth to the poor, lendeth to the Lord.'

"I thank thee that thou hast laid to hand a sufficiency to enable me and mine *to eat our own bread;* even that which, according to the regulations of society, men call our own. Thou only hast a right to call it not so, for we are thine, and all that thou hast given us; but of thy free bounty and kind providence 'thou hast enabled us to provide things honest and of good report in the sight of all men,' and to give a portion to them who need.

"I trust thy Spirit has directed my judgment in the de-termination I have taken to set apart, from time to time, this portion, according as thou prosperest us in business, and preservest us in health and ability to pursue it. I bless thee for indulgent, encouraging appearances, that since I began the practice thou hast added to my stock, and that which I have given has never straitened, but thou hast prospered me more and more. My poor's purse has never been empty when called for, neither has my family purse. Of thine own I give thee, and bless thy name for the privilege.

"Grant direction with respect to whom, and how much to give."

The following meditations will afford refreshment to every christian heart.

" ' As ye have received the Lord Jesus, so walk in him, rooted and built up in him, and established in the faith, as ye have been taught, abounding therein with thanksgiving.'

" Yes, just so, and no other way shall any poor corrupted creature attain holiness, in the very same manner that he received the Lord Jesus at first. He is ' the Alpha and Omega, the first and the last, the beginning and the end.'

" O Lord, my Savior, my complete Savior, and in whom I am complete! I received thee as my expiatory sacrifice, by whom atonement was made for my sins; by whom reconciliation was made; I reconciled to God, and God to me. I was then delivered from the power of darkness and translated into the kingdom of God's dear Son, and have redemption through his blood, even the forgiveness of sins. This same blood must cleanse my daily spots, must cleanse my very best services; this same blood must cleanse my conscience daily, and give me confidence in God, as my reconciled Father. By this same peace-speaking blood I daily present myself in his presence, and know that he sees no iniquity in me so as to condemn me.

" O Lord, I receive thee as my justifying righteousness, disclaiming all confidence in my own works, throwing them aside as filthy rags. I place my sole dependence upon an imputed righteousness; *that* righteousness, wrought out by thee as my surety, in thy holy, meritorious life and death; believing thy testimony, that ' the wages of sin is death, but the gift of God is eternal life, through Jesus Christ our Lord.' Just so must I go on, trusting in, resting upon, rejoicing in the Lord my righteousness. 'By one man's offence many were made sinners, so by the obedience of one shall many (and I among others) be made righteous. Christ is the end of the law for righteousness,' therefore I walk at liberty, free from all dread of condemnation. Not as a slave, not as a servant, not as an hireling, not as a probationer; but as a son and heir of God, to whom the inheritance is made sure. I have received the seal of the testament, ratified and made sure by the death of the testator. All the blessings contained in this Bible, the records of the well-ordered covenant, are mine; and, O glorious truth! the testator died to ratify and insure this testament; but he lives again, the glo rious executor.

" O Lord, I received thee as my king : depending up on promised strength, I swore allegiance to thee, and to thy government. Just so, my dear sovereign Master, must I go on: rejoicing in its privileges, subjecting myself cheerfully to its restrictions: studying with care its positive commands, and setting myself to obey : submitting with meekness to its discipline : claiming thy kingly power to subdue the corruptions of my heart, to defend from foes within and foes without: and when thou callest me to fight, to arm me for battle, and lead me on to victory.

"I received thee as my divine Savior, as *the cove-nant of the people :* the covenant arranged, ratified, and fulfilled; to me a covenant of free gift. Receiving thee, I received all the promises in their fullest extent, as le-gally made over and confirmed to me by the irrevocable gift of Deity: and in thee, as my Savior, dwelleth all the fulness of the Godhead bodily; yes, dwelleth in him for his people, his ransomed; dwelleth in him as our head; we are united to him, one with him, as *he and the Father are one*, and being one with him, we are complete in him. He is the head, we the members; he is the vine, we the branches; he is the foundation and *chief corner-stone*, we the building. Thus let us walk in him; rooted and built up in him; filled with the knowledge of his will, in all wisdom and spiritual under-standing; walking worthy of the Lord, unto all pleasing —being fruitful in every good work, and increasing in the knowledge of God; strengthened with all might, ac-cording to his glorious power; unto all patience and long-suffering, with joyfulness; for it is he 'who work-eth in us both to will and to do of his good pleasure;' and although 'of ourselves we can do nothing, yet we can do all things through Christ strengthening us;' and he has promised, 'that as our day so shall our strength be.'

It is well, Lord, it is well. Thou art mine and I am thine: thou art mine with all thy fulness, what can I want besides? Nothing, Lord. Thou hast given me 'the heritage of those that fear thy name;' I am satis-fied with my portion. Amen. Be my God and the God of my seed, and glorify thy name in us."

"October, 1797.

"Psalm 119. 'Remove far from me vanity and lies.' Every deviation from rectitude and truth is sin. Who that knows any thing of the corruption of the human heart, and its strange tendency to stray, to err, yea, even to pervert the plainest, simplest and most obvious truths, but must see the propriety of his joining the Psalmist, and crying out, 'Lord, remove far from me the way of lies.'

"The way of lies, as it respects our judgment and sentiments; as it respects our motives of action, and as it respects our conduct.

"As it respects our judgment: how does every species of error abound; even the serious and earnest seekers of truth differ in many things, which, although they may not prevent their final salvation, mar their progress in knowledge, in holiness, and in comfort. 'Lord, remove far from us the way of lies.' Lead us to the pure, unmixed, unerring word of truth, as it respects our sentiments, and as it respects our conduct. O how many deceive themselves by resting on a speculative knowledge of the truth, or what they esteem such, while their hearts remain unaffected, their tempers unsanctified, and their lives unfruitful. Passionate, stubborn, relentless, unmerciful, implacable tempers indulged and unmortified, must be a way of lies. 'Learn of me,' says the Savior, 'for I am meek and lowly, and ye shall find rest to your souls.' 'The meek will he teach his way, the meek will he guide in judgment.'

"'Remove far from me the way of lies, and teach me thy law graciously.'

"'Teach me thy law graciously,' not the ceremonial and the moral law alone, but the whole of God's revealed will. The Psalmist knew the law ceremonial and moral, but he wants more and more of the teaching of the Spirit of God. 'He,' the Spirit of truth, 'shall take of mine, and show it unto you.' The word of God is ever the same; it contains the whole truth, and nothing but the truth ; every thing necessary to safety, to holiness and happiness : but O the difference between him who reads with a mind enlightened by the Spirit of God, and him who reads with no other assistance than his own poor blinded, darkened reason. 'Teach me then thy law graciously. I will praise thee with uprightness of heart, when I shall have learned thy judgments. Open thou mine eyes, that I may behold wondrous things out of thy law.' The Psalmist thirsted after more and more extensive views of the word of God, and still as his views were enlarged he desired more. Verse 64. 'The earth is full of thy mercy ;' this was one lesson, but still he cries, 'Teach me thy statutes ; thou hast dealt bountifully with me, O Lord, according to thy word:' still he cries, 'Teach me good judgment and knowledge. It is good for me that I have been afflicted, that I might learn thy statutes.'"

" October, 1797.

"I love to feel the kindlings of repentance, self-loathing under a sense of ingratitude, heart-melting with the view of pardoning grace. I love to feel the sprinkling of my Redeemer's blood on my conscience, drawing forth the tears of joy and gratitude in the view of a free pardon. I love to dwell on the seal of reconciliation, while my heart, glowing with gratitude, sinks into the arms of my redeeming Lord, in full confidence of his love and my safety for ever. I love to feel longings after closer communion, after more conformity to his image, more usefulness to my fellow-members of the body of Christ, and to all his creatures. I love to feel deeply interested in the success of the Gospel, in the declarative glory of Jehovah, as manifested in his works of creation and providence, but chiefly in the super-excellent work of redemption: for 'thou hast magnified thy Word above all thy great name.' "

CHAPTER VI.

FORMATION OF THE WIDOWS' SOCIETY—CLOSE OF HER SCHOOL.

In November, 1797, the "Society for the Relief of Poor Widows' with small Children" was instituted at New-York; a society which has risen into great respectability, and has been productive of very beneficent effects. The Lord, in his merciful providence, prepared this institution, to grant relief to the many bereaved families who were left widows and orphans by the ravages of the yellow fever in the years 1798 and 1799.

It took its rise from an apparently adventitious circumstance. Mr. B——, in the year 1796, was one of the distributing managers of the St. Andrew's Society. The distribution of this charity was of course limited to a certain description of applicants. Mrs. B——, interested for widows not entitled to share in the bounty of the St. Andrew's Society, frequently collected small sums for their relief. She consulted with a few friends on the propriety of establishing a Female Society for the relief of poor widows with small children, without limitation Invitations, in the form of circular letters, were sent to the ladies of New-York, and a very respectable number assembled at the house of Mrs. Graham. The proposed plan was approved, and a society organized. Mrs. Graham was elected first Directress, which office she held for ten years.

At the semi-annual meeting in March, 1798, Mrs. Graham made a very pleasing report of the proceedings of the Managers, and of the amount of relief afforded to the poor. The ladies of New-York truly honored themselves and religion by their zeal in this benevolent undertaking, in reference to which Mrs. Graham says, in a letter to her friend Mrs. Walker:

" I mentioned in my last that we had planned a society for the relief of poor widows with small children: the success has been beyond our most sanguine expectations. We have now a hundred and ninety subscribers, at three dollars a year, and nearly a thousand dollars in donations. We have spent three hundred dollars this winter, and nearly all upon worthy objects. The poor increase fast: emigrants from all quarters flock to us, and when they come they must not be allowed to die for want. There are eight hundred in the alms-house, and our society have helped along many, with their own industry, that must otherwise have been there. The French, poor things, are also starving among us; it *would need a stout heart to lay up in these times.*"

In the same letter she informs her of *the first monthly missionary prayer-meeting* known to have been held in the city of New-York.

" The second Wednesday in February we commenced

our *first monthly meeting for prayer* for the Lord's bless-ing on ours, and all the missionary societies. It was far from full; but we must be thankful for the day of small things, and pray, and wait, and hope. The Dutch churches, the Baptist and Presbyterian have united so far as to officiate in each other's churches; they have collected about seventeen hundred dollars, and are look-ing out for two missionaries to send among the Indians, or to the frontiers."

A few months later we find the following *letter to a young man on his joining the church:*

" September, 1798.

" MY DEAR YOUNG FRIEND,—You have now ratified in a public manner that transaction which, no doubt, passed previously in private between you and your God. You have declared your belief of the Gospel, and have taken hold of God's covenant of promise. You have fallen in with his own plan, which he has appointed for the sal-vation of guilty sinners; and rested your soul upon his word of promise that you shall be saved. You have, at the same time, dedicated and devoted your soul, your body, your time, your talents, your substance, your in-fluence, all that you *are* and *have*, to be disposed of at his pleasure, and for his glory, in the world. You are no longer your own. You are bought with a price, adopted into the family of God, numbered with and en-titled to all the privileges of his children. Your motives of action, your views, your interests, are all different from those of the worldling. Whether you eat or drink, or whatever you do, your aim must be, and will be, to do all to his glory. This must go with you, and be your ruling principle in all the walks of life. By your integrity, uprightness, diligence, and disinterested attention to the interest of your employers, you will glorify God and have his presence with you in business. By a due and marked observance of the Sabbath, and attendance on the ordinances, you will glorify him. By regularity, order, and temperance, crowned with an open acknowledgment of God before all who may surround your board, you will glorify him in an especial manner in these days of degeneracy, and, crowned with family worship, you will glorify him, and his presence will be with you, and great will be your comfort. God's interest in the world must also be yours. The good of his church in general, and that of your own family in particular; and Oh, my son, if you would be rich in comfort, follow the Lord fully, and follow him openly; and if you would do it so as to suffer the least from the sneer of the world, do it at once.

"Already you have received congratulations on your joining the church; by those belonging to it; soon will it be known to those who will scoff at it. But christians and worldlings will look for consistency; and, if it be wanting, the last will be the first to mark it. A decided character will soon deliver you from all solicitations to what may be even unseemly, and dignified consistent conduct will command respect. Not but the Lord may let loose upon you the persecuting sneer and banter of the wise of this world, whose esteem you wish to preserve; but, if he do, the trial will be particular, and he will support you under it, and bring his glory and your good out of it.

" And now, my son, suffer the word of exhortation. You have entered the school of Christ, and have much to learn, far beyond what men or books can of themselves teach, and you have much to receive on divine credit, beyond what human reason can comprehend.

"I would recommend to you to read carefully, and pause as you read, and pray as you read for the teaching of the Spirit—the Epistle of Paul to the Ephesians. Read it first without any commentary, and read it as addressed to you, S—— A——. You will there find what may in part stagger your reason; you will find what far surpasses your comprehension; but yet read on, with conscious weakness, and ignorance, and absolute dependance on divine teaching. When you have read it through, then take Brown's or Henry's exposition of it.

"A degree of mystery, my son, runs through the whole of God's revealed word; but it is *his*, and to be received with reverence, and believed with confidence, because it is *his*. It is to be searched with diligence, and compared; and, by God's teaching and the assistance of his sent servants, the child of God becomes mighty in the Scriptures. Let not mystery stagger you: we are surrounded with mysteries; we, ourselves, are mysteries inexplicable: nor let the doctrine of election stagger you; how small a part of God's ways do we know, or can comprehend! rejoice that he has given you the heritage of his people—leave the rest to him; ' Shall not the Judge of all the earth do right ?'

"Jesus took once a little child and set him in the midst of the people, and said, ' Except ye be converted, and become as little children, ye cannot enter the kingdom of heaven,' intimating with what simplicity and docility men ought to receive the Gospel; and the following text also alludes to this: 'Suffer little children to come unto me, and forbid them not, for of such is the kingdom of heaven.' There are many promises made to the diligent searchers after truth, ' then shall we know if we follow on to know the Lord.' ' The secret of the Lord is with them that fear him; and he will show them his covenant.' Yet the highly enlightened Paul calls the Gospel a mystery, and godliness a mystery; ' for now we see through a glass darkly; but then face to face: now I know in part; but then (in heaven) shall I know even as also I am known.' Therefore, while you use all diligence, accompanied with prayer and the expositions of God's faithful ministers, to understand every part of divine revelation, be neither surprised nor disheartened at the want of comprehension, far less attempt to reduce it to human reason, as many have done to their ruin. The Scripture says, ' Vain man would be wise, though born like the wild ass's colt.' ' The wisdom of this world is foolishness with God.'

I. GRAHAM."

Again we have the following merited strictures by one taught from above, on a passage in Pope's Essay on Man.

" 1798.

"' *Glows in the stars and blossoms in the trees.*'

" There the poet must stop: thus far the natural mind, richly endowed with human powers, can go and trace a God of power, wisdom, and beneficence: O that thou hadst had eyes to see, and discern what flesh and blood could never reach; that all these glories dwindle

into tapers, when compared with Jehovah manifested in
the face of Jesus Christ. Every star, every tree, all
vegetating, bursting, blooming life, answer the end of
their creation, manifesting his glory as thou sayest;
but can they tell thee how this God can be just, and
yet justify those who have rebelled against all his attributes; torturing even his fair and beautiful creation,
and bringing it into subjection to their lusts, as thou
hast well sung: murmuring at, and rebelling against
his dispensations in providence; hardening themselves
against his government; perverting every good to their
own misery, and imbibing wretchedness from means of
blessedness: can all that thou hast sung bring into con-
geniality perfection of wickedness and perfection of
holiness, perfection of wretchedness and perfection of
happiness, perfect opposition in nature and principle!
Here thy song stops short. Thou seest the evils and
the misery; thou hast a glimpse of an opposite good,
but all means proposed by thee, ever have proved, and
ever will prove inadequate to the attainment of it : the
very attributes of a just and holy God oppose it:
heaven and earth must stand amazed at the declaration
that God would justify the ungodly !"

In the month of September, 1798, Mrs. Graham's
daughter Isabella was married to Mr. Andrew Smith,
merchant, then of New-York. Her family being thus
settled to her satisfaction, and her health not good, she
was prevailed upon to retire from her school, and to
live with her children.

During the prevalence of the yellow fever in 1798, it
was with much difficulty Mrs. Graham was dissuaded

from going into the city to attend on the sick: the fear of involving her children in the same calamity, in the event of her being attacked by the fever, was the chief reason of her acquiescing in their wish to prevent so hazardous an undertaking. During the subsequent winter she was indefatigable in her attentions to the poor: she exerted herself to procure work for her widows, and occupied much of her time in cutting it out and preparing it for them. The managers of the Widows' Society had each a separate district; and Mrs. Graham, as first Directress, had a general superintendence of the whole. She was so happy in the execution of her trust, as to acquire the respect and confidence of the ladies who acted with her, as well as the affections of the poor.

Her whole time was now at her command, and she devoted it very faithfully to promote the benevolent object of the institution over which she presided. The extent of her exertions, however, became known, not from the information given by herself, but from the observations of her fellow-laborers, and especially from the testimony of the poor themselves. When she had been absent for some weeks, on a visit to her friends in Boston, in the summer of 1800, her daughter, Mrs. B——, was surprised at the frequent inquiries made after her by persons with whom she was unacquainted: at length she asked some of those inquirers what they knew about Mrs. Graham? They replied, " We live in the suburbs of the city, where she used to visit, relieve and comfort the poor. We had missed her so long that we were afraid she had been sick; when she walked in our streets, it was customary with us to come to the door and receive her blessing as she passed."

We next find letters to her female friend near Boston, who was still in much spiritual darkness and despondency.

To Mrs. C——, near Boston.

" March, 1799.

" MY EVER DEAR FRIEND,—I have just read your letter, painful to you to write, but to me as the mother's anguish which precedes her joy. The day will soon break, and the shadows flee away; and the dear Savior, whom you seek, will again comfort his returning prodigal.

" I will do what you desire me, and though I have the highest opinion of our young Timothy J. M., I will pass by him in this case, and lay it before one of the aged christians, Dr. R——rs or Dr. L——n ; at the same time, my friend, I am as sure of their answer as if I were already in possession of it. Who told my friend that she was blind, and miserable, and wretched, and naked ? Flesh and blood never yet taught proud man or woman this lesson.

" My dear friend, there is nothing new nor strange in all you have told me : there is scarce a heaven-taught soul, who has made any advances in the spiritual warfare, but could sympathize with you from experience. What have you experienced more than the Scriptures tell us ? that ' the heart is deceitful above all things, and desperately wicked.' Only the Lord can search it, only he can cleanse it. He takes the prerogative to himself, and he calls it his Covenant that he will make with sinners in Gospel times. You may strive and fight, and resolve and vow—all will not do: you lie at his mercy for holiness as well as pardon. He is exalted

as a Prince to give repentance, and he is the Author and
Finisher of faith. He works all our works in us, and
without him we are not equal to one good thought.
We are his workmanship, 'created anew in Christ
Jesus.' My dear friend, put the work into his hand,
and try to wait on him in hope—hope in every situation ; do more, *trust*.

"You entirely mistake the situation of others ; none
of us have our heaven here : no, sin dwelleth in us;
the very best have their ups and downs. Do you think
your friend is always on the mount ? very far from
it. I am at times so cold, so dead, so stupid, that I can
neither pray, read, nor hear. I have begun the same
chapter over and over, still trying to fix my thoughts,
and as often they wander on every trifle ; but my peace
lies where you will soon learn to place yours, in the
merits of my almighty Savior. My safety depends not on
my frames, but his promise : and when tossed and tempted, dead and lifeless, emptied of every good, perhaps
buffeted like you with abominable thoughts, the fiery
darts of Satan,—casting all on Him, I am safe as when
basking in the sunshine of his love, and tasting what
you have tasted : for you have tasted, and you shall yet
taste the joys of his salvation. I too have proved false
to his covenant, have gone off with the world, and been
intoxicated with its vanities and empty delights, and
have laid up for myself seasons of deep remorse; my
sins have often separated between my God and me, especially in my younger days; the Lord calls to watchfulness and diligence in the use of means, and he generally honors these means, of his own appointing, with
his blessing. When we either trust to these means,

and fancy merit in them, or neglect to use them as his appointment, he generally makes us feel our error, but he does not cast us out of his family; he chastens us, and restores us.

I write hastily, just to say that you have my sympathy and my love; for well I know, the almighty Lord alone can loose your bonds, and give you 'joy and peace in believing.' All my advice may be summed up in this—trust in the Lord with all your heart; at least aim at this; I say aim at it, for this too must be given you. Roll yourself, your doubts, your fears, your sins, your duties, all on him: say, 'Lord, I believe, help my unbelief.' He is an almighty Savior to deliver sinners from sin as well as from punishment. I leave you on the Father of mercies, and will, when the Lord enables, pray for you.   Yours, &c."

To the Same.

"At last, my dear friend, the Lord appears; appears the bible God—' the Lord God, merciful and gracious, long-suffering, abundant in goodness and truth, keeping mercy for thousands, forgiving iniquity, transgression and sin.'

"When was it that the Lord proclaimed this, and took unto himself this name? After Israel, his chosen, had been guilty of that awful sin in the wilderness, of making the golden calf, and proclaiming 'These be thy gods, O Israel;' David takes it up in the 103d Psalm, ' The Lord is merciful and gracious, slow to anger and plenteous in mercy.'—Read on, my dear, then turn to the 130th. This God is your God, and has long been your

God; his work was upon your heart, though y. u could not discern it. In bondage you have long been, but not a willing captive; unbelief kept you in bondage, long, long after your eyes were opened to see your bondage; and even to discern, in some feeble measure, your remedy.

"The Lord has wise reasons for all you have suffered: if not now, you shall in some after-time ' know and consider all the way by which he has led you, to prove you, to try you, and show you what was in your heart, that he might do you good in your latter end.' You did not wait patiently for the Lord your God; you did not in general say, ' Though he slay me, I will trust in him;'—No, my friend has been a great unbeliever, yet hath the Lord, the sovereign Lord, ' whose ways are not as our ways, nor his thoughts as our thoughts,' brought you out of ' a fearful pit, and out of the miry clay; set your feet upon a rock, and established your goings; put a new song into your mouth, even praise unto our God.' Now you sing the 34th Psalm. I do rejoice with my friend; I bless the Lord with her; let us exalt his name together. It is establishing to my own soul. I have long prayed, and long looked for this: I lived in the faith of it, assured that He who had begun the good work, would perfect it in his own time.

"I cannot but regret your want of pastoral food; yet ought I to regret any thing? The Lord himself is your Shepherd. My Bible lies on my lap, and I had turned to the 34th Psalm to know if it contained what I would point out to you; on finishing the last verse, I unconsciously turned my eye on the Bible; the words that met it were, Psalm 32:8, 'I will instruct thee, and teach thee in the way that thou shalt go: I will guide thee with mine eye.' And so it shall be. Amen, my God, Amen. Do as thou hast said.

"Perhaps, my friend, by this time your notes are lowered. It has pleased the Lord to give you a strange sight: Mary Magdalene, a great sinner at the feet of Jesus, pardoned, comforted, and highly honored in after-life.

"This history, accompanied by the Spirit of God, has consoled, strengthened and raised up many bowed-down since that day, many now around the throne, who sing of pardoning love.

"I now wish to say, hold fast the beginning of your confidence. Your experience is that of God's people To rejoice in the Lord at all times is your privilege, but will not be always your attainment. The Lord has done great things for you, whereof I am glad: but, my dear friend, the warfare is not over: you must endure trials as others; engage with ' principalities and powers, and spiritual wickedness in high places,' and, worst of all, a treacherous heart within; which, for all that it has seen and tasted, is yet corrupt and deceitful: the new life which Christ gives to the soul, evidences itself in the desires of the heart and affections. As certainly as the new-born babe desires the breast, as certainly and as evidently does the new-born soul desire union to God, communion with him, and conformity to him in heart, life and conversation. This principle is in its own nature perfectly pure, but the old nature, the law in the spiritual members, is as perfectly corrupt; ' in my flesh dwelleth no good thing.'

"In the order of God's covenant it has not pleased him to deliver even believers, all at once, from sinful inclinations and passions; he has provided for their final complete deliverance, and sin shall not have dominion over them even here; but it is still in them while in the body, and a dying body; and the remains of sin in the soul make the believer's life a warfare, and this world a wilderness; soul and body are diseased; both are redeemed, and provision made for the entire deliverance of both—for the soul at death, for the body at the resurrection; but while in the body, 1 John, 1 : 8, 'If any man say he has no sin, he deceiveth himself and the truth is not in him.' Look at Paul's experience—what does he say of the believer's state? He calls it a warfare, a fight, a captivity for a time: see 1 Timothy, 6 : 12; 1 Corinthians, 9 : 26.

"I write not thus to dishearten you, but as a friend I warn you, lest you fall again into unbelief. Look not within for comfort, for consolation, for confidence. Christ is the end of the law for righteousness, his blood the atonement, and you are complete in him, his grace is sufficient for you, his strength shall be perfected in your weakness, and you shall go on. Grieve for sin you will, grieve you ought; but keep ever in your remembrance 1 John 2 : 1 and 5 : 11.　　Yours, &c."

To the Same.

"January 14, 1800.

"My dear friend says, 'O that I could have the society of some aged, pious clergyman or christian, who had gone through his warfare.' O that you could, in the Lord's hand! I hope it might do you good; yet, after all, the Lord himself must loose your bonds; ay, and he will, and also appoint the means.

"There are two kinds of rest awaiting you, the one in this life, the other will not be attained till the mortal shall put on immortality. When was it that Paul, the great apostle, could say he had fought the good fight? Not till he could also say he had finished his course, and was ready to be offered up; till then, he, like others, had to continue the warfare between grace and corruption; like others, found a law in his members warring against the law of his mind, so that the thing that he would, he did not, and that which he would not, that he did. Notwithstanding this, there is a blessed rest attainable here, rest from the fear of wrath and hell; a rest in Christ as our atonement, our surety, our complete righteousness, our title to eternal life, and all the grace necessary to fit us for it. This is the work of faith, or rather this is faith itself. The soul established in this can rest in all possible circumstances; it depends not on its frames; in darkness, when it is tossed, tempted, wandering, conscious of unhallowed tempers, perhaps of the actual commission of sin, though at such times the warfare between grace and corruption is so strong as to make the christian exclaim, 'O wretched man that I am! who shall deliver me from this body of sin and death?' he can still say, 'The Lord lives, blessed be my Rock;' see the 42d and 43d Psalms. The christian can still say, my Lord and my God; he is sure the conflict will end, and that his God will bring good out of it; he enjoys hope; he feels his state as safe as in the most enlarged frame of mind, when he can pray, praise, love, rejoice. This is a riddle which only christians can understand, and even they require many lessons to comprehend it, many more to practise.

"Have you Newton's letters? See his 2d letter in Cardiphonia. O try to fix your anchor of hope on that sure foundation which God has laid in Zion—Christ himself. Trust him to save you from every evil without you and within you. When your own weakness sinks you, try to be strong in his strength: when guilt disturbs, wash in the open Fountain. But hold fast the beginning of your confidence unto the end.

"Be comforted, fight on, aim at trusting, and you shall, in the Lord's time, also cease from your own works, and rest, with more advanced christians, on the faithfulness of your own God in Christ. See Hebrews, 4 : 9, also chap. 12 throughout. I finish with chap. 13 : 20, 21; my earnest prayer and sure hope for you, my precious friend!   Yours, &c."

Writing to her brother Dr. Marshall, she alludes to the prevalent neglect of the voice of God in his judgments, and notices the death of Washington.

"NEW-YORK, March 3, 1800.

"Here comes a letter of wo from my dear brother, on a subject almost already forgotten in New-York, the yellow fever. Strange as it may seem, the disease, and all that it carried off, seem entirely out of mind. No mention made of the past, no apprehensions for the future. Country retreats are multiplying around, and people appear as if they had made a covenant with death. Potter's Field is filled with our principal citizens; the prison and prison limits with many of the survivors. The rest are *feasting, dancing,* and *revelling* or weeping over feigned wo in the theatre—a few excepted, who have fled for refuge to the hope set before them, whose eyes have been opened to discern the danger and accept the offered Savior: among which number, I dare, through grace, reckon your sister and her children. ' Bless the Lord, O my soul, and forget not all his benefits.'

" The city (indeed the United States) have been swallowed up in the loss of WASHINGTON. The utmost stretch of human eloquence has been called forth in panegyric. His eulogium has been sounded in every possible mode—not excepting our pulpits. The 22d of February, his birth-day, was set apart to his memory. Two of our ministers were appointed to pronounce an eulogium on his character: one of whom was Dr. Mason, the other Dr. Linn. The last I admired; it had its due influence over me; but of my own minister I could form no judgment; the church, the pulpit, the man, the words, seemed so connected with the 'Lord Jesus Christ,' his favorite theme, I could not realize the *mere* orator.

" Great things were said of Washington, and they were due.

" The Lord himself called him by name, girded him, subdued great armies before him, with handfuls, like Gideon. He gave him wisdom in counsel, and prudence in executing justice. A nation blessed him while he lived, and with all the power of language lamented his death. Ah, human depravity! how striking! Bursting with gratitude to a creature—with enmity to a Savior God; to God, who ' so loved the world, that he gave his only begotten Son, that whosoever believeth on him should not perish, but have everlasting life; and to as many as receive him gives power to become the sons of God,' by putting his Spirit within them, and causing them to love and walk in his statutes. But, alas! the carnal unrenewed mind is enmity against God and his Christ. O that men were wise, and could see their disease, and the remedy!

"What misery is in the world at this day! It is only equalled by the wickedness. How does potsherd dash against potsherd, mutually destroying each other! How consoling to the christian ' that the Lord reigns! The Lord sits King among the nations,' even our own Jesus, ' Head over all principalities and powers, and dominions, and every name that is named in heaven and in earth:' all these shakings, turnings, and overturnings, shall prove subservient to the real prosperity of his church."

"1800.

"I have entered into my closet; I have shut my door; I would pray to my Father who is in secret; I would be shut up with my indwelling God: but see the crowds that follow; see my treacherous heart that gives them admission; see my unsanctified imagination going off with them, leaving nothing before thee but a lifeless lump of clay. Help, Lord! Hast thou not redeemed me from vain imaginations? Lord, fill all thy temple: ' Cast out the buyers and sellers:' thyself prepare room for close, undisturbed, holy conference. Grant that, according to the riches of thy glory, I may be strengthened with might, by thy Spirit, in the inner man: dwell in my heart by faith, that ' rooted and grounded in love, I may be able to comprehend with all saints, what is the breadth, and length, and height, and depth, and to know the love of Christ, which passeth knowledge, and be filled with all the fulness of God.' Give unto thy redeemed servant the Spirit of wisdom and revelation. Reveal thyself more and more in my soul; enlighten the eyes of my understanding. Lord, improve, enlarge the powers of the new man. Spirit of the Father and of the Son, do thine office; 'take of the things of Christ and show them unto me;' that I may know what is the hope of his calling, and what the ' riches of the glory of his inheritance in the saints, and what is the exceeding greatness of his power to us-ward who believe, according to the working of his mighty power, which he wrought in Christ when he raised him from the dead, and set him at the Father's right hand, in the heavenly places, far above all principalities, and powers, and might, and dominion, and every name that is named, not only in this world, but also in that which is to come; and hath put all things under his feet, and given him to be the head over all things to the church, which is his body, the fulness of him that filleth all in all. Filled with all the fulness of God! the fulness of him who filleth all in all!' O what things are these! My soul stretches to comprehend, but, weak and feeble, cannot climb those glorious heights, nor dig into these, to me, unsearchable depths. I can only spell after the language of the Holy Ghost, lisp out his own words. I dare not trust my powers of comprehension to vary even the mode of expression.

" Well, it may be best for me; the valley of humility may be safest for me. 'Father, glorify thy name!' Thou hast quickened me; I am not what I was. Thou hast wrought in me a measure of faith and love; thou hast sealed me with the Holy Spirit of promise; thou hast

given me the earnest of my inheritance; the full possession shall come in thy appointed time. Wherefore I
will sing unto Him that is able, and will do exceeding
abundantly above all I can ask, think, or comprehend,
according to that same mighty power that worketh in
us. Unto him be glory in the church, by Christ Jesus,
throughout all ages, world without end. Amen.

"My covenant God, and the God of my house! Thy
Spirit saith, 'If any man lack wisdom, let him ask of
God.' Thou knowest the difficulty and danger of the
present case. We are ignorant of hidden motions and
principles; of Satan's suggestions; of corresponding or
discordant circumstances; of future providences and
events. Lord, give counsel.

"If information and advice be duty on the part of thy
servant, determine on the side of duty, be the danger
what it may; and O! search, try, and deliver from every
selfish or hidden impure motive. Give prudence in the
choice of words, in the time and manner as well as purity in the matter. Save from injuring any of the individuals concerned. And, O! prepare the heart of thy other
servant, to receive this office of friendship with a proper
degree of confidence. Save from unjust suspicions, that
it may be taken as meant in love, in Christian love and
friendship.

"O thou, who knowest all hearts, all motives, all circumstances past, present, and future! overrule for the
manifestation of truth; for the safety and good of thy
servant, and for the closer union of all concerned in
the bands of Christian love, confidence and affection;
and as our covenant God, in whom we trust for guidance in every path of duty, glorify thy name.

"I record this prayer in faith, and wait an answer of peace from thy inward teaching and manifestation in the course of thy providence. Amen."

"1800.

"Psalm 72 : 17. 'His name shall endure for ever: his name shall continue as long as the sun: and men shall be blessed in him; all nations shall call him blessed. Blessed be the Lord God, the God of Israel, who alone doeth wondrous things. And blessed be his glorious name for ever: and let the whole earth be filled with his glory ; Amen, and amen.'

"Again have I and my children been fed with Christ's flesh and his blood at his own table. 'Glorious things are said of thee, thou city of our God ;' and rich the provision of the house of our God; wonderful the scheme that hath made sinful, guilty, rebel sinners the citizens of this holy city, inhabitants of this holy house. Mysterious truth! The city itself, the house of God; the temple of the Lord, in which he delighteth to dwell. Closer yet, more mysterious, yet equally true, ' his body, his flesh and his bones ;' closer still, one Spirit with him. As Mediator Emmanuel, he is the bond of union, whereby the guilty sons and daughters of Adam are made one with the Father, the Son and the Holy Ghost.

"Wonderfully and fearfully are we made as creatures; as a rational creature, who can understand and comprehend himself? How these members were fashioned? How this spark of vital flame was breathed into the lifeless lump or atom? Wonder-working Lord! thou only knowest. Wonderful are all the works of creation ; but O, what are they to thy work of Redemption! To bring worlds out of nothing, to bring light

out of darkness was thy easy work; but to bring good
out of evil, this, this was the wonder! Thousands and
ten thousands of worlds were, and may yet be created
without cost! God says, Let it *be*, and it is; but Redemption! O, who can tell the cost! Blessed Jesus!
God manifested in the flesh! Christ! Babe of Bethle-
hem! Man of sorrows! Victim on the cross! thou only
canst tell—'Blessed be the Lord God of Israel, who
alone doeth wondrous things, and blessed be his glorious name for ever!' Whatever the cost, *it is finished.*
He bowed his head and said, *It is finished!* This finished work is the new testament, which he bequeathed
to his disciples 'the same night in which he was betrayed,' when 'he took bread, blessed it, brake it, gave
it to his disciples, and said, Take, eat, this is my body
broken for you; and took the cup, and gave thanks, and
gave it to them, saying, Drink ye all of it; for this is
the new testament in my blood, which is shed for many, for the remission of sins.'

"The New Testament! O, who can tell the blessings
and benefits contained in this testament, this dying legacy of our dear Emmanuel, purchased and sealed with
his blood! What is the amount of it? What the sum of
blessings contained in it? Behold, God is become our
salvation. This is the amount. God himself, God in
Christ reconciling us unto himself: by his mighty power subduing the enmity that is in us; melting our flin-
ty hearts; drawing us with the cords of love; creating
us anew after his own image, which we had totally
lost; uniting us to himself, even *us*, who were enmity
itself, but now are become one with God, who is love.

This is the work we have this day been celebrating: a given, a born, a living, a suffering, dying, risen, ascended, glorified, reigning Savior! The Lord of Hosts, the King of kings, the Almighty God dwelling with men, dwelling in men, and feeding them with his own body and blood. 'Behold, God is become our salvation, we will trust and not be afraid, for the Lord Jehovah is our strength and our song; he also is become our salvation, therefore with joy will we draw water out of the wells of salvation.' His attributes are the never-failing source; his ordinances the wells of salvation. God himself is ours, all that he is is ours, to bless and to make us happy. Ten thousand springs issue from this blessed source, specified and particularized in his Bible, experienced and celebrated by his saints. Let us drink and be refreshed, rejoice and praise: for O! who can tell the amount of our riches, in having God for our portion! All things are ours, we are Christ's, and Christ is God's."

The Widows' Society met monthly, when the money in the treasury was divided among the managers, for the relief of the widows under their care. Mrs. Graham as directress thus acknowledges God and asks his counsel:

" 1800.

"O my God, I account it an honorable office thou hast given me. I have received it from thee. Enable me to execute it to thee.

"Father of the fatherless, Husband of the widow! make me a fit instrument in thy hand of distributing thy bounty. Give discernment and judgment, tenderness,

g:ntleness, humility and love; let love to thee be the
principle of my every action; lead me in the straight
path of duty; on the matter, the manner, the time, let
·' Holiness to the Lord' be written. I thank thee for this
sum towards the relief of thy creatures; be with us this
evening, and direct our determination as to the division
of it. Amen."

CHAPTER VII.

BENEVOLENT LABORS—MRS. HOFFMAN—CORRESPONDENCE.

The "Society for the relief of Poor Widows with
small children," having received a charter of incorporation, and some pecuniary aid from the Legislature of
the State, the ladies who constituted the Board of Direction were engaged in plans for extending their usefulness: Mrs. Graham took an active part in executing
these plans. The Society purchased a small house,
where they received work of various kinds for the *employment* of their widows. They opened *a school* for
the instruction of their orphans, and many of Mrs. Graham's former pupils volunteered their services, taking
upon themselves, by rotation, the part of instructers.
Besides establishing this school, Mrs. Graham selected
some of the widows best qualified for the task, and engaged them, for a small compensation, to open *day
schools* for the instruction of the children of widows *in
distant parts of the city:* she also established *two Sabbath
schools*, one of which she superintended herself, and the

other she placed under the care of her daughter. Where-
ever she met with christians sick and in poverty, she
visited and comforted them; and in some instances opened small subscription lists to provide for their support.

She attended occasionally for some years at the *Alms
House*, for the instruction of the children there in religious knowledge: in this work she was much assisted
by a humble and pious female friend, who was seldom
absent from it on the Lord's day. In short, her whole
time was occupied in searching out the distresses of
the poor, and devising measures to comfort and establish them to the extent of her influence and means. At
the same time, far from arrogating any merit to herself, she seemed always to feel how much she was de-
ficient in following fully the precepts and the footsteps
of her beloved Lord and Savior, "who went about doing
good."

It was often her custom to leave home after breakfast, taking with her a few rolls of bread, and return in
the evening about eight o'clock. Her only dinner on
such days was her bread, and perhaps some soup at the
Soup House established by the Humane Society for the
poor, over which one of her widows had been, at her
recommendation, appointed. She and her venerable
companion Mrs. SARAH HOFFMAN, second Directress of
the Widows' Society, travelled many a day and many a
step together in the walks of charity. Mrs. Graham
was a Presbyterian, Mrs. Hoffman an Episcopalian.
Those barriers, of which such an unhappy use has been
made by sectarians to separate the children of God, fell
down between these two friends at the cry of affliction,
and were consumed on the altar of christian love.

Arm in arm, and heart to heart, they visited the abodes of distress, dispensing temporal aid from the purse of charity, and spiritual comfort from the Word of Life.

At each annual meeting Mrs. Graham usually gave an address to the Society, with a report of the proceedings of the managers through the preceding year.

In April, 1800, she stated that "again the pestilence had emptied the city; again every source of industry was dried up; even the streams of benevolence from the country failed. Those store-houses, from which relief was issued to thousands in former calamities, now disappointed their hopes; and those spared by the pestilence were ready to perish by the famine. Such widows as had no friends in the country under whose roof they might for a time seek shelter, were shut up to the only relief within their power, even to *that Society* which had formerly saved them in many a strait. They came, were received with tenderness, assisted with food, advice and medicine.

"Four of the society's board, at the risk of their lives, remained in the city, steady in the exercise of their office. *One hundred and forty-two widows, with four hundred and six children*, under twelve years of age, by far the greater part under six, have, from time to time, during the winter, been visited and relieved. *Widow* is a word of sorrow in the best of circumstances; but a widow left poor, destitute, friendless, surrounded with a number of small children, shivering with cold, pale with want, looking in her face with eyes pleading for bread which she has not to give, nor any probable prospect of procuring;—her situation is neither to be described nor conceived. Many such scenes were witnessed during the last winter; and though none could restore the *father* and the *husband*, the hearts of the mourners were soothed by the managers, whilst they dispensed the relief provided for them by their *Father* and their *Husband*, GOD."

In the summer of 1800 Mrs. Graham again visited her friends in Boston, whence she wrote her daughter Mrs. B—— as follows:

"BOSTON, August, 1800.

"I yesterday received my dear J——'s letter, which gives fresh cause for thankfulness. The more my absence is lengthened, the less I am able to support the want of intelligence. Let us bless God together for all his mercies; among those which are temporal, health is the chief; and I believe to most mothers it is more valued in their children than in their own persons. I rejoice with you over our restored J—y. O that our covenant God may give the more important blessing of divine life! You had need to be importunate for this, after the importunity exercised for natural life. I thank God also for the alleviation of your own distress, for our dear D—'s restoration from complaints, less alarming so far as they existed, but which might have been the seeds of serious affliction.

"I could go on enumerating, for causes of thankfulness crowd into my mind; but all are swallowed up in the grand mercy, the distinguishing mercy of redeeming love to our souls. Salvation, not only to me, but to my house! Oh! all words fail here. Read over with me, sing with me, in your heart, the 103d Psalm. O my

God, dare I even sigh in thy presence, under any temporal pain, or hurt of body or mind, with such a Father, such a Christ, such a Comforter, such a richly-furnished well-ordered covenant, such a constitution of grace and providence; O such an *All in all*, even ' all the fulness of God!' My God and the God of my seed, the God of my house; yea, and the God of my prodigal, who shall in heaven, if never on earth, join the song, ' To him that loved us, and washed us from our sins in his own blood, be glory, honor, dominion, power, and praise, for ever and ever. Amen.' O shall a murmur ever pass these lips, shall this unthankful heart indulge even a sigh over any object but sin; shall I shrink from any cross with such a crown? Father, glorify thy name.

"I have been to church; the subject, 'Be not weary in well doing.' Many arguments were adduced for exertion; but the Gospel was wanting. O that my friends could hear our shepherd; he would sound his Master's voice more in unison with their own hearts' experience and views of new covenant provision and gospel motives: except in the Baptist congregations, the Gospel is much mutilated here, and kept out of sight even by the few who are supposed to build upon it.

"Sabbath next brings round your—I will add, my Gospel feast. I will endeavor to meet you to-morrow evening, and to have you all on my heart, then and on the Sabbath, in that one Lord, one faith, one Spirit, one God and Father of all, who is above all, through all, and in all redeemed to himself by Jesus Christ, and sanctified by that one Spirit uniting all. What subjects! I cannot attain to the comprehension, but I experience their truth, and enjoy the comfort of them."

The two following letters, addressed to a young lady whose acquaintance Mrs. Graham made while at Boston, show how tenderly she sympathized with the feelings of the young, and how earnestly she sought their good.

To Miss M——, Boston.

"September 11, 1800.

"There was, my dear Miss M—, something in your countenance and manner, at our last interview, which has dwelt on my mind ever since. Your former attentions, which I also marked, I attributed to the natural benevolence of your heart; but your following a stranger, an old woman, of whom you know so little, and whom you were likely never to see again—to solicit her friendship and an interest in her prayers, spoke a language beyond nature. Either my sweet friend has already chosen God in Christ to be her portion, and his love in her heart powerfully draws her to every one in whom she thinks she discerns his image; or she conceives that this world cannot give her happiness, even in this life; and impressed with the importance of that which is to come, she wishes to cast in her lot among God's people, that she may 'know the good of his chosen, and rejoice in their joy,' and become a partaker of that peace which the Savior bequeathed to his disciples when about to leave them: 'Peace I leave with you. My peace I give unto you; not as the world giveth, give I unto you; let not your heart be troubled, neither let it be afraid.'

"Let me congratulate my friend, which ever of these be the case. If the first, you have (or will soon have) a peace which the world can neither give nor take away; if the last, the Savior stands at the door of your heart and knocks, soliciting that heart which has too long been hunting shadows and vanity. If your soul is dissatisfied with the things of the world, and tired with disappointment, cast a longing eye to the Fountain of happiness. This is the claim of that God whose name is love, 'My son, give me thy heart.' 'Come unto me, all ye that labor and are heavy laden, and I will give you rest.' 'In the world ye shall have tribulation, but in me ye shall have peace.' Be assured, my dear friend, if you could obtain all of this world that your heart could wish for, you would find vanity written on the possession. Nothing short of God himself can give happiness to the soul; and exactly in proportion as man becomes weaned from the world, and his affections centre in God, is he in possession of happiness.

"But how is this to be attained? By God's own plan, and no other. As many weary themselves in vain, hunting the shadows of time; so many great philosophers, sensible of this great truth, that God alone can satisfy the rational soul, also weary themselves in vain, because they will not seek the blessing in God's own way. 'When the world, by wisdom, knew not God, it pleased him, by the foolishness of preaching (what was esteemed so) to save them that believe.' 'I thank thee, O Father, that thou hast hid these things from the wise and prudent, and hast revealed them unto babes.'

"The Savior said, 'Ye will not come to me, that ye might have life. No man can come to the Father but by me. I am the Way, the Truth and the Life.' 'Search the Scriptures, for in them ye think ye have eternal life, and they are they which testify of me.' The Scripture testifies what our own hearts must assent to, that human nature is depraved and corrupt; broken off from God; at a distance from him by sin; enmity against him in his *true* character popposed to his holy law, in its *extent* and *spirituality:* we are also helpless, dead in trespasses and sins. 'O Israel, thou hast destroyed thyself,' (blessed be God for what follows) 'but in me is thy help.'

"The same Scripture which testifies the misery of man, reveals also his remedy; a remedy of God's own providing, by which man may be restored to the image and favor of God, and to that communion with him which is life and bliss. 'God so loved the world, that he gave his only begotten Son, that whosoever believeth on him might not perish, but have everlasting life: for God sent not his Son into the world to condemn the world, but that the world, through him, might be saved. And this is life eternal, that ye believe on him whom he hath sent.' When man becomes convinced that he is lost, helpless, wretched, lying at mercy, and submits to the method of God's own providing; casts himself on the mercy of God in Christ, and, coming to him, rests on his free promise, 'Him that cometh to me, I will in no wise cast out;' disclaiming all confidence in himself, or in his own works, he accepts of God's offered Grace, in God's own way, a FREE and FINISHED salvation. This is the record of God, that he giveth unto us eternal life, and this life is in his Son: who, of God, is made unto us wisdom, and righteousness, and sanctification, and complete redemption. Believing this, according to his faith it shall be. Christ shall be in him, 'a well of water springing up to eternal life.' He will shed abroad his love in his heart, and, according to his promise, give him ' power to become a child of God.' The Holy Ghost, the Comforter, shall be given unto him, to teach him the knowledge of the Scriptures, and to become a principle of holiness in his heart. Then shall he find that wisdom's ways are ways of pleasant ness, and all her paths peace; then shall he experience the blessedness of ' that man whose God is the Lord;' then is the way open for communion and converse with God the Father, Son, and Holy Ghost.

"If, my dear Miss M—, I have made myself understood, you have my view of God's method of making his creatures happy; and I believe he will make us to know that he is a sovereign God, and that there is no other name, or method, by which men can be saved, but the name of Christ Jesus. But, take nothing on my word, nor the word of any creature; search the Scriptures; read the first eight chapters of the Romans, the whole of the Ephesians; stumble not at mysteries— pass them over, and take the milk for babes; pray for the teaching of the Spirit; and let me recommend to you the advice of Mr. Newton, in his Omicron's Letters, a book well worth your reading. ' Lay not too much stress on detached texts, but seek for the sense which is most agreeable to the general strain of Scripture.'

"My dear Miss M—, I am now old, and I hope have done with the world; but I have been young and drunk deeply of youth's choicest pleasures. I was blest with the best and most indulgent of parents; I was the wife of a man of sense, sentiment, and sensibility, who was my very first love and lover; and that love ripened and improved with years. My children were good and healthy; love, health, peace and competency blessed our dwelling. I had also, in early life, taken hold of God's covenant, and tasted his covenant love; and devoted myself to his service, which was in my mind a principle of moderation, compared with mere world lings; but very far was I from that non-conformity to the world which the precept of the Gospel requires. Had I kept close to my covenant God, enjoyed his bounty with thankfulness, occupied my talents, devoted my time to usefulness and communion with him; had I prayed against corruption within and temptation without, the Lord would have directed my steps and held up my goings, and I should have continued to inherit the earth, and should not have been diminished. But this was very far from being my conduct; the bent of the natural, unrenewed heart, is still opposed to God; and the best are sanctified only in part, while in this life; the law in the members still wars against the law of the Spirit of life in the mind. The goodness of God, which ought to have been a powerful motive to gratitude, love and diligence, was misimproved; I enjoyed the gifts, and forgot the Giver; 'hugged my comforts to death.' Many, many light chastisements, my dear, my kind, my indulgent heavenly Father exercised me with; I had many repenting seasons under his strokes; many manifestations of pardon I received; and many fresh and solemn dedications of my heart, life, and substance did I make; but no sooner was ease and comfort restored, than my heart *turned aside like a deceitful bow;* my whole life, from fifteen till the thirtieth year of my age, was one continued succession of departure and backsliding on my part; of chastening, forgiving, restoring, and comforting on the part of my God.

"He did not cast me off, but dealt with me according to the constitution of his well-ordered covenant—Psalm 89:30. 'If his children (Christ's) forsake my law and walk not in my judgments, if they break my statutes and keep not my commandments, then will I visit their transgression with the rod, and their iniquity with stripes. Nevertheless, my loving-kindness will I not utterly take from him, nor suffer my faithfulness to fail; my covenant will I not break, nor alter the thing that is gone out of my lips.' This is the Covenant (made with Christ as the head of all who believe) of which I took hold in early life; my God kept me to my choice, and manifested his own faithfulness and the stability of his covenant. When lighter afflictions proved ineffectual, he at last, at one blow, took from me all that made life dear, the very kernel of all my earthly joys, my idol, my beloved husband. Then I no longer halted between two opinions; my God became my all. I leave it as my testimony, that he has been a father to the fatherless, a husband to the widow, the stranger's shield and orphan's stay. Even to hoar hairs and to old age he has carried me, and *not one good word has failed* of all that he has promised. 'He has done all things well,' and at this day I am richer and happier than ever I was in my life. Not that I am yet made free from sin, that is still my burden; want of love and gratitude, indolence in commanded duty, self-will and nestling in the creature. But my heart's wish and earnest desire is conformity to the divine will. The bent of my will is for God; and if my heart deceive me not, my God is the centre of my best affections. It is by grace that I am what I am, and the same grace engages to perfect the work begun.

"This God is my God; he will guide me even unto death, through death, and be my portion to eternity. This God I recommend to my friend; and this well-ordered covenant, this all-sufficient Savior, for your acceptance; the Bible for your guide; pray to God for his Holy Spirit to lead you to the knowledge of the very truth as it is in Jesus. Accept this as a testimony of friendship, and believe me yours in love,

"I. GRAHAM."

To the same.

"November 2d, 1800.

"You have, I find, been the child of affliction: she is a stern, rugged nurse; but blessed often are the lessons she teaches. I have, (says God,) chosen thee in the furnace of affliction. It is God's ordinary way of drawing sinners to himself, either to dry up or embitter the streams of worldly comfort, that he may shut them up to seek that comfort that depends not on any transitory source.

"I have no doubt but you shall yet sing with the royal Psalmist, 'It is good for me that I have been afflicted; for before I was afflicted I went astray, but now I have kept thy word. Blessed is the man thou chastenest, Lord, and makest to learn thy ways.' Many are the texts to the same purport; take them for your consolation as a part of God's well-ordered covenant.

"You have met with a late bereavement, which has entered deep into your soul. We are not called to stoicism, but to tenderness of heart and spirit. Jesus wept with the two sisters over a brother's grave. But still the christian's spirit must be resigned, and say, and try to say with cheerfulness, 'not my will, but thine be

5*

done.' And, O my friend, great will be the wisdom and happy the acquisition, if every new bereavement enlarge the room for divine love in the heart, and be filled up with that most noble, most blessed of principles. Seek not, my friend, to replace friendship with any mere worldling; beg of God to fill up the vacuum, then will you be a great gainer.

"Why hesitate to join the church? Let not a sense of unworthiness keep you back—a deep sense of unworthiness is one grand part of due preparation; and no worthiness of yours can give you any title to that 'New Testament in Christ's blood, which was shed for the remission of sins.' Worthless, vile, empty, helpless is every son and daughter of Adam's race: but it was for the ungodly that Christ died; it was while we were without strength; his name was called Jesus, because he should save his people from their sins. In that day, that great day of the feast, Jesus stood among a mixed multitude, and cried, 'If any man thirst, let him come to me and drink—whosoever will, let him come and take the water of life freely.'

"If conscious at the time it is the supreme desire of your soul to be washed in his blood, clothed with his righteousness, sanctified by his Spirit,—go—and take this water of life freely; go as a *sinner* to a *Savior;* go at his command, put honor on his appointment, and repeat the dedication of all that you *are, have,* or *can* have, over the symbols of his 'body broken for you,' his 'blood shed for you;' go, trusting in his mercy, and leave all to his management, believing that *he will* shed abroad his love in your heart, order your footsteps in his ways, and in due time perfect his image in your soul. Keep close to him in the use of means, but look beyond the means for life and power. I commit you to our God and Savior, and· pray that he may be to you 'wisdom, righteousness, sanctification,' and 'complete redemption.'

" I am, my dear Miss M. your ever affectionate, I. G."

In March, 1801, the health of her daughter Mrs. B— requiring a sea-voyage and absence from care, Mr. and Mrs. B—— sailed for Britain, and the following letters were addressed to them during their absence:

" March 23, 1801.

" MY DEAR CHILDREN—This is mortifying to us all that you should be anchored half a mile from us, and there lie for hours—but even this, trifling as it may appear, has its end to answer in *His* scheme, without whom 'not a sparrow falls.' I have retired with my Bible, to commit you, and all my cares and concerns, afresh to that God whose goodness and mercy have followed us through life; who is my God, your God, and the God of our children; who answered my prayers in opposition to my inconsistent conduct; took you out of my idolatrous management into his own more merciful guidance. He has done all things well, and he will perfect his own work.

" Now, may ' the Angel that redeemed you, be with you, keep you in the hollow of his hand and as the apple of his eye;' be with you on his own ocean, and command the billows not to touch you; carry you to the bosom of your dear native country, where a large proportion of his body live in him and by him; bless you, and make you a blessing wherever his providence shall carry you, and restore you with blessings to us, in his own time. Amen."

"This, my dear children, is a day of storm, wind and rain; O that the prayer of our dear pastor, and I hope of many present, may be with you, and be answered to and for you—Lord, be with that family, who now, on the mighty ocean, desire an interest in our prayers. May he whom winds and waves obey, preserve them in this tempestuous season; may they see and improve his wonders in the great deep; may the blessings of the everlasting Gospel preserve their souls in peace, conduct them in safety to their destined port, and restore them to us, enriched with the blessings of thy well-ordered covenant.

"I sent two notes for the Dutch churches, enclosed to Mr. B.; one for Wall-street, to Mr. A., and one for the Brick church, to Mr. M. I watered all with my tears.

"Oh! how it blows and rains! O my children, how my poor heart aches for you; if not in danger, yet sick, and in much discomfort. I gave a note in the old church in the afternoon, supposing the congregation on this dreadful day to be different. Mr. M. prayed: 'The Angel of thy presence be with them; give them much of the consolations of thy Spirit. Conduct them in safety to the place of their destination, and restore them, enriched with thy blessing, to worship with us again in this thy house of prayer.' I write on this day merely to record, for your perusal, the prayers of your church. I think you ought, if the Lord conduct you

safe, to propose public thanks to that God who heard
and answered, if agreeable to Mr. M. Write me how it
was with you on this day. Now I will go to a throne of
grace for you and all of us. O keep close to the Lord;
may he save you from a dissipated, trifling, carnal
spirit; may he sanctify all your comforts, and give you
a just estimation of all you see and hear; may the
christian's portion rise more and more; and the world
and its vanities sink in your view."

"April 10.

"What the Lord is going to do with his and my children I know not; but the Samuel Elam has returned to
port with a leak, after being out nineteen days. On
the day of storm she had seven feet of water in her
hold. I hope the Lord, in mercy to you, to his church,
and to me his unworthy servant, has guided you in
safety, and that the prayers of his church were answered in your behalf. O! my children, what would be the
situation of my heart had I not confidence of your being within the ark. I desire to rejoice over all my
fears, for this unspeakable consolation, that nothing
can hurt you. I experience for you what I did in my
own case, when darkness and tempest added to the
horrors of many, while our vessel kept dashing on the
rock; I, too, expected her to go to pieces every moment; but the idea was ever with me, 'in the bosom of
God's ocean, I shall find the bosom of my Savior.'
On the night of the 29th of March I dreamt my dear
J—y fell over-board, and I saw her floating on the billows, supporting herself by her little chair; this is the
state of my mind; yet I am thankful, and enjoy much

peace. The Lord has given me what I have asked--
the salvation of your souls. In a little time we shall
all be gathered around his throne. Well may I leave
to him all intervening circumstances, as well as who
goes first, and how. O how he blesses my latter end,
how he sooths and comforts my old age; far other
things have I merited, that my soul knows; but he has
not only pardoned, but comforts, and draws a veil over
my transgressions, covering them from the world's observation. What can I say? He is God, a God of mercy."

                                        " April 17.

" I have brought the reality near me, that mine eyes
may never behold you again on earth. I can say, even
of that, *it is well;* but the idea of the horrors of tempest, a leaky vessel racked by the storm, and sinking
by inches; sickness, nervous timidity, and the sufferings to be undergone before the entrance to the haven
of rest be attained, is my chief disquietude, I will not
even say *distress,* because when these horrors (horrors
they are to mere nature) dart across my mind, filling
my soul with momentary anguish, Satan too seeking to
distract my mind, the Spirit of the Lord lifts up a standard against him, and comforts me with his own word,
the everlasting promises suited to every possible circumstance in the believer's lot. Thousands of times
have I grasped that promise, ' Leave thy fatherless children on me, I will preserve them alive.' I pleaded it for
the life of their souls; He answered my prayers; he
has given them life, and they live to him. Yes, I see
the fruit, and though iniquities still prevail against them,
he still purges away their transgressions; kindles their

repentance ; humbles their souls ; lays them prostrate in penitential confession ; washes them afresh in the open fountain ; restores to them the joys of his salvation ; seals their pardon by shedding abroad his love in their hearts, and making them ' walk in the path of righteousness for his own name's sake.'

" Thus he carries them on *from strength to strength* by various means of his own appointing, and some terrible things in righteousness, in the course of his providence ; in all which he is sovereign, but ever consistent with his new covenant name, as proclaimed to Moses on the Mount ; as manifested in the character of God dwelling with us in our own nature, in whom mercy shone prominent ; by which mercy ' they shall appear in Zion, before God,' in due time.

"Is it so ? Is this God my God, and the God of my seed ? Is he himself become our salvation ? Are we heirs of God and joint heirs with Christ ? Is our life hid with Christ in God ? When he appears, shall we (I and the children which he hath given me) in very deed appear with him in glory ? Is all this so ? and shall I tremble at the approach of any of his providences ? Shall I not say when it has taken place, ' The will of the Lord be done,' especially when clothed with love ? I trust that as my day, so shall my strength be, and in the interim I have the same confidence for you ; 'for he giveth power to the faint, and to them that have no might he increaseth strength.' "

" April 25.

" The wind roars and howls in my windows, though not facing the storm, and the white waves in the river picture in my mind the foaming billows of the ocean. The name of our God is my consolation : 'though the waters roar and be troubled, though the mountains shake with the swelling thereof, there is a river the streams whereof shall make glad the city of God. God shall help her, and that right early.' 'When I walk about Zion, and go round about her, when I tell the towers thereof, mark her bulwarks and consider her palaces,' my heart rejoices that 'this God is our God; he will be our guide even unto death ;' and O the joy that my children are the citizens of this Zion, and the heirs of all the promises by virtue of the new testament in Christ's blood! A covenant of works it was to our Surety, and his heart's blood finished the requisites of it. It is now a testament to you, sealed by the same blood. Wherever in his word I meet the character, the providence, the work of God, I read my own and my children's interest. I hope your experience shall be in Psalm 107 : 28. If not wholly, it shall terminate in Psalm 23 : 4. Though you 'walk through the valley of the shadow of death, you shall fear no evil,' for this God, who is your guide even unto death, shall be with you, 'his rod and staff shall comfort you ;' and our darling Jessy he shall carry as a lamb in his arms, and hide her from the horrors, in his bosom. I dwell much on these subjects, and I feel comforted, whatever be the event.

"If the Lord has carried you safe through, and you live to read this in the body, know that our God continues to bless us abundantly in health, peace and plenty, as to temporals; we also experience the peace of his covenant, and have tastes of the bread and of the

water of life. Thanks, all thanks to our new covenant
Head for the stability of the covenant; we change, but
he changeth not. He himself is the covenant given to
the people, and because he lives, his people shall live
also, in spite of Satan and his colleague Sin in our
hearts; sin may, and does bring his people into captivity, but it shall not keep them in bondage for ever. The
time of deliverance ' shall come, when they shall revive
as the corn.' Oh! is it not a well-ordered covenant, and
sure !"

Her next letter gives an illustration of fidelity in a
difficult and, it is to be feared, much neglected duty.

" May 10, 1801.

" MY DEAR CHILDREN,—Last evening was preparation
Sermon. Mr. Y—— preached a very excellent sermon
from the Song of Solomon, ' Who is this that cometh
up from the wilderness leaning on her beloved ?' First
the wilderness of this world, next the church coming up,
then the attitude leaning, and on whom; I thought the
simile well supported, and practical, as he went on. His
application was rich on the christian's support, where
he brought into view many of the names of Christ.

" After sermon we witnessed a most affecting scene;
two female members rebuked and restored to the communion of the church. Never, never did our dear Mr.
M—— shine so bright in my eyes; many tears were
shed. I knew nothing of it, and wondered to what he
was leading, when he addressed the congregation, after
sermon, upon christian walk, watchfulness, and temptation, and the distress occasioned in christian society,

when any of the members were left to fall into open
and aggravated sin. Such was the case in our own
congregation; two (naming the offenders) had been
so far left; but while deeply wounded by the sin and
scandal, he was consoled by their penitence: he assured
the congregation that they had given great evidence
of deep contrition; and were now come forward to acknowledge their crime before their offended and grieved brethren, and to give all the satisfaction in their
power, by submitting to the censure of the church in
this public manner, which, although painful to him,
he must pronounce according to God's appointment.
'Them who sin before all, rebuke before all.' He then
asked them to rise—scarce an individual turned to look;
many were weeping while he laid before them their
guilt in strong, yet tender terms; and finished by expressing his approbation of their thus submitting to
the rod, and exhorting them to humility and redoubled
watchfulness. Then again he addressed the members,
requesting them to receive into their christian love
and affection their repenting, returning sisters; that
they would treat them with tenderness, and restore
them in the spirit of meekness, considering themselves
as also in the body and subject to temptation. 'Let no
one put them in remembrance of the sin which the
Father of mercies has blotted out, nor open those
wounds which he has closed.' 'He doth not chide continually, nor retain his anger for ever.'

"May the Lord bless the discipline of his church;
may he meet us to-morrow with multiplied pardons;
may he melt our hearts to contrition, heal our backslidings, and manifest himself as married unto us; may

he bring us into his banqueting house and his banner over us be love; may his grace be magnified and his name glorified; and may he send a portion to my dear children—yea, a *Benjamin's portion;* may he open wide the leaves of that New Testament, and let them read their rich inheritance and rejoice in their portion.

"Farewell, my dear children. The Lord bless you, keep you, guide you, and cause his face to shine on you, prays your affectionate mother."

The following to the same, was written while on a visit to a worldly friend:

"May 21, 1801.

"I would fain begin to hope that my children are now on, or near the green fields of Albion. Many a severe gale has agitated them, and tried their faith and confidence before this day. But as He who sitteth on the clouds, commanding and governing the elements, is their own God in covenant, who loves them, careth for them, and perfects what concerns them, I hope they have had much of his presence: I hope they have found, even on the boisterous ocean, amidst the horrors of the swelling deep, agitated with winds and tempests, all things necessary to life and godliness in these great and precious promises, accompanied by divine power, by which they are made partakers of divine life, and escape the pollution that is in the world through lust. I hope they are enriched in experience, and advanced in the divine life, by all they have suffered, and all they have tasted of divine support in their sufferings; that Christ is still more precious, his word more tried, and

their confidence in him more established; if so, great
is their gain. And our darling J. being a sharer in the
suffering, shall, at her God's hand, be also a gainer,
though it be not evident to our perception. O how rich
is the Christian! how inexhaustible his portion! his
table is ever furnished, his cup ever full; all is blessing,
no curse mingled—*that* our Surety took to himself;
prosperity and adversity, sickness and health, light and
darkness, all, all shall bless us, work for our good, turn
to our profit, and end in the glory of God and our un
speakable, inconceivable happiness.

"I have been here a week yesterday; all vegetable
nature glows and shines in the perfection of beauty;
flowers, shrubs, trees, grain, grass, falling waters turning the busy mill, the brook murmuring on its way to
the ocean, fit emblem of eternity, all glorify their Creator; and although no such birds as in Britain charm
the listening ear, we have some sweet chirpers of his
praise; and what is wanting to the ear, is made up to
the eye, for in beauty they excel.

"These I may enjoy; with these hold communion;
for, Oh! spiritual death holds all within these walls in
dismal bondage; not one symptom of life appears, but
death, as the dry bones in the valley of vision. Why do
I not wrestle more for the Spirit to breathe on them? I
do pray: but Oh! formal! formal!"

To the Same.

"June 17, 1801.

"My dear Children—Difficult it is for me to exercise patience; the 23d of this month will make three
months since you waved the handkerchief on board the

Mars, off the Battery. I had made up my mind not to give way to expectation short of three months; they are nearly past; how many events take place in that space of time! how many duties ought to be performed! how many sins are really committed! how guilty to wish to annihilate the time that a certain event may come round! For every moment of time we must account, and not one moment of it can we recall. Much you have seen; much you have suffered; much, perhaps, also enjoyed: for the Lord can give songs in the night, and in a dungeon. 'Surely his salvation is near to them that fear him'—to *them* there is no want. The Lord is their Shepherd, he feedeth them in green pastures beside the gently flowing waters; if they wander, he restoreth them, perhaps with the rod, but it is the rod of love; they need not be afraid to enter even the valley of the shadow of death; their Shepherd is with them, and his rod (rod of support) and staff shall comfort them.

"I hope this has been a profitable time to you both; that you have seen more of the evil of sin, and of your own hearts, their deceitful double turnings and windings to cover and conceal the enemy of God and your own souls: more of the extent and spirituality of the divine law, fulfilled indeed in every jot and tittle by your Surety; but still doubly binding on you as a rule of life in the hand of your Redeemer, who hath bought you to himself, and taken you into his own hands, that you might be a holy people to himself, delivered not merely from the penalty and curse, but from the power and indwelling of sin. I hope you have seen more of the unsearchable riches of Christ in all he has done and is now doing for your and his church's happiness, and of those exceeding great and precious promises by which you are made partakers of the divine life, and privileged to escape the pollution that is in the world through lust; more of the faithfulness of God, as a God in Christ, pardoning sin and reconciling you to himself; and day by day, teaching you by his word, Spirit, and providences.

"I am but just beginning to see that I am blind; my own character opening upon me as a sinner, in heart and tongue, and conduct, against my God, my neighbor, and my own soul; how comes it then that I am at ease in God's world; in health, in peace, in comfort, all in an extraordinary degree as to temporals; and as to spirituals, though grieved with self, my joy in Christ also abounds. Can I believe it? what can I say? what can I render to the Lord for all his gifts to me? Nothing can I but just take the cup of salvation, calling upon the name of the Lord, and remain an eternal debtor to his grace for spirituals and temporals."

"June 26.

"By this time you are already in port, on earth or in heaven. Blessed alternative! Ought I to be sad, who can say, 'or in heaven?' Oh no, I trust grace will be given to acquiesce in his most blessed will; a most gracious will it has been to me and mine.

"I wrote you in my last, that our dear Mr. M——leaves us next month for Britain; his errand is to state the situation of this country, as greatly in want of ministers and the means of educating ministers. Many of his people are dissatisfied, as he has two congregations to supply, and a large family of his own. Why should he be the man? For my own part, I think he is the very man; and I am thankful to feel a degree of disinterestedness. Though I love my minister, value his ministry and his person, I hope the general interest of Christ's body is more dear to me, and of infinitely more importance than my private comfort, which, after all, I do not believe can suffer by parting cheerfully with its apparent food to Christ, who himself is the sum and substance of all that any minister can be instrumental in conveying. All means are alike to him, or no means. I therefore rejoice in his will, and pray that the Lord may prosper him, give him 'a double portion of his Spirit,' and favor in the eyes of all whose influence is necessary to advance the Redeemer's kingdom in America.

"Our friend Mrs. K—— is gone, she died suddenly: both Mr. and Mrs. T—— died at their country seat; he first.—She fancied she was getting better. The physician advised her not to ride, as she could not stand the fatigue; she had more faith in air and exercise: the last day she went out she fainted getting into the carriage, and again coming out; and died in the afternoon. She lived near us, yet I never saw her, nor offered one kind office towards the salvation of her soul, which, if lost, leaves me not innocent of her blood, and if saved, as I hope it may be, my sinful neglect is not the less. What a picture in them of the vanity of all under the sun; and in me of the evil of procrastination, for I meant to visit her. O my Savior! is this the return I make for the millions of pardons which thou hast past on my account; sparing even the rod, and blessing me with health, restored limbs, and mercy on mercy, com-

fort on comfort? I want words to paint my abominable
ingratitude, indolence and cruelty; and yet, O yet I
am spared, and my mercies are spared, as far as I know
—but trial may be at hand. Perhaps I write what my
children may never read. Well, even then, mercy,
mercy shall be my song; for I sing the song on earth
which they sing in heaven. I am just going to town to
attend preparation sermon. Our feast is on Sabbath."

"July 17, 1801.

"What shall I render to the Lord for all his mercies?
mercies temporal, mercies spiritual, mercies eternal,
multiplied mercies! The one thing that I asked of the
Lord has been answered in full, and O, how much added! God himself become my salvation, and the salvation of my house; how unspeakable the blessing! Although chastisement and affliction were the means of
correction and sanctification, or even the vengeance
taken on my inventions, yet, as a God, he at the same
time pardoneth. For Oh! my character is ever the
same with backsliding Judah and treacherous Israel.
Glory to that name which is ever the same, and changeth not. 'The Lord, the Lord God, merciful and gracious, long-suffering, abundant in goodness and truth,
forgiving iniquity, transgression and sin.' This was his
name among a stiff-necked people, an idolatrous, ungrateful people; this is his name to me alike in character. O how he has magnified this name to me, a backslider in heart and life; multiplying pardons while I
have multiplied transgressions: still he has been last
with me, healing my backsliding; restoring my soul;
leading me to the open fountain; giving faith to wash,

and joy and peace in believing; not only so, but in this
land of drought, this vast howling wilderness, this vale
of tears, ' where man is born to trouble as the sparks
fly upwards,' my cup with temporal comfort is full and
running over; all his creatures minister to my comfort;
and as days and nights roll on, his daily providence
adds, and diminishes not.

"I had hardly hoped to see the faces of my children
again; for he commanded, and raised the stormy winds
and lifted up the waves of the sea; they mounted to
heaven and sunk again to the deep; death with all its
natural horrors surrounded them; the deep yawned to
devour them; but God, their own God, was at hand,
their anchor of hope, their ark of safety, their hiding
place till the calamity was past; ' they cried to him,
and he saved them out of their distresses; he made the
storm a calm, and the waves thereof still, and brought
them to the desired haven.' This trouble was not unto
death, but for the glory of God and the exercising of
your faith, for the manifestation of his power and goodness, and the enriching of your experience.

"O then ' let us praise the Lord for his goodness
and for his wonderful works to the children of men.
Let us exalt him in the congregation of his people, and
praise him in the assembly of the elders.' "

" October 23, 1801.

" Surely, surely my heart feels grateful for the time,
though this, like every other good motion, will, like the
morning dew, soon pass away.

" My children not only preserved through the tempestuous storms that threatened death with circum-

stances shocking to nature; but my poor sick child preserved during a long and fatiguing journey: that journey made comfortable, yea, delightful, by the warm reception of many kind friends, dear to nature, and many doubly endeared by grace; among the last, the mother and sisters of the kindest and best of husbands; they receiving her as their own flesh and blood, as well as their fellow-member in Christ; blest with a measure of health to enjoy all, and a measure of grace to profit by all; eyeing by faith the dear invisible hand of a covenant God—preserving, leading, guiding through every step—his love the marrow of the whole, and their charter for safety, even amidst the dangers of prosperity.

"Is not godliness gain? profitable for this life as well as that which is to come. What is the portion of the worldling? even in this life " shadowy joy or solid wo," without a balance to the first, or consolation in the last; no sure footing in the one, nor support in the other; distanced from the fountain of happiness by nature, prosperity incrusts their hearts and increases their carnality; nestling in their worldly comforts, they forget they are the creatures of a day, that an endless eternity lies before them, and only the feeble uncertain thread of life between them and that curse under which they were born. Not so the child of God; all things work together for his good; *all things;* his standing is not in himself; his footsteps are directed by infinite wisdom; he is kept by the power of God, through faith, unto salvation. Nothing can separate him from the love of God. His life is hid with Christ in God: there is cause to rejoice always; his privileges are boundless, infinite, for God himself is become his salvation.

"Have we then any cause for fear? Yes, my children, yes; though nothing can rob us of our charter, there is another side to be beheld. In Christ we have all things richly to enjoy, but we have not all in possession: what we have is by faith; all is secured by our Surety for eternity. We shall overcome by the blood of the Lamb: but by the constitution of the Covenant we must enter into that rest, that perfect rest, through great tribulation. While our eternal salvation is secured by our Surety, it hath pleased Infinite Wisdom to appoint another connection, which shall exist while we remain on earth: even the connection between our steadfastness, consequently our comfort, and the means of grace which he hath appointed; making the first to depend in a great measure on our diligent use of the last, insomuch that a great number of the promises are proposed conditionally. Many exhortations are given in this view, and also many threatenings. 'They that wait on the Lord shall renew their strength,' &c. 'Seek and ye shall find, ask and ye shall receive, knock and it shall be opened unto you.' 'Abide in me; as the branch cannot bear fruit of itself, no more can ye, except ye abide in me.'

"Close, intimate, near communion with God, is to be sought by means of prayer, meditation, and reading. If the christian be careful to husband time, and set apart a portion for God, and set about these duties, he will not always miss communion; and this prepares him for other duties, and arms him against temptation; as the promise is concerned to keep him in perfect peace whose mind is stayed on Him. 'If ye, being evil, know how to give good gifts to your children, how much more will your heavenly Father give his Holy Spirit to them that ask him.' 'So shall ye know the Lord, if ye follow on to know him.' 'Delight thyself in God, he will give thee the desire of thine heart.' 'Nevertheless, I will be inquired of by the house of Israel,' &c. 'If his children forsake my laws and go astray, I will visit their faults,' &c. 'Watch and pray, that ye enter not into temptation.' 'But thou, when thou prayest, enter into thy closet,' &c. 'Thy Father, who seeth in secret, shall reward thee openly.' All is laid before us in the Scriptures, in the view of comfort during our pilgrimage, as well as the certainty of our inheritance in the end; the ground whereon we stand, our danger, and the means of safety. See Ephesians, 6: 11.

"There is provision made in the Covenant for great comfort, consistent with human frailty and imperfection, but not with carelessness and negligence. While, therefore, we rejoice in the Lord, we have good reason to join trembling with our exultation. While standing high in comfort, to take heed lest we fall, through the deceitfulness of sin. We carry about with us 'a body of sin and death; ' the devil, as a roaring lion, walketh about, seeking whom he may devour.' 'We wrestle not with flesh and blood, but with principalities and powers,' &c. &c. We live in a world lying in wickedness; the captives of sin and Satan exerting every faculty to banish all thoughts of God, death, and eternity; contriving, with unwearied industry and amazing ingenuity, new gratifications for body and mind in endless variety, suited to all constitutions, all tempers and dispositions, and to those in all circumstances. Of these, the most rational are the most subtle, and, in the hand of the enemy, the most calculated to keep men ignorant of themselves, their misery, and of the great salvation: and, alas! by these he often *spoils* unwary christians, who, though heirs of heaven, heirs of God, and joint heirs with Christ, are, during their minority, subject to like passions with themselves, and ever in danger of being spoiled of their comforts when off their guard.

" With the people of the world christians have much to do: they are fellow-members of society with them; they have many duties to perform to them, with them, and by them; many of the things of the world are necessary to them, many of its pleasures lawful; for 'the earth is the Lord's and the fulness thereof,' and he gives them of it as his wisdom sees good for them. That which he gives them they gather in the same manner, and in society, with the world, by industry and diligence in their lawful calling and business. Keeping near the Captain of salvation, and armed in his whole armor, they are safe. When off their guard, the vigilant enemy gains some advantage, and they get into trouble. O how many gracious names our dear Redeemer has assumed in his word, for our comfort, our meditation, our spiritual exercise! how pleasant and delightful in the light of his countenance to analyze them! Beside the names peculiar to himself as God-man, how many has he condescended to take from among men, and the natural comforts and safe-guards of men! our Shepherd, our Rock, our Ark, all the relations in life, and ends with our *All in all*. But I must have done, that I may tell you that goodness and mercy follow us in this family also."

"July 28, 1801.

"My dear pastor Mr. M. sailed for Britain. I thank thee, good and kind Shepherd of Israel, for all those providences, which seemed small things at the time, that hedged me into that congregation; for all the benefits and comforts I enjoyed under the ministry of thy aged servant now before thy throne, and that thou preparedst thy young servant to fill his place when the time of his departure came.

"I thank thee for all the endowments of our young pastor, of nature and grace. I thank thee, that thou hast kept him faithful to Him who has called him, and for the precious treasure thou hast put in that earthen vessel.

"Now, Lord, that thou hast called him to leave his family and his flock, to travel to a foreign land in the service which thou requirest, go with him, prosper him, overrule all his concerns for thy glory, the good of his soul, of the church in general, and his own little flock in particular. Amen. Glorify thy name."

CHAPTER VIII.

JOURNAL AND LETTERS—LADIES' SCHOOL FOR POOR CHILDREN.

"November 22, 1801.

"Isabella Smith (a grand-child) is very ill; she appears to be in a stupor. Two physicians are attending, but 'my eyes are to the Lord.' She is his own, given to him by faith, as a covenant God in Christ for her in particular, for ourselves and our children. I desire not to draw back, but, the Lord strengthening me, to give up at his call. If it be his will to spare her, she is still his own, to be done by, with, and for, as his infinite wisdom may see fit, for his own glory and her eternal interest. If he is about to remove her out of the world, she is his own; out of the mouth of this babe will he perfect praise; with that company of whom is the kingdom of heaven, she shall join in the song of Moses and the Lamb, 'to Him that redeemed us, and washed us from our sins in his own blood, to him be glory, honor, dominion, and power.'

"O Lord, one petition I prefer—if it be thy will to take her out of the world, take her in thine arms and carry her through the dark valley; grant to her a gentle and easy passage, and an abundant entrance into thy kingdom; and tune our hearts to sing—'The Lord gave, and the Lord hath taken away, blessed be the name of the Lord.' Amen."

"November 23.

"This day the dear Isabella joined the church triumphant, and took her place among that company which Christ has pronounced blessed. I yesterday asked of the Lord that he would take her in his arms and carry her through the dark valley, that he would give her a gentle and easy passage, and an abundant entrance into his kingdom. He heard my prayer; it was indeed soft and gentle; not a struggle, not a groan—and the affliction which brought down the frame was moderate throughout. I was enabled to resign the Lord's own into his own hand, in the faith that he did receive, and would keep that which I committed to him.

"My soul is satisfied—more than satisfied; I rejoice, and congratulate the lovely babe on her early escape from a world of sin and sorrow, to the arms of her dear Redeemer, and to perfect blessedness with him."

"November 24.

"It is done—finished—the soul with God, the body in the tomb. It is all well—yes, our Covenant God, thou doest all things well. I firmly believe thy mercy is over all thy works. *Goodness, mercy,* yea, loving-kindness has marked thy every step. I believe it now. I shall see it soon.

"Now, our God, follow this bereavement with thy purifying, sanctifying grace. Enable us all to search and try our ways. Lead our souls into a knowledge of the secret corruptions of our hearts, that we may confess and mourn over them, wash in the blood of Christ, be pardoned, restored, and get a great victory. Enable us through life to abide in Christ; to keep close to thee, transacting all our affairs with thee, before they come into the view of the world. Let thy wisdom and thy Spirit, in connection with thy providences, be our counsellors. O keep us in a dependant frame of mind, humble and watchful. Strip us of all self-confidence. May we at the same time be strong in the Lord and the power of thy might; rejoicing in thee, the God of our salvation, 'the strength of our heart, and our portion for ever.' Glory, glory, glory to Father, Son, and blessed Spirit. Amen, and Amen."

" December, 1801.

"It is my earnest desire 'to grow in grace, and in

the knowledge of our Lord and Savior Jesus Christ.' It is my desire 'to love the Lord my God with all my heart, with all my soul, with all my strength, and with all my mind; and to love my neighbor as myself,' so as to do to him whatever I could expect from christian principles in him, on an exchange of circumstances.

" It is my desire to ' give all diligence to add to my faith virtue, to virtue knowledge, to knowledge temperance, to temperance patience, to patience godliness, to godliness brotherly kindness, to brotherly kindness charity, that these things being in me and abounding, I may be neither barren nor unfruitful in the knowledge of our Lord and Savior Jesus Christ.'

"I desire to grow in grace day by day, to profit by every ordinance of God's appointing, and by every providence; and I pray, Lord, I pray that thou wouldst grant me my desire, so as that I may become more spiritual, more discerning in the Scriptures, more fruitful in good works: that thou mayest increase also my humility. Open to my view more of the extent and spirituality of thy divine law; the majesty, purity, holiness, of thy nature; the exceeding sinfulness of sin; the hidden corruptions of my own heart, and my inability to search them out, and to crucify them; give me also more just views of my past life, that I may ever be convinced that I am, what I really am, 'the very chief of sinners and the least of all saints:' and that it is entirely of grace that I am what I am. O make out this promise to me; I will record it in thine own words: Ezekiel, 16 : 62. 'I will establish my covenant with thee: and thou shalt know that I am the Lord.' I confess myself the character described in the two fore-

going chapters; and though thou hast chastened me
ten thousand times less than my iniquities deserve even
by the constitution of the new covenant, thou hast
chastened me. Now, O Lord, most merciful and gracious, who 'pardonest iniquity, transgression, and sin,'
for thy name's sake, do to and for me as thou hast
said—'I will establish my covenant with thee: and
thou shalt know that I am the Lord. That thou mayest
remember, and be confounded, and never open thy
mouth any more because of thy shame, when I am pacified towards thee for all that thou hast done, saith the
Lord God.' Amen."

To Mr. and Mrs. B——, in Britain.

"December 7, 1801.

"I have received my dear J——'s three letters from
Dingwall: fresh matter of praise to our Covenant God.
You have had your season of affliction; and now you
have a season of refreshing, a resting-time. The cup
of the christian is always more or less mixed. Your
afflictions have ever been mixed with much mercy, and
now your season of rest is also mixed. I well know
that no temporal comfort can compensate the absence
of your justly beloved D——. He, however, who is
the God of both, who goes with him and stays with
you, can not only support, but comfort. The omniscient, the omnipresent, the omnipotent God is our
God, and the God of our house; all that he is is ours,
to bless us. 'Behold, God is become our salvation.'
Every endearing name known among men he takes
to himself, to inspire us with pleasing confiding love:

every name that connects the idea of protection, to keep our minds in quiet peace, in the assurance of safety. *Father, Husband, Brother, Friend, Prophet, Priest, King, Physician, Help, Health, Light, Life, Counsellor, Guide, Sanctuary, Anchor*—but I should fill my sheet. I said it all at first : *God* is ours, and ours with the knowledge of all our backslidings, which he heals; our wanderings, from which he restores us, and our sins, which he forgives; one of his names is *the God of pardons.* He delights in mercy. Are we not his witnesses? What has our whole life been, but sin, backslidings, and wanderings? What have his dealings with us been, but pardons, healings, restorations? Therefore we remain, as at this day, with our desires towards him, and our faces Zion-wards. What he hath begun he will perfect, and in a little while our eyes shall behold him, our hearts shall enjoy him, ' we shall be like him, and see him as he is.' "

To the same.

"December 26, 1801.

"I rejoice over my dear children, and bless our gracious God that he has led them a sweet and most delightful sojourning among his churches, animating their spirits by their mutual communion; blessing them, and, I hope, making them blessings. I pray the Lord may make our dear D. an instrument among others of spreading his Gospel, building up his Church, and pulling down the strong holds of Satan; and that you may be in your place a help meet for him, in this as in every thing else. May the Lord˙choose his path and direct his steps, and yours with him. Women were helpers of the apostles and others in Paul's days: at the same time care must ever be taken not to obtrude in any respect. I pray that you may be kept spiritual and humble: eminence in God's service is truly desirable, if the heart be kept humble. If the Lord open the eyes to behold more of the extent and spirituality of his law, the holiness and purity of his nature, the evil of sin, and its contrariety to all that is in God; and if he turn the eyes inward to the hidden corruptions of the heart, when it is evident to the soul that all is of grace, then may eminent services be safe.

"'I abhor myself, and repent in dust and ashes,' was the exercise of Job; and justly so. Job, who was eyes to the blind and feet to the lame, a father to the poor, and the cause which he knew not he searched it out: when the ear heard him, it blessed him; when the eye saw him, it gave witness to him; who withheld not the poor from his desire, nor caused the eye of the widow to fail; the stranger did not lodge in the street, but he opened his door unto the traveller: all this was true as far as the external act, and as he then thought, with a proper temper of heart, Job could justify himself before his fellow-sinners, blind like himself; but when God comes to deal with him, how different his views! Then it was, 'Behold, I am vile, what shall I answer thee! I will lay my hand on my mouth:' even with the very best there is cause for this exercise, could we see in the same light.

"How deceitful is the human heart! how unfaithful the conscience! how little do we know of the sins of our daily walk! We are called to watch and pray, that we enter not into temptation; to walk with God in close, intimate communion: 'whether we eat or drink, to do all to his glory:' to consult him in all the affairs of life, narrowly observing his providence in connection with our circumstances; weighing all in his presence, requesting him to determine our wills and direct our steps. We ought not to say 'We will go into such a city,' and do this or that; but 'If the Lord will.' How inconsistent our conduct with these rules! How often do rashness, precipitation, and self-will accompany our determinations and movements! And how often do His goodness and wisdom overrule our folly; save us from our own pits, and prevent the evil that might be expected! At no time does he deal with us as we sin, though sometimes he stands by and allows us a taste of our folly: then we are in trouble, we dig our pits and fall into them, but we cannot deliver ourselves. O what a God! who, even at such a time, says to us, 'Call on me in the time of trouble; I will deliver thee, and thou shalt glorify my name; thou hast destroyed thyself, but in me is thy help.' Blessed help! mercy to pardon, goodness to restore, wisdom to guide, faithfulness to carry through and perfect what concerns us, overruling our very follies, and causing them to teach us to profit. This is God's way, according to many declarations of himself in his word, and the experience of all his redeemed.

"Blessed then is the man that trusteth in the Lord; they truly are a blessed people whose God Jehovah is. "

"February, 1802.

" MY DEAR, MY BELOVED CHILDREN,—I trust the Lord is your support; I know you are in trouble; it cannot be that opportunities have been wanting all this time; nor can it be that my children have been negligent: No, no; I cannot suppose it. My children are in trouble, they could not write that they were otherwise, and therefore remain silent until they can write the issue. It is proper, and sure the Lord feeds me with comfort. O the comfort of knowing that the Almighty God is their own reconciled Father by an everlasting covenant! Christ the Mediator and Surety, their Advocate, Brother and Friend; the Holy Ghost their Teacher, Guide and Comforter. It cannot be ill with my dear children, who are also God's dear children. My Father, I know it, thou chastenest for their profit. I know not where they are, nor how they fare. I know not what to ask for them; but thou art every where present, thine eye is upon them, thou knowest all their wants, all their burdens, all their bereavements, or whatever tries them. O let thy sensible presence be with them! open wide the leaves of that New Testament in Christ's blood, and let them read their rich legacy, their unsearchable riches in Christ! give them confidence in thy wisdom and goodness, and sweet acquiescence in all thy dealings with them. Thou hast spared in mercy, perhaps now thou hast taken in mercy: yes, thy tender mercies are over all thy works, and a large ingredient in every cup thou puttest into the hand of thy children. It is well, it is well!

"Since writing the above, I have received my dear D.'s letter, second copy, by the way of London. The Lord is your God, and the God of your seed. John the Baptist leaped in the womb when the salutation of Mary sounded in his mother's ears; he was then a living soul, and an heir of salvation at that moment. If your babe was conceived in sin by the first covenant, he is an heir of grace by the second. Think it not hard; no, you do not think it hard that you have conceived him in sickness, carried him in sickness, and suffered the pangs of birth without the succeeding joy to make you forget your anguish. All this shall be for the glory of God, and that is what you seek; believe it now, you shall see it soon. I do sympathize; my fond heart had embraced a sweet babe added to the family for one taken. The Lord has taken this also; it is his due; I shall soon leave the mortal and join the immortal; five have joined the head, six remain; and one I know nothing of, more than that I cast him on the Lord, and look for mercy. I thank my God that he gave you the grace of resignation, and supported you in the solitary confinement. Alas! my child, did you listen for the voice of your babe? Oh, what a suspense! but let me stop—he had reached maturity ere that time; without the fight, obtained the victory; he is of ' the travail of the Redeemer's soul; children are God's heritage, the fruit of the womb his reward.' Rest then in the Lord; this is to his glory, both without and within your soul."

"May 20, 1802.

"MY DEAR CHILDREN,—Here am I in my little room, surrounded with every comfort, and as the provision of my God, I value all; but there lies the chief, *my Bible*, the Testament of my dying, risen, ascended, reigning Savior, bequeathing to me eternal life, executed in full, and made as sure as the promise and oath of God. The influences of the Holy Ghost on my mind, taking of the things of Christ, and showing them unto me; opening wide the leaves of that New Testament, in which I read unsearchable riches, and my title to them sure; yes, sure, even to me, a base idolatrous Gentile, a rebel against the eternal King, my Creator, Preserver, Provider; a backslider in heart and in life. What has such a one to do with a holy God? He hath said, only return; and he himself hath turned to me, chastened, convinced, restored, comforted. 'His ways are not as our ways, nor his thoughts as our thoughts; but as the heavens are above the earth, so are his ways above our ways, and his thoughts high above our thoughts,' and his plans above our conception. For although it is for ever true, that 'he is of purer eyes than to behold evil, and cannot look on iniquity;' that his law has denounced a curse upon the transgressor who keepeth it not in every jot and tittle; it is for ever true, that this God is unchangeable in his nature and purposes. What he hath said, that will he do. It is for ever true, that I am all I have said, and worse, a sinner in heart, tongue, and practice. Yet am I a beloved child, a justified one, an heir of God.

"Here is the Testament, here is my charter with the seal of God upon it—JESUS! thou art the Secret of the Lord! thou art the Lion of the tribe of Judah, the root and offspring of David! Thou hast prevailed to open this book of secrets, to loose the seven seals, and lay open its mysteries. Thou, Lamb of God, the appointed and anointed to the great work! in our room, and in our nature, thou hast sustained the curse. Thou hast obeyed the law; thou hast drunk the last drop of the last vial of that wrath which would have sunk my soul in the endless depths of misery; and I never could have expended one drop, but sunk deeper and deeper under it. O not unto me, not unto ministers, not unto any creature be the praise. As for me, I am, in a word, all that is vile in myself; ministers, providences, afflictions are just what God makes them; without his blessing they will not only pass without profiting, but Satan and corruption will make them ministers to themselves. Worthy is the Lamb that was slain, for he has redeemed me with his blood. Worthy is the Lamb to receive power, and riches, and wisdom, and strength, and honor, and glory, and blessing—to him, to him alone, be the praise; who, of an heir of hell hath made an heir of heaven, by a substitutional righteousness wrought out in his own person: mine by free gift, in which I am completely justified. To this work let nothing be added, with this work let nothing be mixed.

"There is another work going on by the same Spirit of truth; also his purchase and gift—Sanctification. In this I am called to occupy, watch, strive, fight. Life is given; means of support and growth provided; weapons of warfare—all things necessary to life and godliness: these are promised to the diligent use of means; and poverty, stagnation, discomfort threatened to the indolent. O how sovereign and gracious has my God been in his dealings with me in this respect also. For a sluggard have I been in the days of youth and the prime of life; yet to me hath he given the comforts promised only to the diligent. Here I sit on the verge of three-score; my heart in some good measure loosened from the world, although in full possession of it. Health, ease, plenty, elegance, friendship, respectability;

old age welcome, death unstung become a familiar friend, the messenger of my Father to fetch me home to those mansions which my Redeemer has taken possession of in my name. My hope is strong for my offspring. Stately have been his steps of mercy towards them already, and he saved them from their mother's snares; he heard and answered my prayers, for his name's sake, and overruled my practices; he is my God, and the God of my children; the God of my children's children to the latest generation; my cup is full of comfort, temporal and spiritual. O praise him, praise him, for he is your God, and the God of your offspring also!"

" June 4, 1802.

"Making allowances for the difference of time, and supposing my dear children in health, all about them is in a racket. This is his Majesty's birth-day; and you are at this moment, perhaps, set in some social company, by invitation, to honor the anniversary, to repeat the wish of long life, health and comfort to the lawful Sovereign of Britain.

"Here sit I in my dear little room, with a lovely landscape in view; B —— M.'s park in velvet verdure; the full grown trees scattered thin to display the carpet, and in full foliage; the clump of willows weeping to the very ground, with a gentle wave agitated by the zephyr; while the other trees keep their firm, majestic posture; the Hudson river covered with vessels crowded with sail to catch the scanty breeze; some sweet little chirpers regaling the ear with their share of pleasure. I think I never heard any little warbler in this land sing so sweet as those which now salute my ear.

'These are thy glorious works, Parent of good.'

"Can all the philosophic ingenuity of London, this evening, produce such a scene? The gardens no doubt will be glorious, but the ground-work is also 'God's; but why say I that in particular? All is his; the very notes that warble through so many guilty throats are his creation; all the art of man cannot add to their number. Sweet bird, thy notes are innocent, O how sweet! Lovely trees! ye who stand erect, and ye who weep and wave; I wish no brighter scene. The shadows lengthen fast, so do yours and mine, my Sovereign;* a few, a very few anniversaries, and we must change the scene; change to where no courtiers flatter, no false meteors blaze; where shadows flee away, realities appear, and nothing but realities will stand in any stead.

"O may we meet! for me, I nothing have, I nothing am. But one there is, who was, and is all that the mind of saint or angel can conceive of glory and of happiness; and he is mine, and I am most blessed. Lengthen on, ye shadows, until all is shadow on these orbs of flesh. Then, O then,

'My captive soul set free
From cloggish earth which oft has made me sigh,
Ascends the eternal hills, as seen to see,
As known to know, and grasp the Deity.'"

"1802.

"Our friend B—— has now proved how far it is safe to leave the fate of eternity unsettled. He is gone to

* Mrs. Graham received a pension as a British officer's widow until her death.

the state of the dead: with whom his soul is gathered, He only knows whose mercy none ought to limit; he is gone to his own place; if without a Surety-righteousness, which he sought not after in health, we know where that place is; but after reading of a thief on the cross, nothing with God is impossible. My mind is much impressed; that sentence rings in my ears, so often repeated, "I am determined to do all the good I can, and leave the rest to God. I have no time to search." Oh! oh! one thing is needful.

> ' Life's a folly, age a dream
> Borne along the common stream
> Earth's a bubble light as air,
> If my rest be centered there.
> How can that be solid joy
> Which a moment may destroy.'

"Mr. B—— was seized with the fever in its most malignant form; for him every genius was exerted, and the medical store ransacked for the healing balsam, but in vain. The Judge calls for the soul, and the body must, at his command, dislodge its tenant; how awful, if no Surety was at hand, if he must stand naked—we know the rest; did I say, we know? O no! What can we know of that wrath which in the garden of Gethsemane, when no murderous hand was near, no high priest, no council or cross, wrung the blood through every pore of the pure, the innocent Lamb of God, supported by Godhead. ' If such things were done in the green tree, what shall be done in the dry?'"

Another of her grand-children was shortly after removed by death; his illness is noticed in the following meditation :

"August, 1802.

"Ezekiel, 20 : 32, 'And that which cometh into your mind shall not be at all that you say, we will be as the heathen, as the families of the countries, to serve wood and stone.' Verse 35, 'And I will bring you into the wilderness, and there will I plead with you face to face.' 36, 'Like as I pleaded with your fathers in the wilderness of the land of Egypt, so will I plead with you, saith the Lord God; and I will cause you to pass under the rod, and I will bring you into the bond of the Covenant.' 43, 'And ye shall remember your ways, and all your doings, wherein ye have been defiled, and ye shall loathe yourselves in your own sight, for all your evils that ye have committed; and ye shall know that I am the Lord, when I have wrought with you for my name's sake, not according to your wicked ways, nor according to your corrupt doings, O ye house of Israel, saith the Lord God.'

"It is good, yes, Lord, it is all good; too often have we said, 'we will be as the heathen, to serve wood and stone.' Often hast thou chastened, often have we confessed, often resolved that we would walk more softly, more tenderly, more circumspectly before thee. But, alas! when thy hand is removed, when thou healest us, and restorest to us health, comfort and our pleasant things, we *wax fat and kick*, nestle in our comfort, abuse thy gifts, and lose sight of the giver. Alas, Lord! thus it must ever be with us, when we keep not near to thee; we cannot walk one step alone without stumbling. Thou knowest these naturally wicked hearts, that they are deceitful above all things, they betray us before we are aware. Blessed, ever blessed be our God for his well-ordered covenant! Blessed for the discipline of it! O Lord, we are again in the wilderness, and under thy chastising rod: for weeks past, we have ' eaten no pleasant bread;' thy rod is still suspended over our pleasant, our dear child; the streams of life ebb, he sickens, he dies, if thou interfere not. But the issues of death are in thy hand, and our eyes are towards thee. In vain are all means, all medicines, if thou impart not the healing virtue.· Thy weeping servants seek the healing virtue from thy waters, thy seas, thy purer air. All nature is in thy hand and ministers thy pleasure; to some conveying health, to some disease. An herb to be boiled in simple milk, as the figs for Hezekiah's boils, has been proposed? O let this prove the appointed means or direct and point out that which thou wilt bless, and let our hearts and tongues give the glory to thee.

"We deserve this bereavement; but, Lord, what do we not deserve? Even according to the constitution of the covenant of grace, and consistent with thy pardoning, saving mercy, and all thy long-suffering, wert thou to take vengeance on our inventions, by exercising all thy threatened chastisements, should we ever be out of the furnace? But even in this view, thou never hast dealt with us as our iniquities deserved. 'He will not always chide, neither will he keep his anger for ever.' Thou hast, in thousands of instances, 'cast our sins behind thy back, into the midst of the sea; blotted them out, to remember them no more for ever. Thy ways are not as our ways, nor thy thoughts as our thoughts.' We may plead, 'deal not with us as we sin; but according to the multitude of thy mercies blot out our transgressions. Pardon our iniquity, for it is great.' Affliction is

appointed, but it is 'in measure, when it shooteth forth.'
O debate with it, and according to thy promise 'Stay
thy rough wind in the day of thine east wind.' Lord,
say *it is enough*, give the blessing, and by this measure
shall iniquity be purged, and the fruit be to take away
sin. All means are alike in thy hand, and any measure.
In holy sovereignty and consummate wisdom thou
afflictest, and in thy hand afflictions yield the peaceable
fruits of righteousness: the hearts of thy people are
melted, and they sing of mercy and of judgment, and
glorify thy name. But, O Lord, a look, such as thou
gavest to Peter, will melt our hearts and restore our
backsliding souls. The announcing of our pardon by
the same power, will make them overflow with love. If
thou but call us by name as thou didst her who sought
thee at thy sepulchre, with the same power we shall
recognize our Savior and worship him.

"O Lord our God, ever faithful to thy promises,
thou hast said, 'Whatsoever ye ask in my name, believing that ye receive, I will do it.' O Lord, I ask not
the life of this child on this ground. I have through
life asked one thing of thee, and that will I seek to obtain while life and breath remain, and reason and grace;
I will seek it, seek it with importunity, holding fast
by thy promise to do it, and believing that it shall be
according to my petition. Make good to me this thy
promise, in a spiritual and eternal sense. Be my God,
and the God of my children, and of my children's children to the latest generation. Let my children according to the flesh, be thine by regeneration of the Holy
Ghost: it is a great boon; but hast thou not said, 'Open
thy mouth wide, I will fill it?' Father, do as thou hast

said: this is my one petition, and I cannot be said nay. I ask for myself, my children, and my children's children, to the latest generation, the life which Christ died to purchase, and lives to bestow, that we may be made one with him, and our life hid with him in God. Amen, and Amen.

"But, O my Father! thou hast said, 'Be careful for nothing; but in every thing, by prayer and supplication, with thanksgiving, let your requests be made known unto God.' I ask with submission to thy holy will, if consistent with thy glory, his good and the good of the parents, the life of this child; that thou mayest spare him for our comfort, but first for thine own glory; that thou mayest give the different branches of this family a joyful meeting, a full feast of grateful thanks to thee for all thy mercies; and our hearts may rejoice before thee for the abundance of comfort. Shouldst thou, in thy adorable wisdom, otherwise determine, thy blessed and thy holy will be done. Wash the soul of this child in the blood of Jesus, clothe him with thy righteousness, sanctify him by thy Spirit, and fit him in every respect for thy kingdom. And, O my divine Redeemer, I renew my petition which thou didst so evidently grant in the case of our dear Isabella; take him in thine arms of mercy; soften and shorten the parting pangs, and carry him gently through the dark valley, and give him an abundant entrance into thy heavenly kingdom, to join the hosannas of thy little children, of whom thy kingdom is partly made up: and O sanctify the affliction to all concerned; direct our discipline according as thine all-seeing, heart-searching eye sees we need; that it may bring forth the peaceable fruits of righteousness, and 'the fruit of affliction be to take away sin,' and the glory of all redound to thee, Father, Son, and blessed Spirit! Amen, and Amen."

" September, 1802.

"'What manner of persons ought we to be in all manner of holy conversation?'

"'O give thanks unto God, for he is good, and his mercy endureth for ever.'

"'How precious are thy thoughts unto us, O God; how great is the sum of them.'

"'Were we to count them, they are more in number than the sand. When we awake we are still with thee.'

"'The Lord is gracious and full of compassion, slow to anger, and of great mercy.'

"'The Lord is good to all, and his tender mercies are over all his works.'

"'All thy works shall praise thee, O Lord, and thy Saints shall bless thee.'

"'Never hast thou dealt with us as our iniquities deserve, nor rewarded us according to our transgressions.'

"'Who is a God like unto thee, who pardoneth iniquity, and passeth by the transgression of the remnant of thy heritage. He retaineth not his anger for ever, because he delighteth in mercy.'

"'He will turn again, he will have compassion upon us, he will subdue our iniquities, and thou wilt cast all our sins into the depths of the sea.'

"'Let Israel hope in the Lord, for with the Lord there is mercy, and with him is plenteous redemption.'

"'And he shall redeem Israel from all his iniquities.'

"'The Lord hath done great things for us, whereof

we are glad. The Lord hath turned our captivity, filled our mouth with laughter and our tongue with melody.'

"Thomas (her grandchild) is restored to perfect health. Thou hast heard our petitions, and continuest to us all our pleasant things.

"It is a time of prosperity; thou givest us the 'upper and the nether springs;' thou blessest my children 'in their basket and in their store;' and while the riches of many are making to themselves wings and flying away; while many are sinking from affluence to poverty, falling on the right hand and on the left, by thy most manifest providence thou hast preserved them from the wreck. O teach them to acknowledge thy hand in all this, and to say and feel, 'not unto us, O Lord, not unto us, but to thy name be the glory. It is God that giveth power to get riches.' O enable them to honor thee with 'their substance, and with the first fruits of all their increase.'

" 'In the day of prosperity let them rejoice,' but let this joy be in the Lord. O let thy gifts ever, ever lead them to the Giver, and fill their hearts with gratitude, their mouths with praise; and let their very actions be worship, while they acknowledge thee in all their ways, and thou directest their steps. May they be as 'a city set on a hill, which cannot be hid, and their light shine before men, that they seeing their good works, may glorify their Father who is in heaven.'

"And now, O Lord, we wait for thy blessing in the restoration of our dear D. and I. B. and J. 'Thou hast shown them great and sore adversities,' and thou hast manifested thy power to save. 'When they passed through the waters thou wast with them, and through the rivers they did not overflow them. When they walked through the fire they were not burnt, neither did the flames kindle upon them. For thou art the Lord their God, the Holy One of Israel, their Savior.'

"'Thou didst stay thy rough wind in the day of thine east wind, and in the multitude of their thoughts within them did thy comforts delight their soul. Thou humbledst them under thy mighty hand, and thou hast in the multitude of thy mercy exalted them in due time.'

"In all their sojourning thou hast been with them; and in fellowship with thy church greatly hast thou comforted them. Thou hast given them favor in the hearts of thy people, and made 'the stones of the field to be at peace with them.' And now, O Lord, restore them to their friends and christian society, and to their place which thou hast in thy goodness given and preserved to them. Here may they be thy witnesses, that 'thou art the Lord, and besides thee there is no Savior.'"

"September, 1802.

"This day has the Lord our God answered our prayers, and enriched us beyond the ordinary lot of humanity. D. and I. B. and J. are restored to their preserved places, and to the bosom of their family. 'We are as men who dream; our mouths are filled with laughter, our tongues with melody; the Lord hath done great things for us, whereof we are glad. Thou hast turned our captivity as streams in the south. We sowed in tears, we have reaped in joy. Bless the Lord, O our souls;' ever true and faithful is his word, 'They that go forth weeping, bearing precious seed, shall doubtless come again rejoicing, bringing their sheaves with them.'

"'O Lord, from thee is our fruit found;' may our sheaves be many and weighty, thou working all our works in us, to thine own glory and our blessedness. Amen."

"1802.

"Dear brother Pero,* happy brother Pero, thy Jesus, in whom thou trustedst, has loosed thy bonds, has brought thee to that rest which remains for the people of God; thou drinkest of the pure river that maketh glad the city of our God; of that blessed Fountain from which issue all the streams which refresh and revive us weary pilgrims. But a little while ago, and thou wast weary, dark, and solitary; thy flesh fettering and clogging thy spirit; thy God trying thy faith, hope, and patience, which he had previously implanted, watered, and made vigorous, to stand that trial more precious than gold that perisheth, though it be tried by fire, and was made manifest to the glory of that Savior who leaves not his people in any case. If need be, they are in heaviness, through manifold temptations; but he knows how to deliver them, having himself been tempted.

"Thou hadst a taste of his cup; like him thou didst endure the contradiction of sinners; like him thou didst experience the desertion of friends: even thine old mistress, whom thou lately didst esteem as a sister in Christ, and to whom thou didst look for fresh com-

---

* Pero was an elderly man of color whom Mr. Andrew Smith had purchased, and made free.

Pero had previously been a freed man of Christ. He had been for some time in ill health; Mrs. Graham kindly attended on him, and read the Scriptures to him: he died by the bursting of a blood-vessel, at an hour when none of the family were with him. Mrs. Graham, in humility of spirit, reproaches herself in this exercise, for having been absent from him, without inquiring into his situation, for one hour.

munications from and through that written word, which she could read and thou couldst not, Oh! how did she prove as a broken reed unto thee? how did she neglect thy necessity, and her own opportunity of bringing forth fruit in its season? Thou hast been no loser. The Lord passed by the slothful servant, the unfaithful steward, who neglected to give thee thy meat in due season, and himself took her place; took thee from that household which was not worthy of thee, and led thee to those mansions of bliss which himself purchased and prepared; set thee at that table which shall never be drawn, where thou shalt feast on all the fulness of God, and drink of those pleasures which are at his right hand for evermore. No need of old mistress now; no need of any earthly vessel now, nor of that written word which thou didst so highly prize. The Word made flesh, has removed the veil that shaded the glory of the God-man from thine eyes; flesh and blood could not behold it; of this he has unclothed thee—left it with us to look upon and mourn our sin. Thee he has introduced into the full vision of eternal day, where thou knowest as thou art known, and seest as thou art seen. O that full communion enjoyed between a holy soul and the perfection of holiness! O that Light of Life! that Ocean of Love! that inconceivable blessedness! How hast thou out-run us, brother Pero? How distanced us in a moment? Oh, could I not watch with thee one hour! Oh that I had received thy last blessing, instead of which, conscious offence, deserved rebuke, painful compunction wring my heart; and perhaps the rod of correction may be suspended, and now ready to fall on my guilty head.

"Father! O my Father! Am I not still thy child?

still thy adopted? Have not I an Advocate with thee, Jesus Christ the righteous, whom thou hearest always? does not the blood of Christ cleanse from all sin? yes, O yes. This is my universal remedy; thousands and ten thousands of times have I experienced its efficacy. Father, I again apply; blessed Spirit, do thine office! Wash me and I shall be clean, purge me and I shall be whiter than snow. I confess my sin, I acknowledge mine iniquity. Thou didst bring to me an old disciple, near and dear to his and my Savior; thou didst require me to minister unto him all that he needed; the honor was great, the opportunity valuable. Thou didst empty thy servant for a time, thou didst hide his comfort, that I might, through thy written word, draw living waters for him, and give him to drink. O the honor! O the negligence! Thou didst send the call for thy disciple to come up to thee; in thy providence thou didst make it first known to me, that I might be instrumental in conveying to him, through the same channel, oil and trimming for his lamp. Great was the honor! dignified the service! but lost to me for ever. I passed by on the other side. Blessed, blessed Jesus! thou good Samaritan, who pouredst the oil and wine into his wounds, and tookest him, not to an inn, but to those mansions in the skies, which thou, with thine own blood, purchasedst for him; sanctify, O sanctify to me this thy providence; pardon my neglect. Savior, wash me in thy blood, and sanctify and bring good out of even my transgression. By thy grace, let it be a means of stirring me up to more watchfulness, that I may meet the opportunities afforded me in thy providence, to occupy till thou come."

" The lovely plant which the Lord had blasted, which brought down our hearts with grief, which he had restored and clothed with smiling health and comfort, again sickened, declined, wasted ; every means proved ineffectual ; the Lord refused the healing virtue. He was brought to town to be near the physicians, but the Physician of Israel aided them not. Disease increased ; with pain, sickness, convulsion, much he suffered, and long ; he had a taste of the bitterness of sin, but no part of the curse: *that* the Redeemer drank and expended ; and having by his atoning blood purged this little one from his sins, and perfected all his redeeming work in his soul, he received him into his own heavenly abodes. It is well, all well. Amen."

Mrs. Graham lived alternately with her children, Mrs. Bethune and Mrs. Smith until 1803, when Mrs. Smith removed from New-York. After that time she made her home with Mr. and Mrs. Bethune until her departure to her heavenly home. They loved her not only from natural affection, but for her superior worth. They believed that her prayers brought a blessing on the family, as the ark of God did to the house of Obed-Edom.

" March, 1803.

" I read this day the 36th chapter of Ezekiel, and pleaded God's promises from the 22d verse to the end, for myself, for my children, and for my children's children ; for the church of God throughout the world, in particular for this country, for Britain and Ireland, France and Germany, where his name was once known,

and his Gospel flourished. That the Lord would 'build
the waste places and repair the breaches;' that he would
'purify the sons of Levi,' fill all pulpits with able, faithful ministers of the New Testament, who 'shall declare
the whole counsel of God;' and that wherever his name
is recorded, the Holy Ghost might fill the place, and
convince the hearts of preachers and hearers, of sin, of
righteousness, and of judgment; might 'take of the
things of Christ and show unto them;' and that the great
Head of the church might regulate and overrule all these
breaches, differences, and shakings in his churches.

"O Lord, I am ignorant; I know not the mind of the
Spirit of promise as thou knowest it. The promise of
the fruit of the tree, and the increase of the earth, of the
corn, the wine, and the oil is thine, as are all others.
I am ignorant how far this refers to spiritual prosperity,
how far to temporal. I ask, O Lord, covenant provision,
the fruit of the seed sown in the hearts of men by thine
own Spirit; and that thou mayest build the ruined cities
of thy churches, and fill them 'with men like a flock, as
the flock of Jerusalem in her solemn feasts; so shall
the waste cities be filled with flocks of men, and they
shall know that thou art the Lord.' Thy fair, thy rich,
thy beautiful creation is also the fruit of grace. The
wicked possess it, but they enjoy it not. Thy people
are the heirs, but thou, as a wise and merciful Father,
givest them to possess according as thy wisdom sees
safe and good for them. When with the things of this
world they imbibe the spirit of the men of the world;
when they nestle in thy gifts and forget the Giver;
when they enjoy with a carnal spirit, and not with
thankfulness and a due sense of their dependance on

thee, as the God of providence as well as of grace; thou, in mercy as in sovereignty, blastest their pleasant things, mixest their cup of prosperity with wormwood and gall, or sweepest all away with a turn of thine hand; that thou mayest teach them that man doth not live by bread alone, but by every word that proceedeth out of the mouth of God; that thou mayest withdraw them from sinful purposes, and hide pride from them; that thou mayest open their ears to instruction, and seal it on their hearts; thou dashest to pieces their broken cisterns, that thou mayest lead them back to the fountain of living waters.

"It is good, O Lord, all good; I lay hold upon it; be thou the provider of me and mine; feed us with food convenient for us. Thine own word testifies 'that every creature of God is good, and nothing is to be refused if it be received with thanksgiving, for it is sanctified by the word of God and prayer.' I and the children for whom I pray, possess many, yea, and abundance of temporal good things. O Lord, give suitable grace, grace for grace. Spirit of grace! keep us thankful, humble, dependant, spiritual; enable us to receive all through a covenant channel, as the provision of our Father, by the way, through this wilderness. O may all be sanctified by thy word and prayer, and we enabled 'to eat and drink to thy glory.' Amen.

"Read the 138th Psalm; 'Though the Lord be high, yet hath he respect unto the lowly; though I walk in the midst of trouble, thou wilt revive me. The Lord will perfect that which concerneth me; thy mercy, O Lord, endureth for ever; forsake not thou the works of thine hands.'

10*

"Redeeming work is thy work; regenerating work is thy work; sanctifying work is also thine.

"The first is finished, the second begun, to be perfected in the third. O Lord, I hang on thy promises, which with Christ are all mine, though I have not at all times the savor of them; this is mine infirmity, and often my sin. O keep me looking unto Jesus."

"March 25, 1803.

"Communion Sabbath, Dr. M—— preached from Romans, 6 : 17 : 'But God be thanked that ye were (were in the past time, not now) the servants of sin; but ye have obeyed from the heart that form of doctrine which was delivered you.'

"O Lord, I believe the doctrines of thy Gospel; I know that I am delivered from sin as a master; it hath not dominion over my will, nor entire dominion over my affections; I would be thine, thy servant, thy child, thine in all obedience. I feel this new principle in the desires of my soul. I would do all things to thee, in act and in principle. But, O Lord, the old man is still here, harassing and hindering my new will (which I have received from thee) from acting with freedom and energy. Unhallowed motives steal in, by-ends present themselves; and when outward duty is attained to, there is more of sin than of righteousness. Though entered upon with some measure of purity, yet before it is finished I am at a loss to discern the true principle by which I am actuated. Lord, help me! hast thou not promised to work in me both ' to will and to do of thy good pleasure ?' Is it not the grand end of thy death, that thou mightest purify to thyself a glorious church, 'not having spot nor wrinkle, nor any such thing ;' and shall not I be a partaker ? Art thou not made of God unto thy people, wisdom, righteousness, sanctification, and complete redemption?

"O Lord, my heart pants for redemption from indwelling sin. This depravity of my nature, this opposition, this evil that is ever present with me when I would do good, this indolence, this listlessness, this want of zeal, or else self-will, keenness of temper, impatience, haste: O Lord, there is a host of enemies; gird me, arm me, shield me, lead me forth under thy banner; be my victorious King. 'I will go in thy name, trusting in thy promised strength and grace to help in every time of need.' Glory be to God, Father, Son, and blessed Spirit, for the grace in which I stand. But for grace I had been a willing slave to sin to this hour. By that same grace I shall one day attain to victory. I cast my burden on the Lord, he will sustain until he deliver; I will go up through the wilderness, trusting in the promises, and continue fighting in his strength. 'My soul waits for thy salvation.' Lord, enable me to keep 'looking unto Jesus, the author and finisher of faith.' O give faith in every part of his mediatorial character! May I feed upon him and be strong for this sore fight. Give courage, O Lord; press me forward: may I resolve, and keep the resolution, 'to resist unto blood, striving against sin.'

"I have been a slothful servant in thy family, an idle laborer in thy vineyard, 'an unfruitful branch,' a poor dwarfish member in thy body. Grant, O grant 'a little fruit on the topmost bough.' Oh! at the 'eleventh hour' may I begin to work, to bear some fruit, to the glory of that grace by which my soul is saved from the wages of sin, death, and hell, and made heir, by free gift, of the wages of righteousness, eternal life and glory. I wait for thy salvation!"

There being no public, free, or Sabbath-schools in the city, Mrs. Graham used her endeavors to promote such as would at least furnish education to the children of the widows under her care; and several young ladies offered their services, which she thus notices:

"February, 1804.

"A new thing is on the wheel in the city of New-York. A Society of ladies, organized for the purpose of relieving widows with small children, was new in this country. It is now, by the blessing of God, apparently established. It was entered upon with prayer; it has been conducted thus far with prayer. The blessing of God has rested upon it, and much good has been done by it. Some of us have looked long, and requested of God to open a way by which the children of these widows might be *instructed and taught to read his word,* and by his blessing on it, come to the knowledge of the way of salvation. One means has been attempted of an ordinary kind: twelve children were last week placed at school with Mrs. L——, to be taught to read, and some more are to be placed with another of our widows, for the same purpose. But this indeed is new. A Society of young ladies, the first in rank in the city, in the very bloom of life, and full of its prospects, engaged in those pleasures and amusements which tend to engross the mind and shut out every idea unconnected

with them, coming forward and offering, (not to contribute towards a school,) but *their own personal attendance to instruct the ignorant.* O Lord, prosper their
work. If this be of thee, it shall prosper, and be productive of much good; but if thou bless not, it will
come to nothing but shame. No good can be done but
by thee, for 'there is none good but God;' and what are
all thy creatures, but instruments in thy hand, by which
thou bringest to pass the purposes of thy will: *Christians*, redeemed, enlightened, sanctified, are no more:
'thou workest all their works in them,' they themselves
are 'thy workmanship created in Christ Jesus unto
good works, which thou hast prepared, that they should
walk in them.' Worldlings also are thy instruments:
by them thou workest and bringest to pass the counsels
of thy will; thou puttest into their heart the good thing
which thou workest, and girdest them for the purpose:
though not the children of thy covenant, they are the
instruments of thy providence.

"O Lord, take up this matter; gird these young women to this very purpose, and prosper them in the art
of teaching these orphans of thy Providence. And, O
Lord, hear my more important petition. I am not worthy to be heard. O Lord, I am not worthy to be named
in connection with any good done by thee. 'I am the
chief of sinners,' the chief of backsliders; every thing
in me, of me, or by me, is vile as far as it is mine. All
that is otherwise, all good implanted in me, or done by
me, is thine own; it is grace, free grace, the purchase of thine own Anointed, my dear Redeemer, my
dying, risen, ascended Savior, and the fruit of the Holy
Ghost, 'the sent of the Father and of the Son,' to set

up a kingdom of righteousness in the hearts of the redeemed. Let me, as a sinner saved by grace, to whom thou hast been pleased to give the exceeding great and precious promises; let me, under the sprinkling of the blood of the Covenant, and in entire dependance on my surety-righteousness; let me draw near and present my petition in the name, and for the sake of Him whom thou hearest always. O Lord God Almighty, by this very thing, build up thy Zion. Lay hold of these young creatures, and while they are in the way of thy providence, bring them 'to the house of our master's brethren.' O thou great Teacher, teach thou teacher and taught. Be found of them who seek thee not, and say with power, 'Behold me, behold me, to a people not yet called by thy name,' and out of this small thing in thy providence, bring revenues of praise to thy name as the God of grace. Amen.

"And now, O Lord, for myself, I pray for deep humility; I ask, for his sake who was meek and lowly, to be kept where my place really is, at the feet of all thy servants; and if it be thy pleasure to make me a useful instrument, in proportion make me a humble soul. Let me ever 'remember my ways and be ashamed, and never open my mouth any more because of my shame, when thou art pacified towards me for all that I have done.' O keep me in this contrite frame of mind. In all that to which thou callest me, give me a willing heart, and furnish me with every necessary for thy glory. And now prepare me to speak to these young women *good and acceptable words*. Save me from sacrificing truth, or departing, in any respect, from christian duty; give me such wisdom as may be suited to the occasion:

in all things ' mine eyes are to the Lord; from thee let my fruit be found.' "

"February 17, 1804.

" Saturday the 11th. Twenty-nine young ladies met with Mrs. Hoffman and myself, at Mr. O. Hoffman's, Wall-street, on purpose to receive instructions respecting the school; and having paired themselves according to their mind, I delivered what I had prepared for them: they all seemed hearty in their engagement; and on Monday the 13th inst. Miss L——t and Miss L——n attended at the school-room and commenced teaching thirteen children; four have been added since.

" Again, O Lord, let me request thy blessing on this institution; put thy seal upon it, and mark it for thine own. Gird the teachers for their work, and open the minds of the scholars to instruction. And, O Lord, in thine own time, and by means of thy own devising, provide spiritual instruction for teachers and taught. Is it thy pleasure, Lord, that I attend the children on a day appointed for the purpose? Wilt thou accept of me as an instrument, by which thou wilt do good to the souls of these children; and wilt thou keep me humble and contrite in my own soul? Bless also Mrs. L.'s school; there too let thy work appear; deal with her soul as ' thou dealest with thy chosen;' teach her the way of salvation, and make her a teacher by thine own Spirit. If it be my dear Master's pleasure to use me, I would also attend that school as his instrument. ' Search me, O Lord, and know my heart, try me and know my thoughts, and see if there be any wicked way in me, and lead me in the way everlasting.' "

Mrs. Graham's address to the young ladies above alluded to is given as a specimen of the appropriateness of her addresses on similar occasions, and as an incentive to kindred exertions in every condition of life.

"My dear young Ladies—Every thing new becomes matter of speculation and variety of opinion.

"An association of ladies for the relief of destitute widows and·orphans was a new thing in this country. It was feeble in its origin, the jest of most, the ridicule of many, and it met the opposition of not a few. The men could not allow our sex the steadiness and perseverance necessary to establish such an undertaking. But God put *his* seal upon it; and under his fostering care it has prospered beyond the most sanguine expectations of its propagators. Its fame is spread over the United States, and celebrated in foreign countries. It has been a precedent to many cities, who have followed the laudable example. This fame is not more brilliant than just. The hungry are fed, the naked are clothed, shelter is provided for the outcasts; medicine and cordials for the sick, and the soothing voice of sympathy cheers the disconsolate. Who are the authors of all these blessings? Your mothers, ladies, the benevolent members of this so justly famed Society. But who are these children that idly ramble through the streets, a prey to growing depravity and vicious example? hark! they *quarrel*, they *swear*, and such no doubt will *lie* and *steal*. And that group of dear little creatures, running about in the most imminent danger, apparently without protection, are they under the care of this so justly famed Society? They are; they are fed, they are clothed, their mother's fireside is made warm for them; but no culture is provided for their minds, nor protection from baneful example. These will in time follow that of the older ones, and grow up the slaves of idleness and vice, the certain road to ruin.

"Alas! alas! and is there no help? no preventive? Yes there is! Behold the angelic band! hail, ye virtuous daughters! worthy of your virtuous mothers, come forward and tread in their steps! Snatch these little ones from the whirling vortex; bring them to a place of safety; teach them to know their Father, God: tell them of their Savior's love; lead them through the history of his life; mark to them the example he set, the precepts he recorded for their observance, and the promises for their comfort. And by teaching them to read, enable them to retrace all your instructions when their eyes see you no more.

"My dear young ladies, the sacrifice you have made shall most assuredly meet its reward: but, like your mothers, you will experience much painful banter, you will be styled school madams. Let it pass—suffer it quietly; when your scheme begins to ripen and the fruits appear, who shall be able to withhold their praise? Only be steadfast, draw not back and justify the prophecies of many.

"A great general, in ancient times, in search of glory, landed his troops on the hostile coast, and then burnt all his ships: they must conquer or die. You have, ladies, already embarked in this design; there is no remaining neuter new; your name and undertaking are in every mouth; you must press forward and justify your cause; and justified it shall be if you persevere;

it cannot be otherwise. The benevolence you contemplate, is as superior to that already in operation, as the interest of the soul is to that of the body; and it is your own; the very scheme originated in a young mind in this company. The Society were contemplating mercenary agents—schools for pay, and one is already established.

"But this labor of love! who could have hoped for it? A Society of *young ladies*, in rank the first in the city, in the very bloom of life, and full of its prospects, engaged in those pleasures and amusements which generally engross the mind, and shut out every idea unconnected with self, coming forward and offering—what? not their purses, that were *trash;* but their own personal services to instruct the ignorant, and become the saviors of many of their sex. It is indeed a new thing, and more strange in this age of dissipation, than that institution from which it sprung. May this too become the darling of Providence! May God put his seal upon this also! May he bless and prosper you in this undertaking, bless you and make you a blessing!"

We next have her wrestling supplications for the revival of God's work in the church with which she was connected.

"February 21, 1804.

"O Thou, who art 'Alpha and Omega, the first and the last, who holdest the seven stars in thy right hand, and walkest in the midst of the seven golden candlesticks, who livest and was dead, and art alive for evermore. Amen. And hast the keys of hell and of death. Out of thy mouth goeth a sharp two-edged sword,' by which thou reachest the hearts of the most hardened. O write with power, speak with power, in the heart of the angel of this church. Hast thou not in former days had thy dwelling among them? in days of trouble didst thou not work in them the fruits of labor and patience, so that for thy name's sake they labored and fainted not? Thou blessedst them and gave them peace, and they rejoiced in the light of thy countenance; thou multipliedst them also, so that from a handful they became *two bands.* Alas, Lord, we have, Ephraim-like, ' waxed fat and kicked;' we have left our first love; we have not watched and prayed, as thou gavest commandment, and thou hast left us to enter into temptation; we have forsaken the counsel of our old men, and given heed to flatterers; we have forgotten our dependance on thee, and said, 'Ashur shall save us, we will ride upon horses.' We have set up our idols in our hearts, and put the stumbling-block of our iniquity before our eyes; we have taken counsel, but not of thee, and covered ourselves with a covering, but not of thy Spirit; we have gloried in our own wisdom, and strengthened ourselves in our own strength.

"We are poor, and blind, and miserable, and naked; rich in our fancied wisdom, seeing by our own light, and compassing ourselves about with our own sparks; ' we feed on ashes: a deceived heart has turned us aside.'

"'O Lord, the Hope of Israel, and the Savior thereof.' It is of the Lord's mercies that we are not consumed. To us belong shame and confusion of face, (O cover us with it,) but to thee belongs mercy. Humble us, O Lord, and we shall be humbled; 'turn us, and we shall be turned.'

"It is in our nature to backslide for ever; thou, and thou only, knowest the deceitfulness of the heart; thou, and thou only, canst search it. 'O search us, and try us, and show us what wicked ways there are in us, and lead us in the way everlasting. Deal not with us according to our sins, but according to the multitude of thine own mercies.' We have no other plea; our sins call for judgment, and until thou, thy own blessed self turn us, we are in no situation to receive mercy. Work with us for thy name's sake, establish with us thine own covenant of free, unmerited, undeserved mercy. Then shall we know that thou art the Lord.

"Make us thine by thy own covenant, established in Christ, thy own anointed; the blessed Surety, by thine own appointment; our substitute, on whom it hath pleased thee *to lay the iniquities of us all;* in whose sacred person thou tookest vengeance for all our sins; by whom thy law is fulfilled, magnified, and made honorable; whose doing and suffering in our stead is accepted by Jehovah. 'The Lord is well pleased for his righteousness' sake.' No covenant short of one fulfilled in every jot and tittle could benefit us.

"Thy covenant is well-ordered in all things, and it is sure.'

"Here, O Lord, I take my stand; here I lay my foundation, and on this thy covenant I build; or rather here thou thyself hast laid my foundation, and on this rock hast thou set my soul and built my hopes, thou subduing my enmity. I acquiesce. I will now 'remember the years of thy hand,' look back to thy dealings with thine own nation, whom thou didst 'choose and set apart from all other nations, though of the same blood with all those that dwell on the face of the whole earth.'

"They, like us, destroyed themselves, but in thee was their help. They also sinned, committed iniquity, and did wickedly; they remembered not thy mercy, but provoked thee at the Red Sea, after the great deliverance thou hadst wrought for them, and the wonders thou madest to pass before them in the land of Egypt. Nevertheless thou savedst them for thy name's sake, that thou mightest make thy mighty power known; thou didst repeat thy wonders, and didst dry up the sea before them. 'He fed them with corn from heaven; they did eat angel's food. He clave the rock in the wilderness, and caused waters to run down like a river.' After all, they forsook the God of their mercies; they believed not his promises, nor trusted in his salvation; 'they lusted, and they murmured, and desired to turn back to Egypt. Thou didst chasten them sore for their sin, and didst bring down their heart with grief.'

"'When thou didst slay them, they sought thee, and remembered that God was their Rock, and the most high God their Redeemer. Nevertheless they did flatter with their mouth and lied unto thee with their tongue, for their heart was not right with thee, neither were they steadfast in thy covenant. But thou being full of compassion forgavest their iniquity and destroyedst them not; yea, many a time turnedst thou away thine anger, and didst not stir up all thy wrath.

"'O how many times did they turn back, tempted God, and limited the Holy One of Israel. Yet did

he fulfil all his promises, and by wonders in the sea,
wonders in the desert, wonders in Zoar's field, and in
the camps of their enemies, he led them safely to the
border of his sanctuary, to the mountain which his
right hand had purchased. He cast out the heathen before them, and gave them rest in the land of promise.
Even there they provoked the Most High, provoked
him to jealousy with their graven images.'

"Again thou didst chasten them sore, let loose the
corruptions of men upon them, and suffer them to
fall before their enemies. 'Thou deliveredst thy
strength into captivity, and thy glory into the hands
of their enemies.'

"Yet, O Lord, again didst thou deliver them, and
sentest provision for them by thine own covenant.
'Thou didst choose David thy servant, and take him
from the sheep-folds. Thou broughtest him to feed Jacob thy people, and Israel thine inheritance. So he fed
them according to the integrity of his heart, and guided
them by the skilfulness of his hands.'

"Such are the people with whom thou hast still to
do. Such, O God of infinite mercy! such the God with
whom we sinners have to do! even 'the Lord God,
merciful and gracious, long-suffering, slow to anger, forgiving iniquity, transgression and sin; who will by no
means clear the guilty.' O what could man or angel
have done with this last character of thy name? Thy
covenant makes provision. In Christ Jesus, our blessed
Substitute, all is reconciled. Thy name is one; 'the
just God, and the justifier of the ungodly who believe
in Jesus. This God is our God; we will make mention of
his righteousness, and his only.' By his own covenant,

in his own time, and by means of his own providing, he will revive us. Amen."

"April, 1804.

"'All my desire is before thee,' and it is all contained in thy well-ordered covenant. Many years of vanity, of idolatry, of backsliding, wandering and folly, have passed over my head since I first took hold of thy covenant. How fickle, false, and deceitful have I proved; yet thou knowest, thine own Spirit through all my wanderings testified in my heart, that out of the channel of this covenant there could be neither safety nor comfort; and never, so far as I can remember, have I deliberately chosen to be dealt with by any other. Its corrections and chastisements have reached the deepest sensibilities of my heart. 'Thine arrows stuck fast in me, thy hand pressed me sore; there was no soundness in my flesh, neither rest in my bones, because of my sin; mine iniquities went over my head, were a burden too heavy to bear. I was feeble and sore broken, and roared by reason of the disquiet of my heart. My lovers and friends stood aloof from my sore, and my kinsmen stood afar off. I was ready to halt, and my sorrow was continually before me;' yet even in my darkest, deepest afflictions, when 'deep called to deep,' and thy 'waves and billows were passing over me;' when my 'soul seemed sinking in the mire where there was no standing, I groped in the dark; my heart panted, my strength failed, and the light of mine eyes seemed gone out. I was weak with my groaning; in the night I made my bed to swim with my tears;' yet even then, by that same covenant by which I was suffering, 'light sprang out of darkness,' glimmering hope in the midst of despair. 'I remembered the years of thy right hand; in the multitude of my thoughts within me, (the provision made in this covenant,) thy comforts delighted my soul.'

"I was furnished with a plea, which would condemn, by every covenant but thine, 'Pardon my iniquities, for they are great. Thou, even thou, art he who blottest out transgressions as a cloud, and iniquity as a thick cloud.' Verily, 'thou art a God that pardoneth, though thou takest vengeance on the inventions of thy rebellious children.' 'Vengeance,' not the vengeance of the curse, no; that, O thou blessed Covenant, thou blessed Surety, *that* fell on thy devoted head! Thou by this covenant wast 'made a curse for us.' Thou didst 'tread the wine-press alone, and of the people there was none to help thee.' Thou didst expend the last drop of that cup of vengeance. Every cup put into our hand, though a cup of trembling, is a cup of blessing. I this day take a fresh hold of thy covenant, for myself, for my children, and for my children's children, to the latest generation. For my brother and sister, for their children, and children's children; for the near concerns of our dear D. B.; and for all whom I carry on my mind to thy throne of grace. This is the sum and substance of my prayers. Bring them into the bond of this covenant, and deal with them according to the order of it, and the provision made for them in it, in all possible circumstances. Amen.

"'O God, in the multitude of thy mercies hear me, in the truth of thy salvation.' Truth of thy salvation! Thou only knowest the truth of thy salvation. How little do we know of thy work! Many of those providences which appear to us dark and dismal, are wheels turning round 'the truth of thy salvation;' opening our blinded eyes to the issues of sin, and also delivering from the snares of the devil. 'Deal not, O Lord, with me, and mine, as our iniquities deserve;' this has never been thy way with us; 'but according to thy former loving-kindness,' and to all the long-suffering patience and pardoning mercy which thy aged servant has experienced through her sinful guilty pilgrimage. Thou hast forgiven me all the way from Egypt. 'Leave me not now, when I am old and grey-headed; but when strength and heart fail, be thou the strength of my heart and portion forever.' Amen."

The winter of 1804–5 was unusually severe: the river Hudson was shut by frost as early as November; fuel was consequently scarce and dear; and the poor suffered greatly. Mrs. Graham visited those parts of the city where the poorer class of sufferers dwelt;* in upwards of two hundred families she either found a

* The following notice of these scenes appeared in one of the periodical publications of the day:

"When sorrow shrunk before the piercing wind,
And famine, shelterless, in suffering pin'd;
When sickness droop'd in solitary pain,
Mid varying misery's relentless reign;
Oh then tumultuous rose the plaints of grief,
And loud and strong the clamors for relief!
Then active charity, with boundless care,
From gloomy faces chas'd the fiend Despair,
Dispelled the horrors of the wintry day,
And none that ask'd went unrelieved away.
"Yet there are some who sorrow's vigils keep,
Unknown that languish, undistinguish'd weep!
Behold yon ruin'd building's shattered walls,
Where drifting snow through many a crevice falls;
Whose smokeless vent no blazing fuel knows,
But drear and cold the *widow's mansion* shows;

Bible their property, or gave them one; praying with them in their affliction. She requested a friend to write, first one Religious Tract, and then another, suited to the peculiar situation of those afflicted people. One was called "A Donation to Poor Widows with Small Children," the other, "A Second Visit to Poor Widows with Small Children." And lest it might be said it was cheap to give advice, she usually gave a small sum of money along with the Tracts she distributed. There was at this time neither a Bible nor Tract Society in New-York. Mrs. Hoffman accompanied her in many of her excursions. In the course of their visits they discovered a French family from St. Domingo in such extremity of distress as made them judge it necessary to report their case to the Honorable Dewitt Clinton, then mayor of the city. The situation of this

> Her fragile form, by sickness deeply riven,
> Too weak to face the driving blasts of heaven,
> Her voice too faint to reach some pitying ear,
> Her shivering babes command her anguish'd tear:
> Their feeble cries in vain assistance crave,
> And expectation 'points but to the grave.'
>   "But lo, with hasty step a female form
> Glides through the wind and braves the chilling storm,
> With eager hand now shakes the tottering door,
> Now rushes breathless o'er the snow-clad floor.
> Her tongue soft comfort to the mourner speaks,
> Her silver voice with soft emotion breaks;
> Round the drear hovel roves her moistened eye,
> Her graceful bosom heaves the lengthened sigh.
>   "I know thee now—I know that angel frame—
> O that the muse might dare to breathe thy name!
> Nor thine alone, but all that *sister-band*
> Who scatter gladness o'er a weeping land;
> Who comfort to the infant sufferer bring,
> And 'teach with joy the widow's heart to sing.'
>   "For this no noisy honors, fame shall give,
> In your own breasts your gentle virtues live;
> No sounding numbers shall your names reveal,
> But your own hearts the rich reward shall feel."
>   ALBERT.

family being made public, three hundred dollars were voluntarily contributed for their relief. Roused by this incident, a public meeting was called at the Tontine Coffee-House, and committees from the different wards were appointed to aid the Corporation in ascertaining and supplying the immediate wants of the suffering poor. The zeal of Mrs. Graham and Mrs. Hoffman paved the way for this public-spirited exertion, which, probably, was the means of saving the lives of some of the destitute and friendless.

In the month of August, 1805, Mrs. Graham paid another visit to her friends in Boston, of whom she spoke with much affection and esteem. She used to mention, with peculiar approbation, a Society of pious ladies there, who met once in every week for prayer and mutual edification.

On returning to New-York she again wrote to her friend Mrs. C——, renewing her endeavors for her consolation and establishment in the faith of Christ; and soon after informed her of the dangerous illness of two of her grand-children, one of whom, in the righteous dispensations of an unerring Providence, was taken, and the other left.

To Mrs. C——, Boston.

"Greenwich, New-York, September 26, 1805.

" My dear Friend,—I arrived here on Monday. I found my children in health, but much affected with the death of the amiable youth M——, and the melancholy situation of his bereaved parents.

" The epidemic spreads over the city in every direction among the few remaining in it. All the public offices are here; crowds of the citizens, and houses and stores spring up in a day; all is bustle and confusion, and all seem *mad* on business.

"Parting with my dear friend was most painful, so painful that nothing could alleviate it but the presence of my own children, who could there have been room from deeper sorrows, would have shared it with me. O that I could put my God in my place in your heart! What are earthly friends? How few are steady against all change of circumstances! of these, fewer still have it in their power to supply every link of friendship's chain; a thousand unforeseen incidents disappoint their wishes and frustrate their hopes, rendering abortive their greatest exertions. But there is a *Friend*, every where present, thoroughly acquainted with every circumstance of the heart and of the life; all-powerful to relieve; whose love is invariable, and ever the most tender when every other friend stands aloof; a friend in adversity, 'a friend who sticketh closer than a brother,' whose 'love surpasseth the love of women.' This friend receiveth sinners—casts out none who come to him. He was never known to disappoint the hopes of any poor sinner. He receives them into his heart; he takes all their burdens and cares on himself, pays all their debts, answers all demands against them, and is every way surety for them; they become his own, no one has any thing to say to them but himself. He knows them—how apt to err, to wander, yea, to forget him, and prove ungrateful; all this he knows, but he has made provision for all. He has a rod, and he will subdue their iniquities. He will heal their backslidings, he will bring back and restore his wanderers. He will in due time perfect what concerns them, and present them to his Father purified, without spot or wrinkle.

"In the meantime he requires them to confide in him; to go up through this wilderness leaning upon him; to tell him all their complaints and griefs, and to comfort themselves: and he will impress the comfort by means of his great and precious promises, scattered like so many pearls through his sacred Bible, tabled there, on purpose for us to ground our prayers upon, and delight ourselves in. This is your friend's Friend, and of ten thousand beside. This was the wicked Magdalene's Friend; this, the persecuting Paul's Friend, wicked Manasseh's Friend; the adulterous, murdering David's Friend. And he is your Friend, though your eyes are holden that you see him not. He is leading you by a way that you know not. This is one of his characters, 'I will bring the blind by a way that they know not.'

"I was happy to find your niece was to return with Mr. C——; but, my dear, a painful dread has assaulted my peace, lest Satan get the advantage by means of a stranger in the family, and undo what has been begun. The world may have peace without God; but you shall not. You have, however feebly, taken hold of his covenant, and he will keep you to your choice. 'If his children forsake his laws and go astray,' &c. Psalm 79 : 30."

"November, 1805.

"MY DEAR FRIEND,—This is not our rest; through much tribulation all Christ's disciples must follow him. There is a rest prepared for the people of God: as far as tasted in this world, (and in this world it is tasted,) it consists in a mind resigned to the will of God, in proportion as it can say, 'thy will be done on earth as it is done in heaven.' Christ himself was made perfect through suffering, and all his followers shall be so in their appointed measure. What is our cup to his? O my dear friend, we are ransomed, we are redeemed, and we are fitting and preparing for the purchased inheritance, that perfect rest prepared for the people of God when their warfare is finished. Let him do all his pleasure with us here; let him subdue our iniquities in his own way; let him glorify his name by our sufferings—his glory is ever connected with his people's best interests. We shall one day acknowledge that he has done all things well, and that not one word of all that he has promised has failed.

: "It has pleased the Lord to take from us our dear sweet Rebecca; young as she was, through much tribulation she entered in: I have scarcely seen severer suffering, nor a harder dismission. It is well, the Lord will answer his own ends by it for the good of all concerned, as well as for his own glory. Our dear G. was ill at the same time, and all hope was lost as to him also; for a whole week we looked upon him as dying. A bold measure was taken with him, which succeeded; the Lord had commanded life; it was not thought of for her. God had appointed to her entrance into life eternal. It is all well. Blessed, blessed be his name! for her he has taken and him he has restored, both equally. I. G. S—— was confined at the same time with a broken arm; N. B—— with the fever and pleurisy. Deep have been the wounds in this aged heart, not yet wean-

ed from earth, but tremblingly alive to every thing that
concerns my children. Yet I do give up. I have asked
but one thing with importunity, and by that I abide. I
did not ask for temporal life, but the life which Christ
died to purchase, and lives to bestow; let him answer
my petition by means of his own appointing: by health
or by sickness, by riches or by poverty, by long life or
early death—only let all mine by the ties of nature, be
his by regeneration of his Spirit."

Having felt the trials and the responsibilities of
widowhood, she wrote to her brother's widow, Mrs.
Marshall, in 1805:

" You are now, my dear sister, the only head of your
family. Will you take Joshua's determination ? ' As for
me and my house, we will serve the Lord !' Take hold
of God's covenant for your orphan children as for yourself, and consider them as his, to be brought up for
him. Be a priestess in your own house, and keep up
the worship of God daily in your family, and confess
your Lord and Master before angels, men, and devils.
They who thus honor God, he will honor.

" You are indeed, my dear, arrived at an important
stage of your journey through this great wilderness.
You are now the head of the family, and are to God immediately answerable. No earthly consideration must
make you give up the government of it, nor the prerogative which he hath given you, to counsel, and even beseech your household to serve the Lord. You cannot
give grace; you cannot give life; and where there is no
life there can be no spiritual exercise; but you may use

means, although there is much prudence to be observed to avoid disgust.

"Be faithful then, my dear sister, to your important trust. See that your household remember the Sabbath-day to keep it holy; your children, of course, will accompany you to the house of God, but let not your servants absent themselves from his ordinances, and endeavor, on your return home, to explain and bring home the word that may have been spoken to their consciences. Above all, let it be your constant aim to set before them a godly, consistent example, and be much engaged in prayer for them—I mean for your servants as well as for your children, and God will, in all probability, make you a mother in Israel, the mother of many spiritual children, and turn your captivity into rejoicing, and fill your mouth with songs of praise; or should you not have this comfort, should the night of adversity last to the very valley of the shadow of death, the morning of eternal rest shall then beam forth upon your own soul, and your prayers may be answered for others, when the eyes that wept and the breast that heaved are at rest in the dust. O, then, my sister, possess your soul in patience, and seek to make daily advances in holiness."

CHAPTER IX.

ORPHAN ASYLUM SOCIETY—FOREIGN MISSIONARIES—

LETTERS.

On the 15th of March, 1806, the female subscribers to proposals for providing an Asylum for Orphan Children met at the City Hotel; Mrs. Graham was called to the chair, a Society organized, and a board of direction chosen. Mrs. Hoffman was elected the first Directress of the Orphan Asylum Society. Mrs. Graham continued in the office of first Directress of the Widows' Society, but took a deep interest in the success of the Orphan Asylum also; she, or one of her family, taught the orphans daily, until the funds of the Institution were sufficent to provide a teacher and superintendent. She was a trustee at the time of her decease. The wish to establish this new Society was occasioned by the pain which it gave the ladies of the Widows' Society to behold a family of orphans driven, on the decease of a widow, to seek refuge in the Alms-house; no melting heart to feel, no redeeming hand to rescue them from a situation so unpromising for mental and moral improvement.

"Amongst the afflicted of our suffering race," thus speaks the Constitution of the Society, "none makes a stronger or more impressive appeal to humanity than the *destitute orphan.* Crime has not been the cause of its misery, and future usefulness may yet be the result of its protection; the reverse is often the case of more

11*

aged objects. God himself has marked the fatherless
as the peculiar subjects of his divine compassion. 'A
Father of the fatherless is God in his holy habitation.'
'When my father and my mother forsake me, then the
Lord will take me up.' To be the blessed instrument
of divine Providence in making good the promise of
God, is a privilege equally desirable and honorable to
the benevolent heart.' "

And truly God has made good his promise towards
this benevolent Institution. He has crowned the undertaking with his remarkable blessing. It was begun by
his disciples in faith, and he has acknowledged them in
it. Having for fourteen months occupied a hired house
for an Asylum, the ladies entertained the bold idea
of building an Asylum on account of the Society. They
had then about three hundred and fifty dollars as the
commencement of a fund for the building: they purchased four lots of ground in the village of Greenwich,
on a healthful, elevated site, possessing a fine prospect.
The corner-stone was laid on the 7th of July, 1807.
They erected a building fifty feet square; from time to
time they proceeded to finish the interior of the building,
and to purchase additional ground as their funds would
permit; and such was the liberality of the legislature
and of the public, that the Society soon possessed a
handsome building and nearly an acre of ground, all of
which must have cost them little short of twenty-five
thousand dollars. In that house Mrs. Graham and Mrs.
Hoffman spent much of their time; there they trained
for Eternity the children of those whose widowed dying
mothers they had cheered with the hope that when they

should be taken away, God would fulfil his gracious promise and preserve their fatherless children alive.

Mrs. Hoffman survived Mrs. Graham seven years. Her end, like that of her friend, was PEACE. But though God removed those mothers in Israel, their prayers are still before him, and the Institution continues to prosper. In 1836, the city having extended to where the Asylum was situated, and the property at the same time increased in value, the Society became desirous to remove where the children would enjoy purer air, and have greater convenience for a garden and pasture for cows. With the advice of their patrons, they sold the property for about $39,000; purchased nearly ten acres of ground at Bloomingdale, and on the 9th of June the same year laid the foundation-stone of their present beautiful building.

In the 34th annual Report of the Society, for 1840, we find the following record of God's goodness:

"On no former occasion has the Board of Direction been privileged to make to the friends and patrons of this Institution a more favorable Report than the present. The ORPHAN'S HOME is completed, and the beautiful building on the banks of the Hudson is alike an ornament to the city and a memorial of the liberality of its inhabitants. Within it are found, not only ample accommodations for a numerous family, but a place for the Lord, an habitation for the orphans' God. On the 19th of November last the chapel was opened for religious worship; the services were performed by reverend clergy of different denominations; and a highly respectable and apparently gratified audience attended. All the children, 165 in number, were present, from the infant in arms to the youth who will this day pronounce the valedictory.

" To those who have witnessed the progress of this Institution from the *small frame-house* of 1806 to the noble edifice of 1840, accompanied by the recollection that the door has never been closed against the destitute orphan, how deep must be the conviction of an over-ruling Providence—the truth of the declaration, that ' God is the father of the fatherless in his holy habitation,' and the fulfilment of his gracious promise, ' Leave thy fatherless children, I will preserve them alive !' Nor is the orphan family merely furnished with sufficient accommodation for dwelling and moral and religious education: the grounds afford ample room for exercise and recreation; the garden supplies them with fruit and vegetables; and, there being pasture for several cows, wholesome milk is added to their simple breakfast, while the abounding river invigorates the frame by a saline bath,—and by casting a net into it, furnishes an occasional dinner of fresh fish."

The Society, ever grateful to the founders, have erected a tablet on the wall of the beautiful chapel, which bears the following inscription:

SACRED

TO THE MEMORY OF

ISABELLA GRAHAM,

Who died 27th July, 1814;

AND OF

MRS. SARAH HOFFMAN,

Who died 29th July, 1821.

THEY WERE BOTH FOUNDERS OF THIS INSTITUTION.

TO THEIR PRAYER OF FAITH,

AND WISDOM IN DIRECTING ITS COUNSELS,

THE SOCIETY IS INDEBTED FOR MUCH OF THE SUCCESS

THAT HAS ATTENDED IT.

THEY WERE LOVELY IN THEIR LIVES,

AND DURING MANY YEARS THEY TRAVELLED TOGETHER

THE WALKS OF CHARITY.

"When the ear heard them it blessed them, and they
caused the Widow's heart to sing for joy."

THEY NOW REST FROM THEIR LABORS,

PARTAKERS OF THE BLESSEDNESS OF THOSE

WHO DIE IN THE LORD:

THEIR WORKS DO FOLLOW THEM.

The success which has attended the Orphan Asylum
Society furnishes strong encouragement to attempt
great and good objects even with slender means. God
in his providence will command a blessing on exertions
of this character. It is too common a mistake, and
one fatal to the progress of improvement, that great
means should be in actual possession before great objects should be attempted. Ah, were our dependence
simply on apparent instruments, how small must be our

hopes of success! There is a mystery, yet a certainty, in the manner by which God is pleased in his providence to conduct feeble means to a happy conclusion. Has he not preserved, cherished and blessed his church through many ages, amidst overwhelming persecutions, and that often by means apparently inadequate to this end? We must work for, as well as pray for, the blessing which God has promised to bestow on our sinful race. We must put our shoulder to the wheel, whilst we look up to heaven for assistance, and God will bless those who are found in the path of duty.

In this Asylum the ladies have set no limits to the number to be received; and it has pleased God also not to set limits to the means necessary for their support. The Institution is a great favorite with the public, and is frequently visited by strangers, who are delighted with the cleanliness, health, and cheerful countenances of the orphans.

The Society have received a charter of incorporation from the legislature; they have a handsome seal, with this inscription: IN-AS-MUCH AS YE HAVE DONE IT UNTO ONE OF THE LEAST OF THESE, YE HAVE DONE IT UNTO ME.

For several years it was customary with Mrs. Graham to visit the *New-York Hospital ;* and before the admirable provision since made for the separate care of those mentally deranged, she paid a particular attention to patients of this description.

To the apartments appropriated to *sick female convicts in the State Prison* she also made many visits; she met with some affecting circumstances among this class.

In the winter 1807–8, when the suspension of commerce by the embargo rendered the situation of the poor more destitute than ever, Mrs. Graham adopted a plan best calculated in her view to detect the idle applicant for charity, and at the same time to furnish employment for the more worthy amongst the female poor. She purchased flax, and lent wheels where applicants had none. Such as were industrious took the work with thankfulness and were paid for it; those who were beggars by profession never kept their word by returning for the flax or the wheel. The flax thus spun was afterwards wove, bleached, and made into table-cloths and towels for family use.

Mrs. Graham used to remark that until some Institution should be formed to furnish employment for industrious poor women, the work of charity would be incomplete. It was about this time, that, deeming the duties too laborious for her health, she resigned the office of first Directress of the Widows' Society, and took the place of a Manager. She afterwards declined this also, and became a Trustee of the Orphan Asylum Society, as more suited to her advanced period of life.

The lady to whom the following letter was addressed was MISS FARQUHARSON, a person of genuine piety and worth, whom Mrs. Graham had educated and prepared to become her assistant in teaching. When Mrs. Graham retired from her school, Miss Farquharson declined to succeed her, preferring to accompany and enjoy the society of her patroness and friend. Until 1804 she proved as efficient an assistant to Mrs. Graham in her charitable labors in the Widows' Society and Sabbath-school as she had been in her boarding-schoo!.

During the prevalence of the yellow fever in 1804, she was called to attend her own dying mother, and underwent so much fatigue, that on her return to Mrs. Graham she broke a blood vessel, and for four months was confined to her room, during all which time Mrs. Graham attended her night and day. Her medical attendants prescribed a long voyage and residence in a hot climate as the only means of saving her life. About that time Mr. Andrew Smith was preparing to sail for the East Indies with his family, via England. With them she embarked. She sojourned several weeks in Birmingham, and there the circumstances commenced which eventually led Miss Farquharson to become a Missionary's wife and *the first American Missionary to foreign lands.* Her history has been published by Rev. Mr. Knill, in a Tract entitled "The Missionary's wife."

The London Missionary Society were preparing to establish a mission in the idolatrous city of Surat, but the East India Company would not allow christian missionaries to sail in their ships. The Society thankfully availed themselves of the privilege of sending Mr. Loveless and Dr. Taylor in the American ship Alleghany. They arrived in Madras, June, 1805.

During the voyage an attachment was formed between Mr. Loveless and Miss Farquharson which death only could sever, and introduced her to scenes of usefulness for more than thirty years, for which she was eminently qualified by early training. As soon as Mrs. Graham heard how her friend was going to be employed, she wrote to her as follows:

"MY DEAR SALLY,—Many tears have I shed over

your letter. What a changing lot has been that of my family! The Lord's providences to me and mine have not been of the ordinary kind, and you, as one in it, seem to be a partaker with us. Surely, of all others, we have most reason to say, ' We are strangers and pilgrims on the earth.' Oh that we may drink into the true spirit of that phrase, and enjoy the genuine, firm faith of an everlasting habitation, of living at home with God!

"My dear Sally, take the comfort of this, that it is the Lord who hath led you all the way by which you have gone. Of all persons whom I know, you were, from your temper and disposition, the least likely to travel, still less to continue a traveller. No ordinary means would have led you to leave your friends and religious privileges. And many a pang it has cost me, on reflection, to think how positive I was that you should take the voyage. But it was of the Lord. The physicians urged it as the only chance you had for life, and they had reason; for of all those who were attacked in the same manner, there is not one alive, within my knowledge, at this day.

"The Lord, by wonderful means, called you from your native land, and led you to the very spot where you met Mr. Loveless. The same God, being also his God, led him, by means perhaps equally unforeseen and uncommon, to the same spot, united your hearts to each other, and made you one in his hand, and I trust to his glory. You ask my blessing: I have carried both of you to my God and Savior, and have prayed, and continue to pray, that the Lord will bless you individually and unitedly, give you much sweet communion with himself, and much social enjoyment with him and with one another. May he bless Mr. Loveless as a Missionary, and give him the spirit of his office, and much fruit among the heathen, as seals to his ministry; and may you be a helper with him, and both be blessed and made a blessing.

"I feel my loss. You were a comfort and a help to us all, especially to me: but I do not mourn; I heartily acquiesce. This is not only agreeable to me, as it is one of God's wise arrangements to you and us all, but I think it will be more to your comfort. Religion and conjugal love will sweeten almost any lot. It is the Lord's appointment and his richest earthly blessing.

"My dear Sally, I have ever considered you as my child. You are very dear to my heart. Tell Mr. Loveless he must ever consider me as his mother.

"Your affectionate mother,

"ISABELLA GRAHAM."

In the month of January, 1807, the London Missionary Society, of which Mr. Bethune was a Foreign Director, sent to this country the Rev. Messrs. GORDON, LEE, and MORRISON; the two first to sail in an American ship for the East Indies, and Mr. Morrison for China. These devoted Missionaries shared largely in the hospitalities of christians in New-York, and spent much of their time with Mr. B——'s family. Mrs. Graham took great delight in conversing and advising with them, and though none of her letters addressed to them have come to hand, it is believed she corresponded with them. The following extract of a letter, from Dr. Morrison, indicates the respect and christian affection with which he regarded her.

"On board the Trident, May 24, 1807.

"MY EVER DEAR MOTHER GRAHAM,—I think you were led by the special interference of our gracious Lord, to put into my hands the work which you did, accompanied by the edifying and comforting letter which you wrote me.

"I thank you for telling me what God did for your soul, and join with you in ascribing to the Lord salvation and honor. I had, my mother, from the time of leaving my dear relations and friends, passed through waters deep as the fathomless ocean which I crossed; but with the Lord there is mercy; with him is 'plenteous redemption.' 'He is ready to forgive.' He has restored to me, in some measure, 'the joy of his salvation,' and will not, I trust, take his Holy Spirit from me. This is my prayer. To-day he enabled me, on board of this vessel, to open my lips to teach transgressors his way. O, that sinners may be converted unto him!"

To Mr. and Mrs. B——, at Balston Springs.

"NEW-YORK, August, 1807.

"MY BELOVED CHILDREN,—A husband, wife and child, make a family, and God ought to be acknowledged by them as such. I am anxious that you should meet in your room for that purpose some time every morning.

"If it cannot be accomplished at an early hour, redeem that time in a later, and also before going to rest in the evening. The Lord has honored your family worship with genuine fruits, follow it up in all places. Like Abraham of old, where-ever you pitch your tent, for a longer or shorter period, there raise an altar to the Lord, to that God who has fed you all your life, carried you as on eagle's wings, and will carry you to old age and gray hairs."

To Mrs. Juliet S——, New-York, one of her former pupils.

"Belville, September 16, 1808.

"MY DEAR JULIET,—Since the hour I received your letter you have been little out of my mind. You call upon me as mother, friend, counsellor. Shall conscious unworthiness, or weakness, or ignorance, prevent my answering? No; for God often chooses weak instruments to bring to pass great ends? I have been once and again at a throne of Grace, for wisdom to direct me, and grace to be faithful. If your desire after spiritual knowledge be sincere, and from the Spirit of God operating on your heart, you will bear searching.

"You are a communicant, my Juliet; this presupposes that a very great and an important change has taken place in your mind; that you have been made deeply sensible of what the word of God testifies of every son and daughter of Adam's race. Romans, 3 : 9, 'As it is written, there is none righteous, no not one.' 'Man is born as the wild ass's colt, going astray from the womb.' Job. 'The heart is deceitful above all things, and desperately wicked; I the Lord search it.' 'Having the understanding darkened, alienated from the life of God, through the ignorance that is in us, because of the blindness of our hearts.' Ephesians, 4 : 18. 'Dead in trespasses and sins'. Chap. 2 : 1.

"Your profession presupposes that this chapter may be addressed to you, Juliet, by name. 'You hath he quickened, who were dead in trespasses and sins; wherein in time past ye walked according to the course of this world, according to the prince of the power of the air, the spirit that now worketh in the children of disobedience: among whom also we all had our conversation, in times past, in the lusts of our flesh, fulfilling the desires of the flesh and of the mind; and were by nature the children of wrath, even as others. But God, who is rich in mercy, for his great love wherewith he loved us, even when we were dead in sins, hath quickened us together with Christ; by grace are ye saved, through faith, not of works, lest any man should boast.' Works there are, my Juliet, most assuredly; every quickened soul will live, and bring forth fruits of righteousness; but these works are not attainable but in God's way and order. It follows, 'For we are his workmanship, created in Christ Jesus unto good works, which God hath before ordained that we should walk in them.'

"My Juliet says, 'To you then I look up to teach me.' Let me then bring you to the great Teacher and Prophet of the Church, without whose teaching all human instruction will be ineffectual. We read of two amiable characters coming to Christ professedly for instruction. The first you will find in Matthew, 19 : 16. The young man asks him, 'What good thing shall I do, that I may inherit eternal life ?' Jesus answers him, by referring him to the moral law: the young man, not made acquainted, by the Spirit of God, either with the extent or spirituality of that law, or of the depravity of his own nature, answers, as many in like circumstances still do, 'All these things have I kept from my youth up.' I do not suppose any one could contradict him. It is added that Jesus loved him, and he was a person of attractive character; but Jesus knew that the true principle was not there—supreme love to God, 'with all the heart, with all the soul, with all the strength, and with all the mind:' therefore he gave him a test which proved that the world was uppermost in his heart. He went away sorrowful, and we hear no more of him.

"Of the other person we read in that remarkable chapter, the third of John's Gospel—*Nicodemus*, a ruler of the Jews, and also a teacher. Well knew he the law, as to the letter of it, both moral and ceremonial; he must also have been acquainted with all the Old Testament Scripture types and prophecies, it being his office to expound; and no doubt, among others, was looking for the promised Messiah. Jesus does not send him to either the law or the prophets. This ruler comes with a conviction and an acknowledgment that Jesus himself was a teacher immediately from God; and Jesus immediately takes upon himself his great office, and begins with urging that which is a sinner's first business—' to know himself,' what he is by nature, and the necessity of the new birth. Nicodemus, with all his learning, was a stranger to this doctrine: 'How can a man be born when he is old?' Jesus repeats his doctrine, 'He must be born of water and the Spirit;' baptized with water and the Holy Ghost. 'That which is born of flesh is flesh, and that which is born of the Spirit is Spirit. Marvel not that I said unto you, ye must be born again.' Humble that proud reason that will believe nothing but what it can understand. 'The wind bloweth where it listeth, and thou hearest the sound thereof, but canst not tell whence it cometh or whither it goeth: so is every one that is born of the Spirit;'—a mystery it is; nevertheless it is true.

"Follow out the chapter, my dear: Jesus preaches his

own Gospel, and brings in that beautiful type, the serpent, which he had commanded to be raised on a pole, that those who had been bitten with fiery serpents, whose bite was death, should look upon it and be healed. Read it, my dear, in the 21st of Numbers; and in reference to this, he himself says, 'Look unto me, all ye ends of the earth, and be ye saved.' Except a man be born again he cannot see the kingdom of God. Quickened, renewed in the spirit of his mind, old things pass away and all things become new, new principles, new desires, new pleasures, new ends. The work is God's. The whole plan of Redemption is his from first to last. It is clearly revealed in Scripture, and there is no dispute among christians concerning it. The fall of man, his corruption and depravity; his state under the curse of a broken covenant, and his exposure to eternal misery; his helplessness and total inability to gain acceptance with God; his ignorance of himself—'dead in trespasses and sins,' 'without God and without hope in the world:' this is his situation by nature. But there is good news proclaimed, 'God so loved the world that he gave his only begotten Son' to become the Surety of lost sinners. He took our nature upon him, our sins upon him, our duties upon him: he was placed in our stead; sustained the penalty of the broken law; fulfilled its utmost demands; *redeemed* us; gave us a new covenant, of which himself is the Surety: and 'there is no condemnation to them that are in Christ Jesus.'

" The merits of Christ, exclusive of any thing of ours, are the sole foundation of our hope. Christ is set forth, in Scripture, as the atonement, the propitiation for sins, the one Sacrifice for sin; Christ is the end of the law for righteousness; all is made ours by free gift. 1 John, 5 : 11. All is ready, justice satisfied, God reconciled, peace proclaimed. But what is all this to a thoughtless world insensible of their situation, danger, and need? It is an awful saying, but it is of the Holy Ghost,—if our Gospel be hid, it is hid to them that are lost, in whom the God of this world hath blinded their minds, and darkened their understandings, and hardened their hearts, &c. Therefore the application of this grace is also of God; it is all within his plan; he has appointed means, and commanded our diligence in the use of them. We have his Bible in our hands, his ministers in our churches, who are also pastors and teachers if we apply for their aid in private; we have a throne of grace to go to, and many great and precious promises held up in God's word for us to embrace and plead for Christ's sake: we have many prayers in the Scriptures which we may adopt.

"I acknowledge we are all still dependant for the effect; *that* must be from God himself. But he does honor his own ordinances. He puts forth his power, and convinces of sin; this is his first work. The soul is awakened, aroused, convinced of sin and misery; sins of the heart, sins of the tongue, sins of the life, press upon the conscience which never disturbed before; mispent time, wasted talents, lost opportunities, neglect of God's word and ordinances, so that the soul cannot rest. O, my Juliet, this is a hopeful case. I hope you have experienced something of this. It is one of the surest marks of the operation of the Spirit of God, and a prelude to the new birth. It never takes place without it, for ' the whole need not a physician, but they that are sick.' Only the weary and heavy laden will prize rest, and Christ is the rest they need; only a convinced sinner will or can prize the Savior, and now the Lord opens his mind to understand the Scriptures. He sees the provision which God has made for ruined sinners, by providing a substitute to stand in his room; he perceives how God can be just and justify the sinner who takes shelter in Jesus; he falls in with God's gracious plan; receives the Lord Jesus as God's gift to sinners; trusts entirely in his merit for pardon, peace, reconciliation, and eternal life; resigns his soul into the hands of his Savior, in the faith that he will save it, and devotes himself unreservedly to his service, in the faith that he will give him grace to live to him in all holy obedience. Now, and not till now, according to God's promise, he receives power to become his child; this is God's order, John, 1: 12. Now he receives life and begins to live; but there is yet a great work before him. It hath pleased God in his plan to finish at once a justifying righteousness; it is his own work, and was finished in that awful hour when he announced it in his last words on the cross, John, 19: 30. To this nothing of ours is to be added, with this nothing of ours mixed; it is for ever perfect, it is God's gift made ours in the hour when we first 'believe, receive it, rest our souls upon it.'

"But it hath not pleased God in this plan to deliver the believer at once from indwelling sin. This is the subject of the christian *warfare*, the *race*, the *good fight*. Now the believer receives life, and is called to work. 'Work out your own salvation with fear and trembling, for it is God that worketh in you both to will and to

do.' All the promises in this blessed Bible are his, they
are yea and amen in Christ; Christ himself is his; his
Spirit dwells in him. The believer is united to Jesus
by as real a union as the branch to the vine, the members to the head, the building with the foundation.
Yet sin dwelleth in him, and is to be expunged by constant applications to Christ in prayer; by means of
watching, striving, fighting—fighting under his banner.
In his blessed word we are informed where our strength
lies, what are our weapons, what our armor. But what
can I say on those subjects? the whole word of God is
on the subject of redemption; to this refer the whole
labors of Christ's ministers, and the whole dispensation
of God's providence.

"Are these things so? My Juliet, this is not the
doctrine of any one church. About these subjects there
is no dispute. Presbyterians, Episcopalians, Baptists,
Independents, all agree in these great things. And are
these things so *indeed?* O my Juliet, where is the time
to be spared for plays, assemblies, and such numerous
idle parties of various descriptions? I must stop; the
subject is great, and we have many excellent treatises
on the various parts of it, by able, pious men. It would
be improper to crowd it thus into a letter, unless to in-
stigate to further investigation.

"Farewell! I ever am, my dear Juliet, yours affec-
tionately,   I. GRAHAM."

The delicate state of health to which one of her
grand-daughters was reduced in 1808, made it necessary for her to spend the summer season for five successive years at *Rockaway*, Long Island, for the advan-

tage of sea-bathing. Mrs. Graham went with her, it being beneficial to her own health also. In this place she met with many strangers; the company residing there treated her with much affection and respect. She always attended to the worship of God morning and evening in her room, and was usually accompanied by some of the ladies who boarded in the house. Her fund of information, vivacity of manner, and the interest which she felt in the happiness of all around her, made her society highly valued and pleasing. Few of those ladies who stayed with her at Rockaway for any length of time, failed to express, at parting, their esteem for her, and they generally added a pressing invitation for a visit from her, if ever she should travel near where they dwelt.

The following is one of her sweet meditations while at Rockaway :

"Rockaway, August, 1809.

"Sweet health again returns, which, considering the agitation of my mind, surprises me ; but it is the Lord's pleasure. I did not wish to recover. I was in hopes the Lord was about to deliver me from "this body of sin and death." Lord, reconcile me to thy most holy will. Health is certainly a great blessing. I feel its sweetness. O make me thankful! Great and numerous are my mercies. Every thing pleasant and every thing necessary to life, to godliness, is mine : food and raiment to the utmost desires of nature; the beauties of thy fair creation surround my ordinary dwelling ; my dear little room, my Bible, and books of every virtuous kind, (by grace, thy chief mercy, I desire no other ;) and by the kindness of my children, I possess all as if they were my own personal property. By thy wonderful loving-kindness, thou hast given me, instead of the contempt which I have merited, the love and esteem of thy people, and thou hast made ' the very stones of the field to be at peace with me,' so that wherever I go I meet with kindness."

To Mrs. Marshall.

"New-York, October, 1809.

"I find your letter dated ' *Elderslie*,'—the very name gives a thrill to my old heart; in a moment the various scenes of my youthful days rise before me—the old mansion itself, and all its beloved inmates, every one of whom have now crossed the Jordan of death, leaving me a solitary wanderer in this weary wilderness. Ah, I can at this moment think of spots, by the burnside and the braeside, endeared to my heart by a thousand tender associations. There have I wandered with my beloved, idolized husband, and there has he delighted my heart with professions of love. These were indeed moments of ecstasy; but hush! there are you a widow with very, very different sensations, and here am I a widow with sensations equally different. The Lord has showed us many and sore adversities, but he will bring us up from the deeps below; we are much nearer our Father's house, and I hope proportionably riper for those joys which are at his right hand; and although your letter has brought some pleasing recollections to my mind—days of love and courtship, days, some of solitude, some of disappointment, some of ecstasy— yet I find they were all days of idolatry, therefore to be mourned over, not re-tasted, re-enjoyed with delight. No, no; Father, forgive me."

CHAPTER X.

NEW-YORK BIBLE SOCIETY—ASSOCIATIONS FOR PRAYER—
HAPPY OLD AGE—LETTERS.

· "In December, 1809, a *Bible Society* was organized
in New-York, and about the same time twenty respectable persons united in a Society, to wait on the
Lord, to know *what their hands could find to do, to promote his glory*, to advance his kingdom, to spread the
savor of the Redeemer's name, or in any way to benefit
the souls of their fellow-sinners.

"On Monday a meeting for prayer was instituted in
Hetty-street, and another in Mulberry-street, with
which the presbyterian ministers have agreed to meet
in rotation. It is the Lord! We have heard of revivals
all around, but feared lest the aggravated sins of New-
York might provoke the Lord to pass by, leaving 'our
fleece dry, while the dew wet all around.' Great have
been our privileges; the Gospel trumpet has sounded
in every corner of our city. The Lord's servants have
set before us life and death, assuring us, from God's
word, that 'though hand join in hand, the wicked shall
not go unpunished;' beseeching us 'to flee from the
wrath to come, and lay hold on the hope set before us.'
God in his providence has visited us with mercies and
with judgments: 'stricken us, and healed us;' scattered
us, and gathered us: but alas! alas! we were 'eating

and drinking, marrying and giving in marriage.' Many, very many, wasting their time, health and substance, in all manner of immorality, and our rulers caring for none of these things; yea, many of them practising the same things; and O! God's own saved people sitting still, restraining testimony before men, and prayer before God. What were we to expect but that God should say, ' Why should they be stricken any more; they will revolt more and more; they are joined to their idols, let them alone.' Such, O Lord, would be the case didst thou not deliver us out of our own self-destroying snares. If thou turn us not, we shall never turn; it is in our nature to backslide for ever.

"But is not the time come to pass when 'before thy people call thou answerest, and while they are yet speaking, thou hearest.' Art thou not calling with power, 'Return, ye backsliding children, and I will heal your backslidings?' and hast thou not prepared their hearts to answer, 'Behold we come unto thee, for thou art the Lord our God: truly, in vain is salvation looked for from the hills, and from the multitude of mountains; truly, from the Lord our God is the salvation of Israel.' Hast thou not, O God, prepared the hearts of thy people to pray, and thine ear to hear? Is not this Bible Society, and are not these *associations for prayer*, tokens from thee for good? More and more, Lord, may thy people 'give thee no rest. until thou make Zion a praise in the earth.' 'O the Hope of Israel, and the Savior thereof, be not as a wayfaring man, that turneth aside for a night.' May thy people constrain thee to abide with us for ever, 'to form us a people for thyself, to show forth thy praise.'

"I have just conveyed dear Mrs. A——le to the confines of the eternal world. I trust the dear Redeemer received her spirit. I have a good hope that she is now in possession of the mansion purchased and prepared for her by that dear Savior whose name she professed, and I think, in an humble, steady, quiet way, faithfully followed. She loved the word of God, the house of God, the people of God. She spoke little, but said she had a good hope: asked me to read the Bible different times, and also to pray; said the invitations of the Gospel were sweet to her: observed that the Lord had been very merciful to her in her affliction.

"A few hours before her death she desired me to read that hymn, 'To him that loved the souls of men,' &c. Also, 'Come let us join our cheerful songs,' &c She asked if I thought she would continue long; I said, No, my dear; you will very soon be with Jesus; and encouraged her as the Lord enabled me. She repeated the question some time after, and I gave her the same answer. She then said, 'This night?' I answered, Yes, my love, this night. She bowed her head with a sweet smile, laid it in a reclining posture, and set herself to wait with patience the Lord's time. She was very much oppressed, and breathed with much difficulty. Some time after she asked me to pray, which I did, and begged that the Lord would increase her faith and patience, and, if according to his will, give her a gentle passage and an abundant entrance. In a short time her breathing became short and low; she shut her eyes and gently breathed weaker and weaker, till her God delivered her without motion or groan. I was on my knees praying. I then thanked God for his goodness in this sweet dismission; prayed for the husband, the children, the two young men present, and us all, gave glory to God, and rose to watch to future duty.

"O my God, is not my own death at hand? It is a hard battle. My Jesus! Thou knowest the struggle. I too must drink of this cup; mix it for me, my Redeemer. O let a full sense of free pardon, the recollection of the great and precious promises, a bright view of the joys at God's right hand, as the fruit of thy death, be applied to my soul in that awful hour! Holy Spirit, pour in 'the oil and wine' of thy consolations in that trying hour. O let me not be straitened! 'Open wide to my soul the leaves of that well-ordered covenant,' of which Christ himself is the sum and substance. Redeeming God, may I experience proof in that solemn hour, that 'thy flesh is meat indeed, and thy blood is drink indeed!' O feed me with this living food! may I feel life spring up in my soul, and be assured that I shall 'never die!' O my God! grant one more request. Open my lips, and let them, as well as my heart, be filled with the high praises of my redeeming God.

"I know I am unworthy; the vilest of the vile; but magnify thy grace. I have much forgiven; O let my heart burn with love and gratitude in that hour, and my lips utter its effusions in songs of praise! Amen.

"When the short thick breathing comes, and the slow fetches, sealing up speech and expelling the spirit from its abode, O let me hear or understand thee, saying unto me—'It is I, be not afraid.' "

" 'Come and let us return unto the Lord, for he hath torn, and he will heal us; he hath smitten, and he will bind us up. After two days will he revive us, in the third he will raise us up, and we shall live in his sight.'

" ' O Lord, turn us and we shall be turned, draw us and we will run after thee. Revive us, and we shall live in thy sight.' Thou must ever be first. It is in our nature to backslide for ever: and whenever we see a backslider restored, or a rebel lay down the weapons of rebellion, *there* we may trace thy footsteps, O God of grace.

" No external providence will touch our hard, our deceitful hearts. All that goes under the name of misfortune will but drive us *from* thee, never *to* thee, till thou teach us to profit, and lead us by the way that we should go. Thou callest, ' Return, ye backsliding children, and I will heal your backslidings;' but we have been foolish, sottish children, without understanding, wise to do evil, but to do good having no knowledge.

" Let the days come when the children of America (the earth is the Lord's) shall ' come with weeping, and seek the Lord their God ;' when ' they shall ask the way to Zion, with their faces thitherward:' when they shall come, saying, ' Let us join ourselves to the Lord in a perpetual covenant, never to be forgotten. O the Hope of Israel and the Savior thereof: is not that day and that time come ?' Hast thou not been working on ' the right hand and on the left ?' Thou hast given us pastors according to thine own heart, who feed us with knowledge and understanding: and thou art here and there proving thy Gospel thy power and thy wisdom, to the salvation of sinners; casting down the imaginations of pride, and bringing all into subjection to thy Son Jesus.

" O pour out ' the spirit of grace and supplication ' upon thy living members, that they may wrestle with thee, and ' not let thee go until thou bless us,' until thou make this ' cloud like a man's hand ' cover our heavens with blackness, and issue in a plentiful rain. ' O pour water upon him that is thirsty, and floods on the dry ground; thy Spirit upon our seed, and thy blessing upon our offspring.' O Lord, hast thou not said that thou wilt do it, and that ' they shall spring up as among the grass, and as willows by the water-courses. One shall say, I am the Lord's, another shall call himself by the name of Jacob, and another shall subscribe with his hand unto the Lord, and surname himself by the name of Israel.' Amen, O our God, amen.

" Last week the Lord's young servant, Mr. R——, received to the communion of the church seven adults, Mrs. B—— and her two daughters, Dr. H—— and sister, Mr. C——, and a black woman, servant to Mr. H——. It was a glorious sight, and revived the hearts of God's people who witnessed it. O God of grace, grant that the fruits of righteousness may prove that they are broken off from the wild olive-tree, and grafted into thee, thou living and life-giving olive-tree; from thee must ' their fruit be found.' O cause them to bring forth much fruit! ' Herein is the Father glorified, that they bear much fruit ;' so shall they be Christ's disciples, and attain to the assurance of that happy state. Father, glorify thy name! Amen."

In the year 1810, whilst bathing at Rockaway, she

was carried by the surf beyond her depth, and for some time there was scarcely a hope of her regaining the shore. Her grandchildren were weeping on the beach, and the company assembled there were afflicted but hopeless spectators of her danger. At that moment of peril she prayed to the Lord for deliverance, but acquiesced in his will, if he should see fit to take her to himself in this manner. Able to swim a little, she kept herself afloat for some time: she became at length very faint; and when her friends on the beach apprehended her lost, they perceived that the waves had impelled her somewhat nearer to them. A gentleman present, and her female attendant, stepped into the surf and extending their arms for mutual support, one of them was enabled to lay hold on Mrs. Graham's bathing-gown and to pull her towards them. When they brought her ashore she was much exhausted, and had swallowed a considerable quantity of water. It was some hours before she revived, when she addressed the company in a very serious and impressive manner that affected them to tears. Her health during the following winter was much impaired by the shock it had received.

"ROCKAWAY, June 15, 1810.

"Came here the first of the month, with the children in the whooping-cough. No 'church-going bell' here, but the Lord is every where; and I have found him here, warming my heart with gratitude and contrition, and drawing it out in prayer for his people met to worship in his sanctuary.

"When at a distance from my own people, it has been my practice to join with whatever class of professing christians might be near me. Here it has been with the Methodists, who, I believe, enjoy communion with God. Yesterday I went to a meeting of ———, who lay great stress on good morals; but, O my God! what could I do, shut up with them? Without the finished work of my Savior I could have no hope; without his law-fulfilling righteousness I must stand a law-condemned sinner.

"The preacher yesterday took no text; in the course of his sermon he said the Scriptures were only secondary guides. He began with the importance of thinking of death, and said it could not be possible for a rational being to live carelessly, with thougths of death and eternity in view. Is it so? No; we see sinners die, under the full conviction that they are dying, as thoughtless as they have lived.

"He said, that by constantly attending to the motions of the Spirit and complying with them, christians arrived at a state of perfection even here; and brought in that text, 'He that is born of God cannot sin,' &c. Spoke highly of watchfulness, and avoiding connection with the world; said a real christian could not hold any office of power among men. Paul held one, but he gave it up when he became an apostle. Christ's kingdom was not of this world. Laws and officers were necessary among the men of the world, but not among christians. Spoke of the cross of Christ as consisting in suffering and self-denial. His blood was the Spirit which cleansed from all sin, by delivering all who obeyed him from its power. He named not my blessed Savior, except when he had occasion to mention some of his moral sayings. He said, indeed, that he was

the Light that lightened every man that came into the
world, and the condemnation was, that men would not
receive it; but one word of his blessed Priesthood he
spoke not—but said we were in a state of probation,
and every one would be judged according to his works,
taking into view the advantages he had enjoyed; recom-
mended the reading of the Scriptures, especially the inspired books, the New Testament, and the Prophets;
for it needed no inspiration to write the national his
tory of the Jews more than that of any other nation.
Said the Scriptures were good secondary guides, and
contained excellent lessons and truths.

"When I was coming away he offered me his hand,
saying that I was not a resident there. I answered no,
I was separated from my own people, but wished to
unite with any class of christians who met professedly
to worship God; but confessed I could not live upon
what he had this day delivered. He asked what was
wrong. I answered, he had given some good exhortations; I agreed with him in many things respecting
conduct; but I missed the foundation. He repeated
the Scriptures, 'Other foundation can no man lay,' &c.
I said, Exactly—off this foundation there is no salvation—on this foundation there may be loss, but no condemnation. We have a great and merciful High Priest,
who can have compassion on the ignorant, and them
who are out of the way; and there may be straw, hay,
stubble, which will be burnt up, but the soul itself, being on the foundation, is safe. He said with firmness,
that will be burnt up in this world; 'without holiness no
man shall see the Lord.' I said, True, but why avoid the
tenure of Scripture; read all the Epistles, the Lord Je-

sus Christ, the Gift of God, the Propitiatory Sacrifice, the meritorious law-fulfilling righteousness, is set forth, in every one of them, as that which saves from wrath and entitles to eternal life. He said they were all emblems of our being made holy in heart and life—Christians were baptized unto the death of Christ, and rise with him to newness of life, buried with him, &c. I granted that as one reading of these words. He said every other view was shadow. I said no—the blood of bulls and goats is shadow; Christ himself, his person, his offices, his life, his sufferings, his death, his burial, resurrection, ascension and intercession within the vail, are all substance—the sole foundation of my hope, and my only plea at a throne of grace.

> " Dear name, the rock on which I build,
>   My shield and hiding-place,
> My never-failing treas'ry, fill'd
>   With boundless stores of grace.
> Jesus ! my Husband, Shepherd, Friend,
>   My Prophet, Priest and King,
> My Lord, my life, my way, my end,
>   Accept the praise I bring."

"Rockaway, August, 1810.

"Hebrews is my ordinary, when no other passage of Scripture attracts my particular attention. This is the third morning I have opened the New Testament on the 14th chapter of John, and have fed delightfully on the first three verses. There is at all times a thorn in my heart, keeping me in continual remembrance of my vile, ungrateful backslidings, so that I eat my sweetest morsels with bitter herbs. It was particularly painful to me this morning ; nevertheless, the Lord God, merciful and gracious, repeated on my heart, 'Let not your heart be troubled, neither let it be afraid.' I was arrested at the

4th verse, 'Whither I go ye know, and the way ye know.' I have had many comfortable exercises on the 8th verse, the Redeemer's answer to Philip's inquiry. But this morning my mind was led to a different view of that saying, and which I think was literally included. The Redeemer was going to his Father, and his way lay through death, the death of the cross. The hour was at hand when he was to make his holy and righteous soul an offering for sin, that he might become the Author of salvation to all who obey him. All the sins confessed and pardoned by the sacrifices under the law were laid on this blessed Surety—*they* were only the shadows, *he* was the substance—the real Lamb of God which taketh away the sin of the world was now to be offered up. This was he who said, 'Sacrifice and offering thou wouldest not, but a body hast thou prepared me; in burnt offerings and offerings for sin thou hast had no pleasure; then said I, Lo, I come to do thy will, O God:' by which will we are sanctified through the offering of the body of Jesus Christ once for all.

"He was going to the garden—Oh that garden! Peter had said he was able to drink of that cup and to be baptized with that baptism. Ah no, Peter! that exceeding sorrow in the garden, when no visible hand was upon him, was a cup the least drop of which would have overwhelmed the strongest angel. No strength short of omnipotent could have sustained that hour and power of darkness. It was not the scourge, the thorns, the nails, nor the last pangs of dissolution; through all these he was as a lamb led to the slaughter, and as a sheep before her shearers, dumb. It was a mysterious horror, of which no created being can have any conception. It was this that wrung the great drops of blood through every pore of his sacred body: this that extorted the agonizing prayer, 'Father, if it be possible, let this cup pass from me.' And again, in his last moments on the cross, 'My God, my God, why hast thou forsaken me?' Blessed, for ever blessed be our Jehovah Jesus, who said, 'Not my will, but thine be done!' The will of God was done, and he said, 'It is finished, and gave up the ghost.'

"All his people must follow him by the way of death; nearly all his disciples followed by the death of the cross, and many others after them, supported by his almighty grace, rejoiced that they were counted worthy to suffer for his sake; but they drank not of that cup.

"Some of his people, for holy and wise purposes, have had a taste in the hiding of God's face, but *no curse; that* he himself drank to the last drop: 'He trod the wine-press alone, and of the people there was none to help him.' By his own death he destroyed him that had the power of death, and secured victory to all his followers: he changed its aspect from that of the king of terrors to that of a welcome messenger from their redeeming God, to conduct them to those blessed mansions which he has purchased and prepared for them; neither will he leave them alone with that messenger: 'And if I go, I will come again and receive you to myself, that where I am, there you may be also. I will not leave you comfortless, I will come to you. The world seeth me no more, but ye see me; because I live, ye shall live also. Let not your heart be troubled, neither let it be afraid.' Amen. 'Come, Lord Jesus.'

"Psalm 40 : 6. 'Sacrifice and offering thou didst not desire; mine ears hast thou opened; burnt-offering and sin-offering hast thou not required; then said I, Lo, I come, in the volume of the book it is written of me; I delight to do thy will, O my God: yea, thy law is in my heart.' Heb. 10: 8. 'Above, when he said, Sacrifice and offering, and burnt-offerings, and offering for sin thou wouldst not, neither hadst pleasure therein; which are offered by the law; then said he, Lo, I come to do thy will, O God. He taketh away the first, that he may establish the second. By the which will we are sanctified, through the offering of the body of Jesus Christ once for all. This man, after he had offered one sacrifice for sins, for ever sat down on the right hand of God. For by one offering he hath perfected for ever them that are sanctified. Whereof the Holy Ghost also is a witness to us: for after that he had said before,' (chap. 8: 10, now repeated chap. 10: 16,) 'This is the covenant that I will make with them after those days,' (in consequence of Christ's doing the will of God, fulfilling all righteousness,) 'I will put my laws into their hearts and in their minds will I write them; and their sins and iniquities will I remember no more. Now, where remission of these is, there is no more offering for sin. Having, therefore, boldness to enter into the holiest by the blood of Jesus, by a new and living way, which he hath consecrated for us, through the veil, that is to say, his flesh; and having an High Priest over the house of God; let us draw near with a true heart, in full assurance of faith, having our hearts sprinkled from an evil conscience, and our bodies washed with pure water. Let us hold fast the profession of our faith without wavering; for he is faithful that promised.' Again, 'The Lord sware, and will not repent; thou art a priest for ever after the order of Melchisedec. By so much was Jesus made a surety of a better testament; because he continueth ever, and hath an unchangeable priesthood. Wherefore, he is able to save to the uttermost those that come unto God by him, seeing he over liveth to make intercession for them. Christ glorified not himself to be made an High Priest; but He that said unto him, Thou art my Son, to-day' have I begotten thee, saith also in another place, Thou art a Priest for ever after the order of Melchisedec.' Again, chap. 7: 28. 'For the law maketh men high priests which have infirmity; but the word of the oath which was since the law, maketh the Son, who is consecrated for evermore.' Acts, 10:36. 'The word which God sent unto the children of Israel, preaching peace by Jesus Christ: He is Lord of all. How God anointed Jesus of Nazareth with the Holy Ghost and with power, who went about doing good and healing all that were oppressed by the devil, for God was with him. To him give all the prophets witness, that through his name, whosoever believeth on him shall receive remission of sins.' "

How well she was qualified to give instruction to young disciples, will appear in the following letters to two, who died shortly after of consumption.

To Miss Van Wyck, New-York.

"Rockaway, 1810.

" MY DEAR, MY BELOVED ELIZA,—Mr. and Mrs. B. are here on a vist for one night. I did not expect to see them so soon, or I would have had a letter ready. I expect another opportunity in the course of a few days, when I will send you a long letter, from my heart, and, I hope, dictated by your and my Teacher.

"I learn by my children that you continue much in the same way in which I left you. It is your own God who mixes your cup, and it is to you a cup of blessing; there is no curse in it. Your Jesus drank that cup to the very dregs, that bitter as well as sweet might be to you a cup of blessing. O then, my darling, hold fast by your Redeemer; he is the Lord your Righteousness, and the Lord your strength; he connects your profit with his own glory. You shall in this protracted affliction manifest it, and hold out the word of life to those around you.* You shall witness for him that he is the Lord, and besides him there is no Savior—that 'he gathers the lambs in his arms, and carries them in his bosom—that he is to them a hiding-place from the wind, and a covert from the tempest—as rivers of water in a dry place, and as the shadow of a great rock in a weary land.' That it is he that teacheth them to profit, and leadeth them by the way that they should go, and that in due time he will perfect all that concerns them.   Farewell! Yours with affection,

"I. GRAHAM."

(*To the same.*)

"Rockaway, Sabbath, 1810.

"MY DEAR, MY BELOVED ELIZA,—I wrote you a few lines yesterday by Mr. B. I now propose to fulfil my promise. I expect an opportunity to-morrow or next day, for I saw a great many carriages pass this way to

---

* This prediction was remarkably fulfilled in the experience of this dear young saint; an interesting account of whose illness and death was published in the Christian's Magazine, and afterwards as a Tract.

the tavern, as I suppose, from New-York. It is a common thing with some to come here on Saturday and return on Monday, to spend this blessed day in pastime. You would not, I know, exchange situations with them; you would rather be suffering than sinning.

"It is your own observation that God does all in wisdom; in this wisdom he is pleased to lengthen your day of affliction. Sin, my darling, is the cause of all suffering; but is not always the *immediate* cause. Besides particular chastisement for particular sins, there are afflictions to be filled up in the body of Christ, (his church,) a measure of which, in kind and degree, is appointed by unerring wisdom to each individual member. Col. 1:24. These sufferings bear no part in atoning for sin, nor in redeeming our forfeited inheritance. Christ ' trode the wine-press alone, and of the people there was none to help him.' 'He was made sin for us, who knew no sin, that we might be made the righteousness of God in him; who when he had by himself purged our sins, sat down on the right hand of the Majesty on high.' Heb. 1:3. Again, chapter 10:11. 'And every priest (in the Levitical law) standeth daily ministering and offering oftentimes the same sacrifices, which can never take away sins. But this man, after he had offered *one sacrifice* for sins, for ever sat down on the right hand of God; for by one offering he hath perfected for ever them that are sanctified : whereof the Holy Ghost is also a witness to us; for after he had said before,' (see from verse 5,) 'This is the covenant which I will make with them after those days, saith the Lord; I will put my laws into their hearts, and in their minds will I write them; and their sins and iniquities will I remember no more. Now, where remission of these is, there is no more offering for sin.' Paul says the *Holy Ghost* is a witness, because he copies from the ancient Scriptures the prophecies of Jeremiah, 31 : 31. and Ezek. 36 : 25, and from the Psalm 60 : 7. Your mother will read to you also the 8th chapter of Hebrews, containing the same things, the new covenant, in consequence of Christ, as the surety of sinners, having made full atonement, magnified the law, and made it honorable; therefore there is now no condemnation to them who are in Christ Jesus.

"It has pleased God, my darling, in the adorable plan of reconciling sinners to himself by Jesus Christ, to perfect at once a justifying righteousness for them, and to bestow it upon them as a free gift. ' This is the record, that God hath given to us eternal life; and this life is in his Son.' 1 John, 5 : 11. But it has not pleased him to deliver us at once from depravity; provision is made for final deliverance by the same covenant, and is effected by the same power, but in this believers are called to work. It is evident from Scripture, and the experience of Christians answers to it, that in the hour of believing they pass from death to life, considered as a state. This is the hour of the new birth: they then receive life for the time, and it is their privilege, by the constitution of the new covenant, to ask and receive, from day to day, grace to help in every time of need. To them, and not to the unregenerate, the exhortation is addressed: ' Work out your own salvation with fear and trembling, for it is God who worketh in you, both to will and to do, of his good pleasure.' The means are of God's appointing, in the diligent use of which they go from strength to strength. The grand means is faith in God's promises, of which there are very many in the Scriptures. Believers are to put forth their own exertions, as the children of Israel were called to go out against their enemies, in the faith that God would give them victory and lead them to their promised rest. The battle was the Lord's, and he fought for them; but the means were their exertions. Believers are God's workmanship; but this work he carries on by exercising their natural powers, which he sanctifies to a different end from that to which they were formerly by their own spirit directed. Still the Scripture testifies that 'if any man say he has no sin, he deceives himself, and the truth is not in him;' and, while sin remains, its consequence, suffering, must. The judgments of God, as the moral Governor of the world, are denounced against, and executed upon the workers of iniquity. The children of God experience personal chastisements for personal sins, as a provision of the covenant. Psalm 89:30. And, if I mistake not, there are afflictions experienced by individuals, as members of Christ's body, in which God does not bring into view the personal sins of the sufferer. In this sense I read Paul's Epistle to the Colossians, 1:24. 'Who now rejoice in my sufferings, and fill up that which is behind of the sufferings of Christ in my flesh, for his body's sake, which is the Church.' 1 Thes. 3:3. 'I sent Timotheus to establish you, and to comfort you concerning your faith; that no man should be moved by these afflictions; for yourselves know that we are appointed thereunto.' Phil. 2:17. 'Yea, if I be offered upon the sacrifice and service of your faith, I joy and rejoice with you all ; for the same cause do ye joy and rejoice with me.' 2 Cor. 1 : 6. 'And whether we be afflicted, it is for your consolation and salvation; and whether we be comforted, it is for your salvation and consolation.' There is no conscious personal sin expressed in these sufferings ; on the contrary, Paul says, verse 12, 'For our rejoicing is this, the testimony of our conscience, that in simplicity and godly sincerity, not with fleshly wisdom, but by the grace of God, we have had our conversation in the world, and more abundantly to you-ward.'

"Most of the prophets and apostles suffered martyrdom. They indeed sustained public characters, but the beggar Lazarus, who, in addition to poverty, was full of sores, was carried by the angels from the rich man's gate to Abraham's bosom. And thousands and tens of thousands of redeemed highly sanctified ones have suffered lengthened martyrdom, and perished with hunger, in holes and caves of the earth, unknown in history, except in groups—unseen at the time, except by the eye of the omniscient Jehovah, by whom the hairs of their head are numbered ; their tears are in his bottle ; nor shall one sigh nor one groan perish without its result.

"O my Eliza, what delightful wonders shall open to our view when delivered from these prison-holds of earth !

"I have finished one sheet, my dear Eliza ; I fear it is too much, and may prove too fatiguing, especially as there are many references requiring a stretch of attention. I have been reading the Epistle to the Hebrews, and you have naturally got my thoughts on part of it.

"I remember once of your complaining that you had

made small progress in knowledge, in comparison of a young person that had just left you; but you checked yourself, and said, 'The Lord has given me faith, let me be thankful.' I at that time considered your departure as very near, and advised you to keep your eye fixed on Christ, as your Redeemer and Savior, who had performed all things for you, and would perfect all that concerned you; and added, one hour in heaven will make you wiser than the most enlightened saint on earth. Since that it has pleased your Lord to add many days to your life. He has mitigated your pain, and given you some intervals of ease and composure, and our dear Eliza has grown in that time. Should it please God to spare you for a yet longer season, and continue your intervals of ease, no subject can be so profitable; and I hope your Lord will make it pleasant as that of the contents of the New Testament, which your Savior bequeathed to you, sealed and ratified in his blood. There is a vast variety of precious promises contained in the Scriptures of the Old and New Testament, which are all yours with Christ; for, as a member of his body, 'you are built upon the foundation of the apostles and prophets, Jesus Christ himself being the chief corner-stone.' And now I commend you to your own covenant God, who does and will support you, through life and through death, to that happy land where we shall all meet; and, O then, eye hath not seen, nor ear heard, neither hath it entered into the heart of man to conceive the things he hath prepared for them that love him.

"I am, with much love and affection, yours,

"I. GRAHAM."

To Mr. James Todd, New-York.

"ROCKAWAY, Long Island.

"MY DEAR JAMES,—This will probably be handed you by our mutual friend, Mrs. C——. The thought of her being with you, makes me part with her with less reluctance. You have not been forgotten by either; we have talked much of you, and have united in prayer to your and our God, that he may manifest himself unto you as your reconciled Father in Christ Jesus; and give you 'joy and peace in believing'—that he may give you patience in suffering, and entire resignation to his most holy will.

"It has, my dear young friend, been my earnest inquiry, especially of late years, standing on the brink of eternity, 'What is there within us, or without us, on which a sinner can rest in a dying hour?' If it be a holy life, there is no peace for me. Taking the law of God for my rule, backslider is my name; yet peace I have found, and on the best Security; this blessed Bible is my charter. I have searched it with diligence and prayer, and my mind is confirmed in the following truths:—That the whole world is become guilty before God, and is under his wrath and curse on that account. This is our state: a miserable state it is, and as hopeless as miserable, for any thing we can do merely of ourselves. But I read in this Bible to the full amount of the following conclusions—that in the counsel of the mysterious Triune Jehovah, Jesus Christ, the second person of the incomprehensible Trinity, was sanctified, or set apart to become the Savior of law-condemned sinners, to take their nature upon him, comply with the requisitions of the eternal immutable law of God, and become their surety. Man is a rebel, it is put to his account—a penalty is incurred—He, as their Surety, is made liable. Are they again to be made heirs of eternal life? Perfect obedience is the condition—and of Him, as their Surety, it is demanded. All this being fulfilled, sinners are become his property—he has paid their debt, and merited for them eternal life, all in their own nature, as their Head and representative; so that believers are complete in him. This is the righteousness of God, wrought out by Jesus Christ, in his own person, God-man, as their surety. To this nothing of the believer's is to be added—with this nothing of his mixed; it is for ever perfect; entirely distinct from that holiness of heart and life which is wrought in him in consequence of this. God has declared himself well pleased with this righteousness, and that being himself reconciled, he is in Christ Jesus reconciling sinners to him.

"Hence all the invitations scattered thick in the Old and New Testament, not only to the penitent, weary, and heavy laden, but to the stout-hearted, the backslider, to them that are wearying themselves in their own way. 'Ho! every one that thirsteth, whosoever will, let them come and take of the water of life freely.' Hence all the promises annexed to believing, accepting, receiving, trusting, resting: Christ the Savior is the object—the gift of God to sinners for all the above purposes. The Lord has convinced me that I have nothing in myself on which I can rest; my conscience echoes to his word in all that it asserts of my nature and my state; but this Savior is provided for sinners exactly of this description. I am invited to put in my claim, I believe the record, I rest my salvation on his word; God giveth to me eternal life, and this life is in his Son. Jesus calls me to look unto him, and be saved; I do look unto him, and I am saved. He assures me that those who come unto him shall never be cast out. I do go to him and commit my sinful soul to his keeping; I shall not be cast out. As many as receive the gift of his Son, receive at the same time power to become the children of God. I do receive his gift, and lay claim to his promise. He is my reconciled Father, and I am his adopted child, and he hath sent his Spirit into my heart, by which I can say, Abba, Father.

"I have, my dear James, taken this method of laying before you the grounds of my own hope, because I think it the most simple method, and containing at the same time my counsel to you to lay hold on the same hope. .The warrant is given us in God's own word, as sinners, without respect to fruit or any works of ours. I can, if necessary, give you chapter and verse, to the full amount; but you have those about you who can give it to you by little and little, as your weak state can bear it. This gift is held out to the sinner's acceptance in many places of the word of God, and becomes the sinner's in the moment of believing. Provision is made by the same covenant for his sanctification; but that makes no part of justifying righteousness. Christ is made of God unto him wisdom, righteousness, sanctification, and complete redemption. Try, my precious young friend, to lay hold on this hope, and enter into the rest provided for the believer here. Stretch forth 'the withered hand,' the Lord himself will give you strength. Commit your precious soul into his hands, and

rest assured that he will perfect all that concerns you—
work all his work in you—carry you safely through the
Jordan of death, and put you in possession of the inheritance he has purchased for you. That all this shall be,
is the prayer and firm hope of

"Your affectionate friend,

"ISABELLA GRAHAM."

The two following extracts, addressed to Mrs. C——,
near Boston, present a very gratifying view of Mrs.
Graham in her advanced years, and may well awaken
the desire not only to die the death, but to enjoy the
"fruitful old age" of "the righteous."

"I have, as you know, enjoyed much in life, enjoyed
its dearest, sweetest comforts, love and friendship, with
a heart tremblingly alive to both. Lover and friends of
youth are long since gone, other friendships I have
formed, and have been happy even in these; now I am
shut up with ails and aches. The world (properly so
called) is a dead blank to me; yet I do think I never
enjoyed life more. I would not exchange my present
happiness for the most transporting moments of my life,
(of which I have had a large share,) though thousands
of years were added to enjoy them. I do not mean
barely that happiness which consists in the anticipation
of pleasure beyond the grave; that is indeed delightful;
but I enjoy life now. Books of taste are mine no more:
still less those of science and history; but my dear
Bible! precious subjects! my dear Savior! The height,
the depth, the breadth, the length of the glorious plan of
Redemption open to my delightful perception more and
more, and the Spirit witnesseth with my spirit, that I

have my part in it by the gift of *faith*. I believe the record, that God giveth to us eternal life, and I put in my claim as a sinner. I account it a 'faithful saying, and worthy of all acceptation, that Jesus Christ came into the world to save sinners, of whom I am the chief.' I still enjoy the ordinances of the Gospel: my memory, as you know, is much impaired : I recollect very little of the sermons I hear ; but, I think, I never heard with so much attention. I am delighted, instructed, and fed at the time, and the subjects open to me without my being able to recollect the order or the words of the speaker. O let me recommend this dear Lord to your heart and confidence ; commit all your concerns to him ; mistrust no part of his providential dealings with you ; his wisdom shall manage for you, and you shall one day say, ' He hath done all things well.' ''

"March, 1811.

"I am daily on the lookout ; one year and three months will complete my three score and ten. I do not know one individual alive whom I knew in my school days ; it has been the case for many years. I do not ' long for my dismission, neither am I tired of life ; but nothing in this world, unless closely connected with another, interests me ; and oh! I am tired of sin; still it cleaves to me ; in all things I come short, and many duties neglect altogether; for I still have a considerable share of health, and might do some good, had I will equal to my opportunities; as to the power, it is not in me, but I know I have it in my blessed Head, and for the asking. I cannot but long to be delivered from sin, and sinful apathy in particular, for really my heart must be wickedly fertile, to find out opportunities of moral transgression. Food and raiment are mine without care; my children, under God, care for me. I have my dear little room, my Bible, and books founded on it. I have a dear pastor and christian friends, lively ordinances, and also much of the Lord's presence at times; my cup runs over with blessings, but my gratitude bears no proportion; my zeal for the glory of God and the good of my fellow-sinners seem buried under self-indulgence and apathy. O that the goodness of the Lord may lead me to repentance!

"And now, my dear friend, let me know how it is with you and your dear family. The severe winter is past; how have you got along? with what temporal comfort, and how has the Lord dealt with your soul? Has the barrel of meal or the cruse of oil failed? Does the opening spring cheer your spirits and furnish a song of praise? Does it find you in a situation to dig your garden, sow your seeds, and make provision for future comfort? Has the Lord turned your captivity, and dried up the bitter waters that flowed against you? How are your eyes, after all the briny tears that have steeped them? How are your poor nerves, after all the shocks that have agitated them? All these things have been on my mind; but, from my long silence, you cannot believe it. What are we all, but broken reeds, which pierce the hand when laid hold of for support? There is but one Friend to poor, fallen, miserable man, in the universe. He is mercy; he is goodness; he is truth; he is wisdom; he is unchangeable, and never will fail you; take him to your heart; give it all to him; he only is worthy, no other is."

Her friend Mrs. C. had now experienced new trials, by which she was again plunged into the depth of despondency. In the following we have a noble effort of Mrs. Graham's mind and heart to raise her up to " sit in heavenly places in Christ Jesus."

" June 27, 1811.

"I received my dear friend's letter this day week, and have been answering it ever since. Never was I in such a strait. It contains the effusions of disappointed hopes and anticipations of sore evils; indicates a soul deeply wounded, and taking in christian principles under temptation. Where shall I begin? I have laid it before our compassionate High Priest, I have requested direction. Assist me, O thou blessed Comforter! whose office it is to convince of sin, as well as to minister consolation! Do both, from the heart and by the pen of thy handmaid.

"It appears to me salutary to call your attention first to the sovereignty of God. The silver and the gold are his, and the cattle on a thousand hills; he gives them to whomsoever he pleases; he setteth up one and putteth down another, doing whatsoever pleaseth him 'in the armies of heaven, and among the inhabitants of this earth;' none can stay his hand, or say unto him, what doest thou? He attributes to himself all events; men and other creatures are but instruments. Men's wicked hearts impel them to commit evil, but the events are of the Lord, which he overrules for his own glory, and for the good of his people. 'Him being delivered by the foreknowledge and counsel of God, ye have taken, and by wicked hands have crucified him.' Joseph said, 'ye meant it for evil, but God for good, to save much people alive, as at this day.' The Lord does not often, at the time, give his people reasons for afflicting them, though they can often read them at an after period.

"Job was a holy man; his afflictions from God's own hand were very deep; the teasing unkindness and injustice of his friends made great part of the temptation, and he spoke unadvisedly with his lips. When God did appear, he did not answer his cavils nor give him one reason why he had dealt with him thus; but silenced him with views of his majesty, power and wisdom; of his own meanness and vileness, though correct in his conduct beyond most others. I believe he spoke truth when he said, 'I delivered the poor that cried, the fatherless, and him that had none to help him. The blessing of him that was ready to perish came upon me, and I caused the widow's heart to sing for joy. I was eyes to the blind and feet to the lame. I was a father to the poor, and the cause that I knew not, I searched out.' God allowed the weight of the trial to be upon his spirit, with the conviction of his presumption, till he brought him to his feet. 'Behold, I am vile, what shall I answer thee?' 'I will lay my hand upon my mouth.' 'I abhor myself, and repent in dust and ashes.' These things were written for our example and profit.

"This afflictive providence is now finished, at least so far. What you now possess is the allotment of your God. Set all instruments aside and listen to the holy Ghost—'humble yourselves under the mighty hand of God, and he shall exalt you in due time.' In order to this, I would recommend to you to take a close, retrospective view of your past life, with earnest prayer that God would search you and try you, and show you what wicked ways have been, or now are in you. Go back

to the days of your youth; take a close view of the use
you made of affluence and influence, not comparing
yourself with others; but judging yourself by the law
of God, the only standard of right and wrong, truth and
error. Seek for humbling views of yourself in yourself.
If the Holy Ghost enlighten, you will find sufficient
grounds. Seek for consolation in the free promises of
God, through Jesus Christ, of which there are also abundance, even to the chief of sinners. What I recommend to you has been my own practice, especially in
times of trial; and if health will admit of it, add fasting,
because I think it is the Lord's ordinance. 'The days
shall come when the Bridegroom shall be taken from
them, then shall they fast in those days.'

"Read the third chapter of Jeremiah's Lamentations;
endeavor to come under the feelings of contrition on
account of your sins, and derive consolation from faith
in God's great mercy; ever keeping in view the only
channel through which mercy can flow to sinners of
Adam's race. Take also a view of God's dealings with
his elect nation, in the wilderness; they had nothing but
manna, and were punished for murmuring; while at that
very time the nations in Canaan, the Egyptians, and As-
syrians, were living in all manner of luxury. What was
their whole history but backsliding, threatening upon
threatening? then chastisement, turning, repenting, pardon, reconciliation, and the same round again, every
chastisement severer than the last, while worldlings in
general, have their day to the end; then, says David,
'they are cast down suddenly to destruction.' I wish
you to take a particular view of God's dealings with
them, before Nebuchadnezzar sacked the city of Jeru-

salem. The decree was passed after many warnings, and much long-suffering. How many pauses, as it were, did the merciful Lord God make before he gave them finally up to their enemies; and when the decree was irrevocable, and the chastisement to take place, still he followed them with mercy. See Jeremiah 27 : 12; and chapter 29, the letter which God commanded Jeremiah to write to those who had been carried away captive with Jehoiakim, advising them to build houses and plant vineyards, and to make the most of their situation. Those at Jerusalem were commanded to submit to the king of Babylon, as in that case he would not destroy the city: but no, they stood it out, and the threatened vengeance overtook them.

" The poor were left to take care of the vineyards. Jeremiah remained with them in preference to going with the king of Babylon to be promoted to honor. God offered to take them under his protection and be their God: but no, they would go to Egypt, and put themselves under the king of Egypt's protection. Jeremiah told them from the Lord, that Egypt itself should soon go into captivity. But to Egypt they went and carried Jeremiah with them. See Isaiah's prophecy on this occasion, chapter 35 : 31. Now look at chapter 62 : 24 ; there you see God's judgment and chastening; follow him in the beginning of chapter 63, and view his mercy; in the end of the same chapter again, see his charge against them, but it is followed with mercy, not judgment.

" Thus we learn the character of God. Thus we learn his dealings with his people. They are not called to earthly comfort and prosperity. They ever have been, and still are a suffering people; they are all sinners—

sin brings suffering, and God overrules suffering, so as
to make it profitable to them. Though redeemed by
the life and death of Christ, 'being justified by faith,
they have peace with God;' yet the Lord has not
pleased all at once to qualify them for the purchased
possession. They receive a new birth, new life, and are
called to work out their own salvation with fear and
trembling, with this consolation, that God worketh in
them, both to will and to do, of his good pleasure. This
is not their home, here they have no continuing city;
they are travelling through the wilderness, to the city
and mansions purchased and prepared for them by their
Savior, and must be made holy before they can enter in.
They have many corruptions to be mortified, and many
errors in their estimation of men and things to be corrected. Their hearts require to be made spiritual, humble, tender, resigned, and loving. 'Then shalt thou remember all the way by which I led thee; to prove thee,
and try thee; to show thee what was in thy heart, that I
might do thee good in thy latter end.'

"Besides, all suffering is not the immediate punishment of sin in the individual sufferer, nor for his exclusive profit; it is evident from Scripture, there is suffering for the benefit of the body of Christ—*His Church*,
of which (I think) all have some share. God has wise
ends to answer by all the suffering of his creatures, and
especially of the members of his body. The apostles
rejoiced in this, and so ought we. 'If we suffer with
him, we shall also reign with him.' Paul says 'I fill up
in my flesh that which is behind of the sufferings of
Christ, for his body's sake, which is the Church.'

"Now, my dear friend, look at your real situation,

as a suffering member of a suffering body. Take a view of the saints of God in history, sacred or profane, and compare your own individual suffering with theirs: I am apt to think that, great as it is, it will not rise to mediocrity. I could expatiate on this subject, from what comes every day within my own knowledge. The Lord is working in this way all around me: but of that another time. In your own case, try for a moment to shut out of view every thing without your own family, what you once were, what you once possessed and enjoyed; also what your friends possess and enjoy at this present time; detach yourself from all. What was yours is gone; what you calculated upon is also gone: set all aside, and consider yourself a sinner saved from destruction by grace; in a state of purgation and preparation for happiness; on a pilgrimage with thousands of others your fellow-saved sinners, through the wilderness, to that inheritance which was purchased for you at *such a price.* Your Savior is your leader, protector, provider; also your physician, and the physician of the whole body, perfectly acquainted with the constitution, disposition and temper of every individual. He has made provision for each, all the journey through, and given security that none shall suffer *real* want.

"Bread and water are promised; nothing beyond these, though in general he gives more; to each he gives a portion in hand, to some for a day, some for a week, some for a year, which they calculate upon with more or less probability: none with certainty. Your portion is—for a year; take a view of those whom you know; one with another, I am inclined to think the Lord has still given you your full share of privilege. Look at the ordinary provision he makes for the ministers of his Gospel; most of them with large families; many of those in the country have five hundred dollars, some four hundred, some three hundred, generally ill paid. The Lord puts a blessing in it, he makes it go far; they do what their hands find to do, and get along: so will he do with you, my dear. He will put you upon methods of industry and economy: your one chicken divided into six parts, with a little bit of pork, with the fruit of God's blessing on your industry in the garden, shall both taste sweet and satisfy for the time. Try to be thankful; Moses said of the manna, ' This is the bread which the Lord your God giveth you.' Pray and watch against dwelling on the plentiful tables of others; and when bidden to a feast take your portion, and say, this is from the Lord for the time. Do not let a thought of *misery* or *wretchedness* dwell upon your mind. O no, God is good; you shall not want. O what sweet meals have I and my children made on hot potatoes, nicely boiled and cracked, with salt—not merely content, but they tasted good and savory. There are peculiar pleasures in a life of that kind. You shall yet sing of it.

"Now, my dear friend, I have done with what I had to say on this head. I have had great fears of wounding, lest you should reckon me among Job's friends; but you call me mother, and it is required of a mother to be faithful. I now leave it with the Lord. We are delighted to find you girding up the loins of your mind and setting about active duty. Let us meet at a throne of grace, and look to the course the Lord marks out for us."

To Mrs. G—— Y——.

"MY DEAR MADAM—I have just parted with my dear afflicted friend Mrs. C. she left it in charge to me, that I should write to you in the time of your affliction. Surely I would do any thing whatever that I thought might alleviate either her or your distress. But there are cases to which God alone can speak; afflictions which he *alone* can console. Such are those under which the sufferer is commanded to be ' still and know that he is God.' He never leaves his people in any case, but sometimes shuts them up from human aid. Their grief is too great to be consoled by human tongue or pen.

"Such I have experienced. I lost my only son; I neither know when nor where; and for any thing I know, in a state of rebellion against God. Here at my heart it lies still; who can speak to me of it? neither can I reason upon it. Aaron held his peace. Old Eli said, ' It is the Lord, let him do what seemeth good in his sight.' Samuel in his turn had his heart wrung by his ungodly son. David lamented over his beloved Absalom; but it availed him nothing. Job's sons and daughters were all cut off in one day; he himself lay in deep, sore, bodily affliction; his friends sat seven days and seven nights without opening their mouths, because they saw his affliction was very great; and if they spoke it was to aggravate it; and when God himself spoke, he gave him no reason for his dealings, but charged him with folly and madness. ' Shall he that contendeth with the Almighty instruct him? He that reproveth God, let him answer it.' Then he laid his hand on his mouth, confessed himself vile, and became dumb before God; abhorring himself, and repenting in dust and ashes, instead of the splendid catalogue of virtues enumerated in chapter 29, and complaints in chapter 10, which I make not the least doubt were true, as far as human virtue can reach; but if God charge 'even his angels with folly,' shall man, corrupt, self-destroyed man, plead merit before God?

"But, my dear friend, I do not find in all God's Bible any thing requiring us to acquiesce in the final destruction of any, for whom we have prayed, pleaded, and committed to him, least of all our offspring whom he has commanded us to train up for him. 'Children are God's heritage.' I do not say he has given us any promise for the obstinately wicked; but when cut off, he only requires us to *be still*, to hold our peace. I do not think he takes hope from us. God has set limits to our *faith* for others; our faith must not rest in opposition to his threatenings. We must believe that 'the wicked shall be turned into hell, and all that forget God;' but he hath set no bounds to his own mercy; in that glorious plan of Redemption, by which he substitutes his own Son in the stead of sinners, he has made provision for the chief of sinners, and can now be just and consistent while he justifies the ungodly who believe in Jesus. Short was the time between the thief's petition and the promise of salvation; nay, the petition was the earnest of it. The same was the case with the jailer; I think, too, the publican had the earnest in his petition. Now, instead of laboring to bring my mind to acquiesce in the condemnation of my child, on the supposition of its being for God's glory, I try to be *still*, as he has commanded; not to follow my child to the yet invisible world; but turning my eyes to that character which God has revealed of himself—to the plan of Redemption—to the sovereignty of God in the execution of that plan—to his names of grace, ' The Lord, the Lord God, merciful and gracious, slow to anger, abundant in goodness and truth, forgiving iniquity, and transgression, and sin,' while he adds 'and that will by no means clear the guilty;' I meet it with his own declaration, 'he hath made him to be sin for us who knew no sin, that we might be made the righteousness of God in him.' I read also that 'mercy rejoiceth against judgment,' and many other like scriptures, which, although I dare not ground a belief of his salvation on them, afford one ray of hope after another, that God may have made him a monument of mercy to the glory of his grace.

"Thus God himself consoles his own praying people, while man ought to be very cautious, if not silent, where the Scriptures are silent, as it respects the final state of another, whose heart we cannot know, nor what God may have wrought in it. God hath set bounds to our faith, which can nowhere find solid ground to fix upon but in his own written promise. Yet, as I said above, he has set no bounds to his own mercy, and he has made provision for its boundless flow, as far as he shall please to extend it, through the atonement and merits of his own Son, 'who is able to save to the uttermost all who come unto God by him.' Now, my dear friend, you have my ideas of our situation; if they be correct, I pray that our compassionate Father may comfort you by them; if otherwise, may he pardon what is amiss, and lead you, my dear friend C——, and myself, to such consolation as he himself will own as the work of his Spirit, and save us from the enemy and our own spirit.

" Since writing the foregoing, I feel afraid of what I have said; it is dangerous seeking comfort where the Scriptures are silent; yet while we plead with God to be preserved from error, and try to be *still* before him, he will save us from the subtlety of the serpent, as well as from the rage of the lion. I am, with love,

" Your sympathizing friend,

" Isabella Graham."

" Rockaway, September 10, 1811.

" I have been here four Sabbaths. The first I spent at home, the weather not permitting our going abroad; the second I spent at a Prayer Meeting with the Methodist brethren; the third we rode to Hempstead, where I heard two plain Gospel sermons from Mr. C——, Presbyterian minister; and the last, I attended at the Episcopal church, same place; heard a good plain Gospel sermon from Mr. H——, and witnessed the dispensation of the Lord's Supper.

" To sing the praises of our Redeeming God, and to lift up my heart in prayer with my fellow-sinners, in the comfortable hope that there are other living souls praising and praying with me, refreshes me: to hear the word of God read, and to be led to meditate upon it, however simple and common the exposition, also refreshes me. *I am generally led to pray much for minister and people;* to consider myself as one with them in Christ. However weak his natural powers—however few or small his talents, if I have reason to think that he is taught of God ' that which flesh and blood cannot teach,' I desire ' to esteem him highly for his work's sake.' I thank God for the meanest and weakest of such: I believe they never labor in vain. ' Out of the mouths of babes and sucklings,' in talents as well as in years, ' God will perfect praise.'

" In this new world, thickly settled in many places with natural men ' eating and drinking, marrying and giving in marriage,' while the flood of wrath is hastening to overwhelm them, and none to warn them of their danger, nor point out the ark of safety; shall such men be reckoned of none account, and their labors of no value ? No, the wealth of both Indies cannot balance their work; nor all the talents ever possessed by fallen man, with all the orthodoxy which mere talents are capable of acquiring, without that divine teaching which many of those, thus contemned, possess. That same small discourse, those few plain points, these same things repeated in the same way, contain truths by which sinners may be saved, by which sinners shall be saved.

" Suppose (for it is but a supposition) that these men have made a mistake. They are the Lord's, and in their place by his providence. He will be forthcoming for them, and without miracle. From him ' shall their fruit be found, and his power be manifested by their weakness.' Exert your energies, ye gifted Doctors of Divinity; and may the Lord prosper the means used to produce a ministry which shall render attendance upon their ministrations the interest of both the understanding and the heart. Persuade men who are adding ' field to field, house to house,' thousand to thousand, to provide a competent maintenance for them. If these last remain obstinate, and it be idle to hope that youths of talents without fortune, whatever be their piety, will serve the Church of God at the expense of devoting themselves to infallible penury, and all the wretchedness which belongs to it—is it wise to weaken the hands and discourage the hearts of those ministers already settled pastors, or to furnish their people with arguments in their own vindication for leaving them in want and penury!"

In the year 1811 some gentlemen of New-York established a *Magdalen Society :* they elected a Board of Ladies, requesting their aid to superintend the internal management of the Magdalen House. This Board chose Mrs. Graham their Presiding Lady, which office she held until her decease; the duties attendant on it she discharged with fidelity and zeal. In 1812 the Trustees of the *Lancasterian School* solicited the attendance of several pious ladies, to give catechetical instruction to their scholars one afternoon in every week: and Mrs. Graham was one of those who attended regularly to this duty.

CHAPTER XI.

DEVOTIONAL EXERCISES, AND CORRESPONDENCE.

" February 8, 1812.

" HEBREWS, 11 : 24. 'By faith, Moses, when he was come to years, refused to be called the son of Pharaoh's daughter, esteeming the reproach of Christ greater riches than the treasures of Egypt; for he had respect unto the recompense of the reward; choosing rather to suffer affliction with the people of God, than to enjoy the pleasures of sin for a season.'

"'All that will live godly in Christ Jesus shall suffer persecution; the natural heart is enmity against God,' and hates his image wherever found. If individual christians have the favor of individual worldlings, it never is for their piety, that is rather borne with than loved; and too often christians save themselves from reproach by unfaithfulness; that, alas! has been my sin and shame. In all my friendships with worldlings, some of which have been tender, how unfaithful have I been to friendship's highest office! How seldom have I endeavored to rescue my friend from sin and Satan, by leading her to the Friend of sinners, the source of happiness! Contenting my vile, selfish heart, with things pertaining to this life unconnected with that to come, leaving her under the influence of ' the lust of the eye, the lust of the flesh, and the pride of life;' without eyes to see her danger, or friend to warn her of it; and while she communicated with me in things common to both, in all the good she knew, keeping back nothing from me of all she possessed; how often have I concealed my richest treasure, without inviting her to the participation! O faithless friend! O ungrateful, unfaithful—first to that gracious God who opened mine own eyes, arrested my attention, stopped up my path, and turned me to the way of life; and next to my friend, whom I have left to pursue that same way of death, without attempting to lead her to this same sovereign, merciful, gracious Deliverer.

"And what withheld! Shame belongs to the heart governed by such motives; fear of contempt, reproach, or, at most, the loss of a carnal friendship. Of three such friends, now gone to their place, two continued their worldly course to the last, so far as I know; for the third the Lord provided a more faithful friend, who became worker together with the Spirit of God, led her to the Friend of sinners, 'who has compassion on the ignorant, and them that are out of the way.' By him she was received, and in him she found life, light, and peace.

"She soon outran faithless me in the heavenly race; gently chid me for my remissness, but continued my friend and helper. Ever foremost in the race, humble and steady in faith, she looked not back, nor halted. She has long since finished her course, received her crown and reward of grace, and become fruit to the account of that friend who supplied what was wanting in me. I rejoice with them both, give 'glory to God, from whom their fruit was found,' and take shame and confusion for my part.

"How many opportunities have I lost, and from the same sinful, shameful cause! O my Redeemer, what can I say to thee? Words are wanting to express my loathing of that vile, selfish cowardice.

"Didst thou, who art the Creator of heaven and earth; the brightness of the glory of God, the express image of his person, and upholder of all things, suffer shame, contempt, anguish, death for my sake, that thou mightest redeem me from the second death, and purchase for me eternal life; and do I shrink and turn away from the least taste of thy cup, though the curse is extracted and a blessing infused!

"And after all this, art thou 'pacified towards me?' I search in vain for words to express the amazing grace. 'As the heaven is high above the earth, so great is his mercy towards them that fear him,' and toward vile me, who can lay small claim to that character: yet 'as far as the east is from the west, so far has he removed my transgressions from him. Bless the Lord, ye his angels who excel in strength, that do his commandments, hearkening to the voice of his word. Bless the Lord, all ye his hosts, ye ministers of his that do his pleasure; ye ministering spirits sent forth to watch over and minister to them who shall be heirs of salvation."

"February, 1812.

"Dr. M——, John 1, 'Behold the Lamb of God which taketh away the sin of the world.'

"He dwelt chiefly on the substitution of the victim in the room of the transgressor. When a victim was offered for an individual, he was to lay his hand on the head of the animal (by the appointment of God) as a token of his faith that his sins should be transferred to the victim which suffered death in his stead, and that his sins were forgiven and his person accepted. If the victim was for the whole congregation, then the elders, as their representatives, were to lay their hands upon the head of the victim, signifying the same faith. Great was the subject of the plan of Redemption. The Son of God clothed with our nature, given and set apart as a propitiatory sacrifice, the victim upon whom the sins of his-elect were laid, and he sacrificed in their stead.

"The Lamb of God which took away the sins, not only of the Jewish transgressors, but the sins of the elect out of every nation, kindred and tongue throughout the world; on this Lamb of God rests my own individual hope for pardon and for acceptance. I lay my own individual hand of faith on his dear head, confess my sin, and rely upon his sacrifice for pardon and acceptance,

through the atonement made by himself, God's anoint
ed priest."

" Dr. Romeyn,—2 Timothy, 3 : 12, 'Yea, and all that
will live godly in Christ Jesus shall suffer persecution.'
Gone as usual; but it came home to my heart. I have
not suffered persecution, and why? because my life has
not testified sufficiently against a sinful world. Alas!
alas! the world loves its own, and I have been so ac-
commodating (to say the least) as not to disturb it. 'The
carnal mind is enmity against God; is not subject to
the law of God, neither indeed can be;' but the world
saw little in me of that image which they hate, and
enough of assimilation to balance that little. O my God!
my long-suffering, sin-pardoning God! thou knowest
my vile cowardice; with professors a professor of thy
name, with worldlings a seeming worldling. And now
the season is past, the opportunity lost; the time of life
is arrived when the world itself expects to be abandoned. No line of conduct in me will now reprove them;
they account it wise to look out for a better portion,
when the world can no longer be enjoyed; and
through the deceitfulness of their own hearts, and the
suggestions of the ever vigilant enemy of souls, may be
hardened in sin, by hoping to become religious in old
age. Oh! let thy grace prevent it.

"The sinfulness, and O the ingratitude of my past
life rise in magnitude every review I take of it! And
what can I say? Father, forgive! Yes, I dare say, Father,
forgive! I dare say more; thou hast forgiven! This
grief of heart proves that thou hast not sealed me up in
impenitence. Thou rememberest thy covenant with me

in the days of my youth, when thou didst draw me ' with the cords of love and the bands of a man ;' and though no language can express my baseness and my ingratitude, through all my backsliding life, thy covenant stands fast.

" ' I remember, and am confounded, and will never open my mouth any more because of my shame, now that thou art pacified toward me for all that I have done.' And I know that thou art the Lord.

> Contrition dwell within this breast,
> That God within this heart may rest;
> Shame and confusion flush this face,
> And magnify this glorious grace.
> Grace be my theme while I have breath,
> And on my quivering lips in death.
> Angels and fellow-sinners, say,
> Will you not join me in this lay,
> Now, and through Heaven's eternal day ?

" Blessed Comforter! thou seest old age upon me, loss of memory, and a desultory mind ; I cannot retain even the substance of my dear pastor's sermons. I thank thee for the food and refreshment at the time, and often after for refreshing meditations on the same subjects. I commit all to thee ; keep them for me, and feed me with these truths as thou seest I need. O be to me memory, judgment, presence of mind ; for order, regularity, and natural powers are gone. I rejoice in my dear Savior, ' who of God is made unto me wisdom, righteousness, sanctification, and complete redemption.' He shall perfect that which concerneth me, and finish the work he has begun. Therefore I say, all is well."

" Communion Sabbath, May 17, 1812.

" Was much melted under a sense of indwelling sin,

and the deceitfulness of the human heart, and of my own heart in particular. I have been, I think, much in the exercise of contrition for the sins of my past life, and exercised in watching over my words, thoughts, and actions; now that the Lord has delivered me from all necessity to care, having every thing provided for me *necessary to life and godliness*: pleasant food and clothing both for body and mind; my dear room, retirement, fire, candle, attendance; my precious Bible, and precious, lively, spiritual ordinances; a faithful and beloved pastor, who feeds me with truth: I taste it, and I am fed. I am, as the Lord God merciful and gracious has awarded, under the constant influence of shame and confusion for my highly aggravated transgressions; but I also enjoy the full sense of pardon; ' being justified by faith, I have peace with God through our Lord Jesus Christ;' and knowing that I have a ' great High Priest that is passed into the heavens, Jesus the Son of God,' I am enabled to hold fast my profession, comforted by this, that 'I have not a high priest who cannot be touched with the feeling of my infirmities, but was in all points tempted as we are, yet without sin.' I dare come (not very boldly, for I am under much depression) to the throne of Grace, that I may obtain mercy, and find grace to help in time of need. Every time is a time of need with me, for sin still dwelleth in me. I have peace with God, through my dear Lord and Savior Jesus Christ, but am at constant war with myself. I plead thy promise, that thou wilt ' subdue my iniquities;' ' that sin shall not have dominion over me.' And now, Captain of salvation, I renew the fight, but it is depending upon thee to fight for me, with me, and in me.

I will set myself to watch, but I shall watch in vain, if thou keep not 'the avenues of my heart, and the door of my lips.' O clothe me with thy meek and lowly spirit!"

"Sabbath, July 26, 1812.

"Tired of the bustle of Rockaway, and having some subordinate motives for returning home for a time, I embraced this season in particular; having, in the compass of one week, Sabbath, Wednesday my birth-day, and the day set apart both by the General Assembly of our Church and the Governor of our State, for fasting, prayer and humiliation, besides lectures on the same evening. I returned, therefore, on Friday, the 24th.

"Dr. R—— preached from Psalm 27 : 1, 'The Lord is my light and my salvation: whom shall I fear? the Lord is the strength of my life; of whom shall I be afraid?'

"O my God! my merciful and gracious God! what can I say of thy amazing, distinguishing mercy to me? Delivered from all these fears, and able to adopt the text fully, I know of none who have more or greater cause of fear as sinners. My transgressions have been of *crimson* and *scarlet* hue. O my God, thou knowest them, words cannot paint them. My Savior, thou knowest them, for thou baredst them! every jot and tittle was put to thy account, and thou didst cancel all! O that garden! that cry on the cross! the effects were seen on thy sacred body, but who can conceive the mysterious horror which agonized thy sacred soul! But thou saidst, *It is finished*, and finished it is. 'Lamb of God, which takest away the sins of the world!' on thy consecrated head I lay the hand of faith, confess my sins, pray for forgiveness, and believe that I am forgiven.

"July 29th, my birth-day, and the last day of the three-score years and ten of my sinful life. What an exhibition will that day produce, when the secrets of all hearts will be laid open, all my actions and all the springs of them. In all the myriads which shall appear at the bar of God, will there be such a sinner? taking into view the early grace manifested.

"Born, I think, about the seventeenth year of my natural life; previously instructed in the doctrines and precepts of the Scriptures, as far as the natural mind can conceive, by pious parents and a faithful pastor; with milk provided for my spiritual infancy, and richer food set before me for my growth; the leaves of the new covenant were opened to my view, and the fulness treasured in Christ for my supply; to be asked, to be delighted in; and delighted I was, and satisfied. But O! I 'forsook the fountain of living waters, and hewed out broken cisterns that could hold no water.' Where can language be found to depict my ingratitude, my madness, my folly; and where to describe the long-suffering, the compassionate remonstrances; the kindly, fatherly chastisements; the repeated pardons and restorations of my gracious God in days of youth; aggravating my renewed backslidings, bringing upon my sinful soul vengeance for my inventions? What were the sins of Israel and Judah to mine? Mine were committed after the great atonement was made, the adorable High Priest, Jesus, had with his own blood entered within the veil, and was set on the right hand of the throne of the Majesty of the heavens: 'the minister of the sanctuary, and of the true tabernacle, which the Lord pitched, and not man.' The new covenant was exhibited, established on better promises, himself the Mediator. The new and living way was consecrated to the holiest of all by the blood of Jesus; a throne of grace was established, Jesus himself our Advocate and Intercessor. We are now privileged 'to come boldly to a throne of grace, that we may find grace to help in the time of need.' O how aggravated my sin above theirs, having such great and precious privileges and promises, and a 'High Priest who can be touched with the feeling of our infirmities,' who 'was in all points tempted as we are;' who owns us as his brethren and sisters, yea, the very *members of his body*, and his Spirit dwelleth in us.

"I set apart the day for fasting and deep humiliation; took another survey of my past sinful life; confessed particulars on my knees, and made a fresh application to the blood of sprinkling which cleanseth from all sin; took a fresh hold of his new covenant of promise. 'This is the Covenant that I will make with them after those days, saith the Lord; I will put my laws in their hearts, and in their minds will I write them, and their sins and their iniquities will I remember no more.' Lord, do as thou hast said. I rest my immortal soul on thy promise."

"July 30, 1812.

"The day set apart by the General Assembly and State Legislature for fasting and humiliation, confession of sin, and prayer.

"Our pastor read the 2d chapter of Jeremiah, a great portion of which belongs to my own character as an individual; and is laid up as part of that provision which is to support me through the last stage in the wilderness, and through Jordan, over which I must shortly pass;

laid in as a proof of the amazing long-suffering of God, and his readiness to forgive even the vile backslider in heart and life, as proclaimed in chapter 3.

" Sabbath, Nov. 22.

"Zech. 9 : 12. 'Turn ye to the strong hold, ye prisoners of hope.' My Jesus—my hope, my strong hold, my safety, my Savior, my portion, my life, my happiness—yes, my happiness, for safe I am and happy, though sometimes in heaviness, for yet sin dwelleth in me, and in others dear as my own soul; and though I know it is pardoned, and provision made for pardon to the end, yet, O it is bitter, and bitter let it be! I would not have it otherwise. Heal my depravity, O God! take sin out of this heart ; O fill it with love to thee, and to all my fellow-sinners. My dear High Priest! •it can be but a little further to Jordan. My seventy years are run. Does not the Ark of the Covenant appear, going before me ? am I not called to decamp and follow after ? O my blessed, blessed High Priest! keep my eye fixed on thy person, and let me the little further follow thee step by step, foot after foot, without losing one mark all the way to Jordan ; and there let me see thee. Blessed Ark of the Covenant! roll back the waters of terror, stand firm in Jordan, and bid me come unto thee, and set up the stones of memorial in a song of praise in the midst of Jordan.

O then thy glory let me see,
Then cause thy face to shine on me,
And tune my heart, and tune my voice,
And language furnish to rejoice,
That all around may lend their tongue,
And sweetly join my dying song."

"Sabbath, December 8, 1812.

"Psalm 108 : 7, 8. 'Though I walk in the midst of trouble, thou wilt revive me : thou shalt stretch forth thine hand against mine enemies, and thy right hand shall save me.' 'The Lord will perfect that which concerns me : thy mercy, O Lord, endureth for ever : forsake not the works of thine own hands.'

"I will no longer mourn over loss of memory; I think the Lord has more than made it up to me by his sensible presence while hearing and applying the sermon to my heart at the time : not only so, he enlightens my understanding; it opens more to the elucidations of my pastor; and though I forget the words and the order of his discourses, I am instructed in the knowledge of the subject and the Scriptures in general. Shall I deny the grace of God through fear or pride ? I see it not to be my duty. Can I attribute any thing to myself ? No ; 'shame and confusion of face belong to me' for my carelessness and idleness in the use of means during health and strength of body and mind. Never has God dealt with me as I sinned, but according to his own mercy, and in a way of great sovereignty. Let me record his great goodness, his tender mercies, and bless his name.

"Old age is upon me, and some of its infirmities; my memory is much impaired, and my mind, in temporal things and subjects, becomes very desultory. Not so in spirituals : I think I not only hear and read with more intense attention and prompt application, but my mind is more disposed to meditation; and though I cannot remember much of the sermons I hear, yet my mind is often furnished with happy and profitable thoughts on the same subjects; and I find myself instructed without remembering the instructions. This is evidently from the Lord. It appears to me also that I have not lost the sensibility of youth. I often shed tears, not only of compunction, but of gratitude. I seldom commune without tears. I think much of death; am solemnized, but not afraid.

"As far as I know, my confidence rests upon a surety-righteousness, exclusive of every thing in myself. I am not conscious of self-righteousness; I have no complacency in any thing ever done by me. I not only believe that in all things I come short, and that sin is mixed in all I do, because God hath said so, but am sensible of the particular depravity. It is my sincere desire to be stript of every thing that is mine, (sins and duties laid in one heap,) and to be clothed in the surety-righteousness of my Redeemer; all that is mine put to his account, and all that he did and suffered, as the Mediator and surety of the Covenant, to mine.

"I am afflicted with rheumatism, but God gives me patience, disposes me to enumerate my many remaining mercies;—eyes to read his word and ears to hear it preached; hitherto such moderation of pain as very often to be able to attend with fixedness. I have my room at my own command, candle, fire, and attendance; and, O bless the Lord, my soul! much of his sensible presence. In the night when my aches prevent me from sleeping, he gives me some sweet hymn; I sing, my pain is diverted, while my heart is melted and warmed under the expressions, and I often drop asleep with the words on my tongue.

"I am convinced that the provision I have laid in for

my last journey in the wilderness and through Jordan, is selected by the influence of the Holy Ghost. 'He takes of the things of Christ and shows them unto me;' and while he keeps upon my mind my meanness, my vileness, wrings my heart with the retrospect of my backslidings and highly aggravated transgressions, he opens at the same time the leaves of the New Testament and shows me my deliverance from punishment, the Redemption of my soul, and my 'translation into the kingdom of God's dear Son:' I weep and rejoice; I loathe myself, and clasping my Savior to my heart, am at a loss for words to express how precious he is to my saved soul!

'Jesus, I love thy charming name,
 'Tis music to my ear,
Fain would I sound it out so loud
 That heaven and earth should hear.

Yes, thou art precious to my soul,
 My transport and my trust,
My Savior, Shepherd, Husband, Friend,
 No other good I boast.

All my capacious powers can wish,
 In thee doth richly meet;
Not to mine eyes is light so dear,
 Nor friendship's self so sweet.

Thy grace shall dwell upon my heart
 And shed its fragrance there,
The noblest balm of all my wounds,
 And cordial of my care.

I'll speak the honors of thy name
 While I have life and breath,
Then, speechless, clasp thee in my arms,
 The antidote of death.'

"Dr. M—— preached in the evening from Eph. 3: 30. 'For we are members of his body, of his flesh, and of his bones.' It was a rich sermon; I enjoyed it at the time, but cannot recall it. Blessed Spirit! keep it for me, and feed me with the substance of it, as I stand in need.

"Accept of my thanks, blessed Jesus! that, through thy meritorious life and death, I have an interest in the great whole. Accept of my thanks, blessed Spirit! for thus taking the things of Christ and showing them unto me. And accept of my thanks, Father of mercies! for the gift of thy Son, and all these blessings in him.

"'Blessed be the God and Father of our Lord Jesus Christ, who hath blessed us with all spiritual blessings in heavenly places, in Christ Jesus.' Amen."

"GREENWICH, Sabbath.

"Heard Dr. Milledoler preach in the State Prison to the convicts, from Luke, 19: 10.—'For the Son of man is come to seek and save that which was lost.' He addressed them as fellow-sinners, all being by nature lost and dependent on the same means for recovery.

"True, my heart accords. O Lord, thou knowest I stand in my own estimation a sinner, the chief of sinners. These have added to their sin against thee, breach against men, and are suffering the penalty.

"My sins have been chiefly, though far from exclusively, against God, and with many aggravations. That I was born in a christian land, of pious parents, who gave me religious instructions; brought up under faithful, lively ministers, and in religious society; exposed to few temptations but what arose from the corruptions of my own heart, are aggravations, which, perhaps, many are mourning over, as heightening the sin of unbelief in their unregenerated state. But the aggravations— the painful remembrance of which mars my comfort and covers me with shame and confusion even now, though I know that *God is pacified with me*—are as far

14*

above these as the heavens are above the earth. For in that christian land, under those christian parents and faithful pastors, while yet young and tender, I was 'enlightened, tasted of the heavenly gift, was made a partaker of the Holy Ghost, tasted of the good word of God and the power of the world to come.' I was taken from 'the fearful pit and miry clay; my feet set upon the rock, and a new song put into my mouth, even to the amount of, O death! where is thy sting?'—of redeeming love, pardoning grace, new covenant mercy; I had 'joy and peace in believing.' But forgetting my natural character, the extreme volatility of my spirits, my taste for gayety; forgetting the danger of smothering the heavenly spark by indulging to the utmost bound of lawful pleasure; forgetting my continual need of fresh supplies of grace to preserve and feed that new life which could not live on earthly food; forgetting the deceitfulness of my heart, the injunctions of my Bible; I became cold, negligent in the use of means, distant in prayer, lost enjoyment, and my heart, naturally carnal and madly fond of pleasure, got entangled. 'The lust of the eye, the lust of the flesh, and the pride of life' regained their power; other loves usurped the place of that Beloved who had bought me with his blood, and betrothed me to himself! 'that which came into my mind was, that I would be as the families of the countries, serve wood and stone.' Blessed be his name, he said, 'It shall not be.' He brought me in to the wilderness and pleaded with me, caused me to pass under the rod, brought me again into the bond of the covenant.

"O how often hast thou 'wrought with me,' for thy

name's sake! One self-willed step brought with it a train of consequences dangerous to spiritual life, filling even the path of duty with pits and snares, cutting me off from ordinances, pastor, parents, church, country, and christian society; placing me at the same time in the midst of carnal delights; and every thing in my natural temper and dispositions was congenial to them. What saved me? What in heaven or earth could save me but thy covenant? 'Truly thy covenant standeth fast;' therefore I was not lost in the vortex. But 'the Lord God, merciful and gracious, slow to anger, abundant in goodness and truth, forgiving iniquity, transgression and sin,' kept his eye upon me; many a time did he stop up my path. O from how many delusions of my own seeking; how many snares and nets of my own weaving; how many pits of my own digging hast thou delivered me, when wandering, bewildered, on temptation's ground, in the cloudy dark day! How often hast thou sought me out; how often bound me up when broken, strengthened me when sick, and fed me with judgment, and very, very often, thou madest thyself known to me! I knew thy hand when it shook the rod, when it arrested me on some mad career. I knew thy hedge, thy bar; saw not only escapes, but my Deliverer: often paused, turned, and took fast hold of *thy covenant*. I had no afflictions in those days, but every pleasure lawful to be enjoyed, and natural to the heart of woman; but no pastor, no church, no christian society; yet God was there, my Bible, my Doddridge, and other good books. And to my shame and confusion this day, he was not, in the midst of all my idolatry, 'a barren wilderness, nor a land of drought to me.'

I had many Sabbaths; literally the Sabbath was a 'sign between my covenant God and me;' ill spent it often was, but not with company; it was spent in retirement. The Lord did not leave me so far as to give up the Sabbath to the world. Though my heart was incrusted, and spiritual life scarcely discernible, sometimes the Lord met me, and strange to tell, not with threatenings causing terror, but with compunction, melting, turning, and ere the day was over, manifestations of pardon, though not joy; for I was grieved at my ingratitude.

"I did expect affliction long before it came, and my presumptuous heart calculated upon the fruit being the 'peaceable fruit of righteousness, and to take away sin;' but still I held my way, 'gadding about, drinking the waters of Sihor and the rivers of Syria,' and eating the worldling's dainties. Oh! oh! at last it came; yes, it came. 'Thou didst cut off the desire of my eyes with a stroke,' and with that made the world a blank to me. But, Oh! the stately steps of thy providential mercy previous to that trying hour! O my God, I must ever wonder and stand amazed at thy exuberant grace! In consistence with thy covenant, thou mightest have struck me among these worldings, in 'that dry and barren land,' where not one tongue could speak the language of Canaan, nor bring forth from thy precious Bible the words of consolation to my wounded and bereaved spirit; richly had I merited this, but never, no never, 'hast thou dealt with me as I sinned!' Through the whole of my life, from the time that 'the Lord called me out of darkness into his marvellous light;' from the time that he first led me to the Savior, and enabled me to take hold of his covenant,

' Wanderer, backslider, transgressor, rebel, .idolater, ingrate '—and if there be any name more expressively *vile* and *abominable*, that is mine. And from the hour of my birth, through the whole of this refractory perverse life, ' the Lord, the Lord God, merciful and gracious, long-suffering, abundant in goodness and truth, forgiving iniquity, transgression and sin,' has been, and now is, thy name to me.

"No, ye strong-built walls, ye grated windows, ye gloomy cells, ye confine no such sinner as I. And did the Lord take vengeance on my inventions? O no, *Mercy* preceded, *mercy* accompanied judgment; yea, it was all mercy, not vengeance. He brought me and my idol out of that barren land, placed us under the breath of prayer, among a dear little society of Methodists; he laid us upon their spirits, and when the messenger Death was sent for my beloved, the breath of prayer ascended from his bedside, from their little meeting, and I believe from their families and closets. The God of mercy prepared their hearts to pray, and his ear to hear, and the answer did not tarry. Behold, my husband prayeth; confesses sin; applies to the Savior; pleads for forgiveness for his sake; receives comfort; blesses God for Jesus Christ, and dies with these words on his tongue, 'I hold fast by the Savior!' Behold another wonder! the idolatress in an ecstasy of joy. She who never could realize a separation for one single minute during his life, now resigns her heart's treasure with praise and thanksgiving!

"O the joy of that hour! its savor remains on my heart to this moment. For five days and nights I had been little off my knees; it was my ordinary posture at his bed-side, and in all that time I had but *once* requested life. Surely 'the spirit of prayer and supplication·was poured out.' 'The Spirit helped mine infirmities with groanings which could not be uttered,' leading me to pray for that which God had determined to bestow; making intercession for my husband, according to the will of God.

"'O sing unto the Lord a new song, for he hath done marvellous things. His right hand and his holy arm hath gotten him the victory. The Lord hath made known his salvation. His righteousness hath he openly shown in the sight of the heathen. He hath remembered his mercy and his truth toward the house of Israel. All the ends of the earth have seen the Salvation of our God.' Psalm 98."

"Friday, December.

"Sermon from John, 4: 10. 'If thou knewest the gift of God, and who it is that saith, Give me to drink, thou wouldest have asked of ·him, and he would have given thee living water.'

"This is part of my provision laid in for my passage through Jordan. Christ is the gift of God. Christ is the water of life: he is this living water, and the bread of life *given*—given by God, received by the sinner. Life and comfort are experienced, and fruit produced is the evidence; but first of all, this gift must be known, and the soul's need must be known; Christ, the anointed Prophet, taught this woman both, and no other could. 'Search me, O Lord, and try me.' Hast thou not taught my soul its miserable and ruined state by nature; its helplessness as well as misery? Hast thou not also brought me to this living, life-giving water? Oh! hast thou not given me faith to come? faith to drink? and have I not experienced its solacing quality? Has it not satisfied my soul, and in some degree allayed my thirst for carnal delights? Blessed Spirit, "the gift of the Father and of the Son,' pour into my soul repeated draughts of *this living water;* yea, *be in me,* according to my Redeemer's promise, 'a well of water springing up to eternal life,' and cause me 'to bring forth fruit to the glory of the Father.'

"' Other foundation can no man lay, than that which is laid, Christ Jesus.'

" Do I, O my God, seek for or desire any other foundation? Are not all my hopes for time and eternity built on this foundation? Is not Christ all my salvation and all my desire? Do I not embrace thy covenant just as it is? believing that thou givest unto me eternal life, and that this life is in thy Son, whom thou hast given ' to be a Covenant of the people.' Iniquities prevail against me; but thou wilt not only purge them away, but wilt subdue them: ' Sin shall not have dominion over me, for I am not under the law, but under grace.' "

To Miss Walker, Edinburgh.

" New-York, 1812.

" My dear Miss W——— I think is in my debt; but that is no reason why I may not inquire after her health and welfare, and, through her, of that of her brother, sister, and other dear friends yet in their pilgrimage. My dear, dear Mrs. W——— lives in my affections, and surely what concerns her children can never be to me a matter of indifference. Your dear brother's persevering kindness and tried friendship have written gratitude in indelible characters on my heart. 'A friend in need is a friend indeed;' and such was he. I trust the Lord has rewarded and will reward him. I have still in my possession many dear remembrances of your worthy mother; her sensible, pious letters, some of which have proved prophetic, are among my treasures. What a lovely group presses upon my memory at this moment, united to Jesus and to one another on earth, and the union is now perfected in heaven. Your dear mother, Mrs. Brown, dear Mrs. Randall, and Lady Glenorchy, all zealous for the welfare of the widow and orphans, whose way lay peculiarly through *Vanity Fair*, and whose spirits were too much assimilated to the wares there exhibited, and most unworthy of all the care and pains they bestowed upon her. Tell my *then* dear pastor the pilgrim is not lost; he will find her in the 18th chapter of Ezekiel: he may remember that he and dear Doctor Erskine gave me over to the Lord when leaving Edinburgh. Well has He kept the charge, though I have not my part, after all the chastisements and charges received. But he is 'the Lord, the Lord God, merciful and gracious, slow to anger, abundant in goodness and truth, keeping mercy for thousands, forgiving iniquity, transgression and sin.'

"I am now a happy Mary, enjoying the full sense of pardon and the light of his countenance in the meantime, and the full prospect of being soon with him, made like him, and capacitated to praise him.

"I. GRAHAM."

"Sabbath, January 18.

"Dr. R———. 'By grace ye are saved, through

faith, and that not of yourselves, it is the gift of God.'

"All is of grace, all is free gift; or we wicked, wretched sinners, could have no interest in it. Thanks be unto God for his unspeakable gift of Jesus Christ, given for a covenant of the people. Thanks be unto God for the gift of faith, by which we apprehend this covenant, and become interested in him, as the salvation of our souls. Thanks be unto God for life to work; for new principles and new motives, new desires, new hopes, new fears, and, in some measure, new conduct. All of grace, and to the God of grace be all the glory.

"Afternoon. Jeremiah, 9:23. 'Let not the wise man glory in his wisdom, neither let the mighty man glory in his might; let not the rich man glory in his riches: but let him that glorieth, glory in this, that he understandeth and knoweth me; that I am the Lord which exercise righteousness, loving-kindness and judgment in the earth: for in these things I delight, saith the Lord.'

"O Lord, hast thou not taught me by thy word, by observation, and by experience, that 'all flesh is grass, and all the glory of man as the flower of grass?' Alas! how much have I gloried in even more worthless and transient things; but thou hast put a worm in them, which I hope has cut the roots, and they are in a dying state. O let grace supplant them; let me now glory only in thee and thy blessed, gracious, and well-ordered Covenant. Do I understand and know thee, that thou art the Lord which exerciseth righteousness, loving-kindness and judgment in the earth? Dare I say that I, worm as I am, and a sinful worm, am the subject of this loving-kindness, through the righteousness of Christ? Yes, I dare, by the constitution of thine own covenant—*the Covenant of the people*, the Mediator, the guarantee of the covenant of grace, which is all summed up in him.

" When thou givest Christ, thou givest freely all the blessings of the new covenant.

" This is the record, ' That thou hast given unto us eternal life, and this life is in thy Son.'

" I believe the record, and do understand and know that thou art the Lord, &c."

" February 4, 1813.

" My dear grand-children J. and I. B. waited on their beloved pastor Dr. Romeyn, and professed their faith in the Lord Jesus Christ as the Savior of sinners and their Savior, their desire to give themselves to the Lord and to his church, and to be in all things governed by it; to receive the seal of the covenant of grace, commemorate the dying love of their Redeemer the next opportunity, and swear allegiance to him over the symbols of his body and blood.

" Glory to God for this fresh manifestation of his mercy and grace to sinners. Not unto us, O Lord God, but to thy name be the glory. Thou hast made a covenant with thy chosen, and with believers in him ; and thou hast, by thy Holy Spirit, drawn them to take hold of this thy own covenant, and to give themselves to thee to be made the subjects of it. And now, O Lord, remember thy own covenant, and do as thou hast said : ' Put thy laws in their minds, and write them in their hearts, and be unto them a God, and they shall be unto thee a people; be merciful to their unrighteousness, and their sins and their iniquities remember no more.' Give them understanding to know and believe thy laws, memories to retain them, hearts to love them, consciences to recognize them, courage to profess and power to put in practice. O grant that the whole habit and frame of their souls may be a table and transcript of thy law. Blessed Redeemer! gather these lambs in thy arms and carry them in thy bosom. O seal them with the Holy Spirit of promise! They look forward to that feast of love which thou didst institute in that same night in which thou wast betrayed into the hands of sinners. If it may please thee, 'manifest thyself to them as thou dost not unto the world.' Blessed Shepherd, call these lambs by name; may they know thy voice, rejoice to hear it, and follow thee. In all the preparatory exercises speak to their hearts and commune with them in secret. O give them some love-tokens, which they may never forget; and make thyself 'known to them in the breaking of bread.' Exercise their parents with thankfulness and gratitude, and thine aged servant, to whom, in an especial manner, belong 'shame and confusion of face,' while she stands amazed at the stately steps of thy free sovereign mercy and grace to her, and to her children according to the flesh. 'Husband of the widow! Father of the fatherless! Shield of the stranger!' Glorify thy name, magnify thy grace: all these thou hast been to me; give these parents deep humility, if they have received grace to be more faithful than I; yet thy holy eye has seen much short-coming in them also. Glory to thy name for the grace in which they stand, and that thou hast enabled

them to train up these children for thee. Oh! let this
be a heart-searching time with us all; humble us, and
exalt thy name, and magnify thy grace.

"O Lord, my covenant God, all my desire is before
thee ; is it not that thou magnify thy grace in me and
in my family? There are others, Lord, and the residue
of the Spirit is with thee. Put forth thy power in the
heart of I. G. S. and compel him to come in. And O
my dear I. S. and her family; thou biddest me open
my mouth wide. Lord, see, there is much for thee to
do. I praise thy name for what thou hast done, and lay
me at thy feet waiting for further manifestations of thy
mercy, thy sovereign mercy : I have no other plea.

"Work with us, for thy name's sake, and with J.
M——for whom my worthless prayers have been presented to thee, as also a member of this family. O Lord,
he is now gone out into the world ; he is no longer under the control of man ; bring him under thy gracious
control ; call him into thy kingdom of grace, and make
him a willing subject in the day of thy power. Father,
glorify thy name !"

"April, Sabbath, 1813.

"2 Peter, chap. 2, 1st and 2d verses. 'Wherefore,
laying aside all malice, and all guile, and hypocrisies,
and envyings, and all evil speaking, as new born babes
desire the sincere milk of the word, that ye may grow
thereby.'

"Blessed Spirit! thou hast convinced me of the indwelling of every one of these, and also of my helplessness of myself to make successful war against them.
But, O hast thou not led me to the Captain of Salva-

tion for armor, for strength, for wisdom, for power, and is not my dependence for success on thy promise that 'sin shall not have dominion over me;' that thy grace is sufficient for me; 'that as my day so shall my strength be?'"

" May 5.

" Rom. 5 : 1. 'Therefore being justified by faith, we have peace with God, through our Lord Jesus Christ.'

"Blessed, blessed, blessed doctrine! by no other doctrine can I be justified and saved. Christ the gift of God, and faith the gift of God. *All, all* is of grace.

"I have shut my door, desiring to commune with God, but feeling dull and lifeless, ask what shall I read? My Bible lies just at hand, where shall I read? every part is good. I open and find it marked, Psalm 69 : 13. ' My prayer is unto thee, O Lord, in an acceptable time; O God, in the multitude of thy mercy hear me, in the truth of thy salvation.' In an acceptable time—when? 'to-day, if ye will hear his voice.' Nevertheless, I am continually with thee; thou holdest me by my right hand, and ever upholdest me, in the time of need especially.

"'In the multitude of thy mercy hear me, in the truth of thy salvation.' What is the truth of God's salvation? To be the property of Christ by purchase, to have Christ made our property by the Father's gift; to have the Holy Spirit sent into our hearts to enlighten our understandings, to govern our wills, to regulate our affections and tempers, and to be in us 'a well of water springing up into eternal life.' Father, Son, and Holy Spirit, ours by gift and by power! this, O this contains all my asking for myself, for my children and children's children, for my friends and all dear to me. Take us, O Lord, and in 'the truth of thy salvation' give thyself to us! do all the needful for us, and glorify thy name."

" Sabbath.

"Luke 14 : 16. 'A certain man made a great supper, and bade many, and sent his servants at supper time to say to them that were bidden, Come, for all things are ready. And they all, with one consent, began to make excuse.'

"Alas! such are our hearts, that we make idols even of the blessings and bounties of providence; no room is left for Christ, though without him every temporal good is under a curse, and our own persons also.

"O Lord, bless the gracious invitations given to perishing sinners this day; the pathetic and tender remonstrances of thy faithful servant. O, may many of the poor, the maimed, the halt, the blind, from the streets and lanes of the city, and may many from the highways and hedges, be compelled to come, that thy house may be filled. And, O my gracious Father, let these careless ones, who are my flesh and blood, be among the number! Hear, O hear the prayers offered this day for poor self-deluded, self-destroying sinners! awaken them, O Lord, and sweep away all lying refuges, and, gracious God, settie and establish these halters! O bring to the birth, and give life, and love, and zeal to make a full profession to the glory of thy powerful grace, and to the joy and comfort of fellow-members. Let *thy kingdom come.*"

" In my large light closet, within my airy, comfort
able room; the prospect from my windows such as I
have ever delighted in—woods and water, flower-garden
and fruit-trees, and beautiful shrubs of various kinds, all
as much mine as if my own individual property by the
laws of the land in which I live; surrounded with books,
and my children's rich library at my command; enjoying rich Gospel ordinances, under a godly, gifted pastor,
with pious, loving, sensible church members; a carriage to convey me, Sabbath and week days, to places
of worship; children whose desire is that I may enjoy
all these to the full without care or trouble, they caring
for me; with all these a large measure of health, my
eyes see my teachers, my ears hear their voice. Why
then these tears? Are they all for sin? Lord, search
and see. Does no wounded pride, no selfish hurt mix?
Ah! Lord, thou knowest. I have detected much, and
mourn and weep on that account; but I fear there is
yet much lurking and working that I know not.

" I have set apart the remainder of this day for fasting and humiliation on account of past sins which I already know, and for yet further search into what I
know not of at present. Lord, give me heart-searching
exercises. Glory, glory, glory to Father, Son, and
blessed Comforter, that I am forgiven; thy Spirit witnesseth with my spirit that I am forgiven. Thou hast giv-
en me faith in the truth of thy testimony, that the blood
of Christ cleanseth from all sin—that this is thy own provision for sinners—that Christ died for the ungodly—
that while we were yet sinners, Christ died for us—that
Christ hath loved us, and given himself for us—that

' God so loved the world that he gave his only begotten Son, that whosoever believeth on him should not perish, but have everlasting life.' These last words came from thy own lips of flesh. Thou gift of God to a perishing world, and to me, one of the most guilty in it! thou also saidst, ' He that believeth on the Son hath everlasting life.' Thy Spirit witnesseth with my spirit, that to me it is given on the behalf of Christ to believe in him. Philippians 1 : 29. Therefore I have everlasting life. Him who was slain and hanged on a tree, ' Him hath God exalted to be a Prince and a Savior, for to give repentance and remission of sins.' From this exalted Prince I have repentance and forgiveness of sin, and therefore I dare look at my sins ; I look with grief but not with terror. Though forgiven, and though provision is made for forgiveness, sin is still an evil and a bitter thing.

"This day is set apart for mourning. I desire to search, to know more of my vileness, that I may mourn yet more: that while my heart is wrung for my ingratitude, the Lord may make it the means of crucifying my sins, especially that which ' so easily besets me,' that he will give me the prayer of faith that they may be forgiven, and that I may be delivered from their power in my heart ; that I may be clothed with humility, so humble that nothing can hurt me, wearing my Redeemer's yoke, leaning upon him who was ' meek and lowly,' that I may find rest to my soul. Now, Lord, assist me for the rest of the day, and let to-morrow be the beginning of days."

" Ten o'clock at night.

" The day is spent and I look for the blessing. It has not been spent so much in my usual way of retracing, confessing, and bewailing, but with Owen on the subject of indwelling sin, of purification and the means appointed by God. The blood of Christ is the only effectual means not only as atonement for sin, setting us free from condemnation; but also for cleansing, as sprinkled on the conscience by the Holy Ghost, and purging it from dead works. There are means in which we are to exercise ourselves, depending on the Spirit for benefit. We are to work in the faith that God works in us. Mortification is one means, and though the mortification of the body is, perhaps, one of the lowest, I think it is of divine appointment, therefore not to be neglected. I have been also studying the death of Christ, and his previous sufferings; the unbelief, the opposition, contradiction, contempt, and cruel mocking which he endured; and his meekness, patience, and submission under them; healing Malcus' ear, praying for his murderers; that, as the children of Israel were healed by looking to the brazen serpent, I may be healed by looking unto the uplifted Jesus; the Spirit producing the effect. And as the woman with the bloody issue was healed by a touch, exercising faith in the power of Christ, so I may be healed by a look, exercising the same faith, the Spirit producing the effect of conformity to his example, working in me that meek and lowly spirit for which I have been praying. And now, by grace communicated, I hope to watch over my spirit with more success than formerly. I wait for thy salvation."

The following letter shows how Mrs. Graham persevered in her endeavors to guide and benefit immortal souls as long as God gave her powers to be employed.

(*To Mrs. J. W——.*)

"Greenwich, 1814.

"Did not the dove, my dear J——, get into the ark? Yes, Noah put out his hand and pulled her in; both are types of Christ. He is the Ark of safety from the flood of wrath that must overwhelm unbelievers.

"I know not, my dear, the amount of that over which you mourn with so much agony; I know not even if it be sinful, except in the circumstances; you are conscious of sincerity, and you do not now wish to draw back. We can, my dear, do nothing in our own strength; no, not so much as think a good thought. To make any resolution without dependance on God for strength to perform, is sinful; to make any vow without a consciousness of our weakness and dependance on God for strength to perform, is an aggravation of the evil.

"I suppose my J. has sinned; what then? 'If any man say he has no sin, he deceives himself, and the truth is not in him.' And if you suppose that your sin in this is greater than many other sins with their aggravations, you judge wrong. I think that any one *deliberate* sin, wilfully committed with a knowledge that it is sin, is greater than yours in such circumstances. You are bound by your vow, and God will enable you to perform it. Turn, my dear, to the 2d chapter of the Acts of the Apostles, where Peter preaches to the very murderers of our blessed Savior, and charges the guilt upon them, verse 22d; and again in verse 36th, 'Therefore let all the house of Israel know assuredly, that this same Jesus whom ye crucified, God hath made both Lord and Christ; and when they heard this, they were pricked in their hearts.' Read on, my dear; Peter exhorts even them to repent and be baptized in the name of Christ, for the remission of sins. I make no doubt but many have made vows in a rash manner; but, so far as I know, you have vowed only to serve the Lord; this you are bound to do with or without a vow; and if the Lord makes this vow the means of keeping you watchful, and humble, and firm in avoiding what you have vowed against, it will, by his overruling Spirit, prove a blessing.

"'You do not know where to look for comfort!" To Jesus, my dear; not to yourself, not to any creature. 'Look unto me and be saved, all the ends of the earth, for I am God, and there is none else.' Isaiah 45 : 22. 'O Israel, thou hast destroyed thyself, but in me is thy help.' Hosea, 13 : 9. and chapter 14. Take a view, my dear, of the character of God in his dealings with his perverse Israel, after they had made the molten calf, and sinned otherwise grievously against God. He, at the intercession of Moses, forgave their sin, and proclaimed that wonderful name, which to this day is the encouragement of convicted sinners, and mine in particular. Exodus, 34 : 5. And the Lord passed by him (Moses) and proclaimed, 'The Lord, the Lord God, merciful and gracious, long-suffering, abundant in goodness and truth, keeping mercy for thousands, forgiving iniquity, transgression and sin.' And how can God do this, whose law is, as himself, immutable; and who adds, 'that he will by no means clear the guilty?' Look now to the 53d chapter of Isaiah, where you will find your Redeemer standing in your stead. In the 30th chapter is another amazing display of God's forgiveness. The prophet begins the chapter with, 'Wo to the

rebellious children!' and lays grievous things to their
charge, till you come to the 18th verse, where he says,
' Therefore will the Lord wait, that he may be gracious
to you; therefore will he be exalted, that he may have
mercy upon you; for the Lord is a God of judgment,
blessed are all they that wait for him.' Once more
look at the proclamation, Jeremiah, 3 : 12. God has
provided a sacrifice of sufficient value to atone for
our most aggravated transgressions, and a righteousness answerable to the uttermost extent of his holy law.
Both are made over to the sinner by free gift. 2 Cor.
5 : 21, ' He hath made him to be sin for us, who knew
no sin, that we might be made the righteousness of God
in him.' *In him*—He, our Surety, having fulfilled all
righteousness for us, *as* our Surety and Representative.

"You fear that it is not the hand of the Lord that is
upon you. I do think that it is, my J——. It is the
peculiar office of the Spirit to convince of sin, and I do
think that he is at this time dealing with your soul. But
why look so much at your vow? you have sinned, my
J——, in heart, lip, and life. ' Thou shalt love the Lord
thy God with all thy heart.' O my J——, what prosti-
tuted affections! what mispent time! While God says,
' Whether you eat or drink, or whatsoever you do, do
all to the glory of God,' what self-indulgence and
self-will, instead of self-denial! Listen to the voice of
convictions, listen to it as the voice of mercy, leading
you to Christ the great propitiatory Sacrifice, ' the
Lamb of God which taketh away the sins of the world.'

"Go to Christ, my dear, as a sinner; tell him you
commit your sinful soul into his hands; say, Thou hast
bid me look unto thee and be saved? Savior, I do look

unto thee for salvation. Wash me in thy blood, clothe
me in thy righteousness, sanctify me by thy grace,
accept of me as thy pardoned, saved child; and be a
Surety for me for good, that, having vowed to thee
that I would be thy servant, I may perform my vow;
furnish me with both will and power to devote myself
to thee every day of my life. Try, my dear, to rest on
Christ; put your trust in him; if you do he will not
disappoint you: as your faith, so shall it be unto you.
Now, faith is a saving grace; thereby we receive and
rest upon Christ for salvation, as he is offered to us in
the Gospel. Do as you have said: wait his appointed
time, in the use of means, till he manifest himself to you.
I am hurried for time to get this to town. Farewell.
I will pray for you,   ·   I. GRAHAM."

                              " 1814.

    "JOEL, 2:2. 'A day of darkness and gloominess, a
day of clouds and thick darkness, as the morning spread
upon the mountains.'

    "Not in temporals, nor in the means of grace; every
thing that earth can afford is gathered into my present
cup; it is full and runs over with earthly good, and a
large measure of health to enjoy it. Moral temporals are
also mine in no common degree: friendship, society at
my choice, and respectability in it. Rich means of grace
within my reach, my Bible, and books of every kind
and great variety at my hand, of instruction and of devotion. Mine eyes see my teachers, and my judgment
approves their doctrine as corresponding with that sure
word of testimony 'given me as the test of all human
writings.' Yet it is a day of darkness and of gloom.

    "Isaiah, 50: 10. 'Who is among you that feareth the

Lord, that obeyeth the voice of his servant, that walketh in darkness and hath no light? Let him trust in the name of the Lord and stay himself upon his God.'

"To trust in the name of the Lord, and to stay myself upon my God, is still my privilege, and though with little life and little comfort, my experience. My mind is so desultory! My Bible, and helps derived from men's deductions and experiences, seem useless; they are not blessed as means to fix my heart; trifles of every sort pass and repass often; while my eyes read the words, my mind is gone in a dream on some other subject; my heart remains unimpressed, my mind uninformed; the same in prayer, especially in secret and in the family; less so in the sanctuary.

"I seem, as to apprehension, left to my own dark, dismal, carnal self; naked faith on the finished work of my Redeemer is all that supports me; and that as a bare preventive of fear and source of a hope that 'I shall yet praise Him who is the health of my countenance and my God.' I know his covenant stands fast, I have taken hold of it; I do at this cold and stupid moment place my confidence in it. Christ is God's covenant; God's gift to sinners; I believe it; he is the Lamb of God which taketh away the sin of the world; I believe it; I believe on the Son for all the purposes for which God has sent him into the world; therefore I have everlasting life; I believe the record that God gave of his Son; that God hath given to me eternal life, and this life is in his Son, not in me, but in union with him. 'He that hath the Son hath life; he that hath not the Son hath not life. John, 5.

"I thank thee, my God, that thou hast not left me to

cast away my confidence in Christ. I have life in him, and no life but as I have it from him. Thou seest how it is with me. Thou art my reconciled Father in Christ, but thou hast shut me out from thy presence. I do not enjoy thee; my poor heart is tossed from trifle to trifle. It has been my way through life to destroy myself, and thy way to deliver me. Thou hast been very gracious to me in my old age. I have enjoyed much of thy presence in thy sanctuary and in my private hours; and although sin has dwelt and does dwell in me, I have enjoyed thy forgiving grace, and have tasted thy love, far beyond what I have for weeks past. ' Search me, O God, and know my heart; try me and know my thoughts; and see if there be any wicked way in me, and lead me in the way everlasting.' Show me wherefore thou contendest with me. Am I living in the indulgence of any known wilful sin ? or in the habitual neglect of any known duty ? Lord, ' it is not in man that walketh to direct his steps.' I know I have been unthankful, unwatchful, idle; alas! this is my ordinary course ; but it is not the ordinary course of my Lord God, merciful and gracious, to mark iniquity against me, but to forgive me daily, to lead me to the blood of sprinkling, to give me contrition, and to restore me to his favor by giving me ' joy and peace in believing.' Help, Lord! give me heart-searching exercises. I read thy word, I set about that to which thou callest me. I set apart this day for fasting, but the gracious exercises are not in me. Come, O come, and be with me! Exalted Prince, give repentance and remission ; in thy light let me see light.

"JOEL, 2 : 12. ' Therefore now turn ye unto me with all your heart, with fasting, with weeping and mourning; rend your heart and not your garments, turn unto the Lord your God; for he is gracious and merciful, slow to anger, and of great kindness, and repenteth him of the evil.' O do I not know thee by this name? has it not been thy name to me throughout this wide wilderness, ' pardoning iniquity, transgression, and sin ?" Thou hast prepared a prayer for me—' turn me and I shall be turned, for thou art the Lord my God.' Jer. 31 : 18. I look to thy new covenant in the same chapter; it is all promise, I can do nothing in it. Christ, by thine own appointment, answers for my part, or rather I have no part. I can render nothing to the Lord for all his benefits to me. I will put forth the withered hand to ' take the cup of salvation, and call on the name of the Lord.'

" *Ten o'clock.* The day is spent—I have confessed, and endeavored to turn to the Lord with mourning, but with little sensibility.

" I attended meeting in the evening, heard two excellent discourses on the priesthood of Christ, and joined in two prayers and three hymns with more fixed attention than has been my attainment lately; for this I thank thee, my God. Many have been the beginnings of days and of months which thou hast afforded after backsliding. O add this to the number! Psalm 143. ' Hear my prayer, O Lord; give ear to my supplication; in thy faithfulness answer me, and in thy righteousness. Enter not into judgment with thy servant, for in thy sight shall no flesh living be justified.

" ' My spirit is overwhelmed within me, my heart within me is desolate. I stretch out my hands unto thee; my soul thirsteth after thee, in a thirsty land. Hear me speedily, O Lord; my spirit faileth; hide not thy face from me, lest I be like unto those that go down into the pit. Cause me to hear thy loving-kindness in the morning, for in thee do I trust; cause me to know the way wherein I should walk, for I lift up my soul unto thee. Deliver me, O Lord, from mine enemies! I flee unto thee to hide me. Teach me to do thy will, for thou art my God. Thy Spirit is good; lead me into the land of uprightness. Quicken me, O Lord, for thy name's sake; for thy righteousness' sake bring my soul out of trouble. I wait for thy salvation.

This heart my Jesus bought with blood,
   It is his honest claim;
O seize it, fix it, Savior God,
   To give it is my aim.

Take full possession of this heart,
   And here set up thy throne;
Command each idol to depart,
   And make it all thine own.

O dare I not to thee appeal,
   That 'tis my first desire,
That on this heart thou stamp thy seal
   And grave it with love's fire?

To fix this heart to stray no more
   I ev'n would quit the clay;
Would hasten on to Jordan's shore,
   And plough the wat'ry way.

Nor fear nor dread my soul should move,
   With Jesus in my heart,
Each passion swallow'd up in love,
   I'd court the friendly dart.

The resurrection and the life
   In death itself he'll prove,
And whilst he closes mortal strife,
   Breathe his own life of love.

Then boast not, monster, of thy sting,
   Nor of thy vict'ry, grave;
In th' arms of God's anointed King
   I dare thy fiercest brave.

CHAPTER XII.

CLOSING LABORS FOR THE POOR—SICKNESS AND DEATH.

During the last two years of her life Mrs. Graham found her strength inadequate to so extensive a course of visiting the poor as formerly; there were some distressed families, however, that experienced her kind attentions to the last. She would occasionally accompany the Rev. Mr. Stanford on his visits to the State Prison, Hospital, and to the Magdalen House. This gentleman was the stated preacher employed by "the Society for the support of the Gospel among the poor," and devoted his time to preaching in the Alms House, Hospital, State Prison, Debtors' Prison, &c. with great assiduity and acceptance.

Mrs. Graham now spent much of her time in her room, devoted to meditation, prayer, and reading the Scriptures; she seemed to be weaning from earth and preparing for heaven. Prayer was that sweet breath of her soul which brought stability to her life. Genuine humility was obvious in all her sentiments and deportment. Religious friends prized her conversation, counsel, and friendship; sometimes they would venture on a compliment to her superior attainments, but always experienced a decided rebuke. To her friend Colonel L——, who expressed a wish to be such a character as she was, she quickly replied with an air of mingled pleasantry and censure, "Get thee behind me, Satan." To a female friend who said, "If I were only sure at last of being admitted to a place at your feet I should feel happy." "Hush, hush," replied Mrs Graham, "There is ONE SAVIOR." Thus she was always careful to give her Divine Redeemer the whole glory of her salvation.

This example of humility, self-denial, and sensibility to the imperfection of her conduct, is the more to be valued, as it is so difficult to be followed. Flattery is too commonly practised; and there is no sufficient guard against its dangerous consequences, except a constant and humbling recognition of the spirituality of the law of God, and our lamentable deficiency in fulfilling it. Pride was not made for man : " I have seen an end of all perfection," said the Psalmist, " but thy commandment is exceeding broad." It was by cherishing this sentiment, by studying her Bible, by searching her heart and its motives, and, above all, by grace accorded of heaven in answer to her prayers, that Mrs. Graham was enabled to maintain such meekness of spirit, such an uniformity of christian character throughout her life. May all who read her history be directed to the same sources of true peace and genuine happiness !

In the spring of 1814 she was requested to unite with some ladies in forming a *Society for the promotion of Industry among the Poor*. This was the last act in which she appeared before the public. A petition, signed by about thirty ladies, was presented to the Corporation of New-York, praying that they would assign them a building in which work might be prepared and given out to the industrious poor, who being paid for their labor, might be saved the necessity of begging, and at the same time cherish habits of industry and self-respect. The Corporation having returned a favorable answer, and provided a house, a meeting of the Society was held, and Mrs. Graham once more was called to the chair. It was the last time she was to preside at the formation of a new Society. Her articulation, once strong and clear, was now observed to have become more feeble. The ladies present listened to her with affectionate attention; her voice broke upon the ear as a pleasant sound that was passing away. She consented to have her name inserted on the list of managers, and to give what assistance her age would permit in forwarding so beneficent a work. Although it pleased God that she should cease from her labors before the House of Industry was opened, yet the work was carried on by others and prospered. Between four and five hundred women were employed and paid during the following winter. The Corporation declared in strong terms their approbation of the result, and enlarged their donation, with a view to promote the same undertaking for the succeeding winter.

In the month of May, 1814, a Report was received from Mr. Stephen Prust, of Bristol, in England, of the Society for establishing *Adult Schools*. Mrs. Graham was so delighted with a perusal of it, as immediately to undertake the formation of such a school in the village of Greenwich. She called on the young people who were at work in some neighboring manufactories, and requested them to attend her for this purpose every Sabbath morning at eight o'clock. This was kept up after her decease as a *Sunday School, and consisted of nearly eighty scholars.* She was translated from this work of faith on earth, to engage in the sublimer work of praise in heaven.

For some weeks previous to her last illness she was favored with unusual health and much enjoyment of religion; she appeared to have sweet exercises and communion in attending on all God's ordinances and appointed means of grace. She was also greatly refreshed in spirit by the success of Missionary and Bible Societies, and used to speak with much affection of Mr. Gordon, Mr. Lee, Mr. May, and Dr. Morrison, with whom she had been acquainted when in New-York, on their way to missionary stations in India and China.

Mrs. Graham was very partial to the works of Dr. John Owen, Rev. William Romaine, and Rev. John Newton, and read them with pleasure and profit. One day she remarked to Mr. B——, that she preferred the ancient writers on Theology to the modern, because they dealt more in italics. "Dear mother," he replied, "what religion can there be in italics?" "You know," said she, "that old writers expected credit for the doctrines they taught, by proving them from the word of God to be correct: they inserted the Scripture passages in Italics, and their works have been sometimes one-half in Italics. Modern writers on Theology, on the contrary, give us a long train of reasoning to persuade us to their opinions, but very little in Italics." This remark of hers has great force, and deserves the serious attention of those who write and those who read on theological subjects.

On the two Sabbaths preceding her last illness she joined in communion at the Lord's table. On the 10th of July, 1814, at Greenwich, and on the 17th at her own church in Cedar-street. On each week preceding these seasons she attended three evenings on religious exercises; on Thursdays at the Orphan Asylum, on Friday evenings the preparation sermons, and on Saturday evenings at the prayer-meetings. She appeared lively, and expressed comfort in those religious seasons, and continued actively useful until the very day on which her illness commenced.

On the morning of the 17th she attended the Sabbath-school with her daughter and grand-children. Thus the Lord was pleased to direct that she should lead her children's children into the walks of usefulness before she took her flight to heaven, and impose a pleasing obligation on them that they should follow her steps. Of the same date is the last meditation in her diary.

"July 17, 1814.

" *Communion Sabbath.* 1 Peter, 1 : 8, 9. ' Whom having not seen, ye love; in whom, though now ye see him not, yet believing, ye rejoice with joy unspeakable and full of glory: receiving the end of your faith, even the salvation of your souls.'

"I had requested to be brought to my Lord's banqueting house, and to be feasted with love this day. I ate the bread and drank the wine, in the faith that I ate the flesh and drank the blood of the Son of man, and dwelt in him and he in me. Took a close view of my familiar friend Death, accompanied with the presence of my Savior, *his sensible presence.* I cannot look at it without this; it is my only petition concerning it. I have had desires relative to certain circumstances, but they are nearly gone. It is my sincere desire that God may be glorified, and he knows best how and by what circumstances. I retain my one petition,

" Only to me thy count'nance show,
" I ask no more the Jordan through."

Thus she arose from her Master's table, was called
to gird on her armor for a combat with the King of
Terrors, and came off more than conqueror, through
Him who loved her.

On Monday she appeared in perfect health and visited and gave religious instruction to the orphans in
the Asylum.

On Tuesday, the 19th of July, she complained of not
feeling well, and kept her room; on Thursday her disorder proved to be a cholera morbus, and her children
sent for a physician. She thought this attack was
slighter than in former seasons. On Saturday, however,
she requested that Mrs. Chrystie might be sent for;
this alarmed Mrs. B——, knowing there existed an understanding between those two friends, that one should
attend the dying-bed of the other. Mrs. Chrystie was a
very dear friend of Mrs. Graham. For upwards of
twenty-four years they had loved each other, feeling reciprocal sympathy in their joys and their sorrows; the
hope of faith was the consolation of both, and oftentimes it had been their delightful employment to interchange their expressions of affection towards Him,
' whom having not seen, they loved, and in whom, though
they saw him not, yet believing on him, they rejoiced
with joy unspeakable and full of glory.' On Mrs. Chrystie's entering the chamber of her friend, Mrs. Graham
welcomed her with a sweet expressive smile, seeming
to say, "I am going to get the start of you, I am called home before you; it will be your office to fulfil
our engagement." When she sat by her bedside, Mrs.

Graham said, "Your face is very pleasant to me, my friend."

During Saturday night a lethargy appeared to be overpowering her frame. On Sabbath morning she was disposed to constant slumber; observing Mr. B—— looking at her with agitation, she was roused from her heaviness, and stretching her arms towards him and embracing him, she said, "My dear, dear son, I am going to leave you; I am going to my Savior." "I know," he replied, "that when you do go from us, it will be to the Savior; but, my dear mother, it may not be the Lords' time now to call you to himself." "Yes," said she, "now is the time; and Oh! I could weep for sin." Her words were accompanied with her tears. "Have you any doubts, then, my dear friend?" asked Mrs. Chrystie. "Oh no," replied Mrs. Graham; and looking at Mr. and Mrs. B—— as they wept, "My dear children, I have no more doubt of going to my Savior, than if I were already in his arms; my guilt is all transferred; he has cancelled all I owed. Yet I could weep for sins against so good a God: it seems to me as if there must be weeping even in heaven for sin."

After this she entered into conversation with her friends, mentioning portions of Scripture and favorite hymns which had been subjects of much comfort and joy to her. Some of these she had transcribed into a little book, calling them her "victuals" prepared for crossing over Jordan; she committed them to memory, and often *called them to remembrance as her songs in the night* when sleep had deserted her. She then got Mr. B—— to read to her some of these portions, especially the eighty-second hymn of Newton's third book:

> " Let us love, and sing, and wonder;
> Let us praise the Savior's name !
> He has hushed the law's loud thunder,
> He has quenched Mount Sinai's flame;
> He has washed us with his blood,
> He has brought us nigh to God." &c.

Mrs. Graham then fell asleep, nor did she awaken until the voice of the Rev. Dr. Mason roused her. They had a very affectionate interview, which he has partly described in the excellent sermon he delivered after her decease. She expressed to him her hope as founded altogether on the redemption that is in Jesus Christ: were she left to depend on the merit of the best action she had ever performed, that would be only a source of despair. She repeated to him, as her view of salvation, the fourth verse of the same hymn:

> " Let us wonder; grace and justice
> Join, and point at mercy's store;
> When, through grace, in Christ our trust is,
> Justice smiles and asks no more;
> He who wash'd us with his blood,
> Has secured our way to God."

Having asked Dr. Mason to pray with her, he inquired if there was any particular request she had to make of God by him; she replied that God would direct; then as he kneeled, she put up her hands, and raising her eyes towards heaven, breathed this short but expressive petition, " Lord, lead thy servant in prayer."

After Dr. Mason had taken his leave, she again fell

into a deep sleep. Her physicians still expressed a hope of her recovery, as her pulse was regular and the violence of her disease had abated. One of them, however, declared his opinion that his poor drugs would prove of little avail against her own ardent prayers to depart and be with Christ, which was far better for her than a return to a dying world.

On Monday the Rev. Mr. Rowan prayed with her, and to him she expressed also the tranquillity of her mind, and the steadfastness of her hope, through Christ, of eternal felicity.

Her lethargy increased; at intervals from sleep she would occasionally assure her daughter, Mrs. B——, that all was well; and when she could rouse herself only to say one word at a time, that one word, accompanied with a smile, was "Peace." From her there was a peculiar emphasis in this expression of the state of her mind: "Peace I leave with you, my peace I give unto you," had been a favorite portion of Scripture with her, and a promise, the fulfilment of which was her earnest prayer to the God who made it. She also occasionally asked Mr. B—— to pray with her, even when she could only articulate, as she looked at him, "Pray." She was now surrounded by many of her dear christian friends, who watched her dying bed with affection and solicitude. On Tuesday afternoon she slept with little intermission. This, said Dr. Mason, may be truly called "falling asleep in Jesus." It was remarked by those who attended her, that all terror was taken away, and that death seemed here as an entrance into life. Her countenance was placid and looked younger than before her illness.

At a quarter past twelve o'clock, being the morning of the 27th of July, 1814, her spirit gently winged its flight from a mansion of clay to the realms of glory, whilst around the precious remnant of earth her family and friends stood weeping, yet elevated by the scene they were witnessing. After a silence of many minutes they kneeled by her bed, adored the goodness and the grace of God towards his departed child, and implored the divine blessing on both the branches of her family, as well as on all the Israel of God.

Thus she departed in peace, not trusting in her wisdom or virtue, like the philosophers of Greece and Rome; not even like Addison, calling on the profligate to see a good man die; but like Howard, afraid that her good works might have a wrong place in the estimate of her hope, her chief glory was that of " a sinner saved by grace."*

After such examples, who will dare to charge the doctrines of the cross of Christ with licentiousness? Here are two instances of persons, to whose good works the world have cheerfully borne testimony, who lived and died in the profession of these doctrines. It was faith that first purified their hearts, and so the stream of action from these fountains became pure also. Had not Christ died and risen again, all the powers of man could never have produced such lives of benevolence, nor a death so full of contrition, yet so embalmed with hope. Hallelujah : " unto Him who loved us, and washed us from our sins in his own blood, and hath made us kings and priests unto God and his Father : to him be glory and dominion for ever and ever. Amen."

* This was Howard's epitaph, dictated by himself.

At the next weekly prayer-meeting which she had usually attended, the circumstances of her death were made subjects of improvement. On the 16th of July she was a worshipper with her brethren and sisters there, and on the evening of the 30th they were called to consider her by faith as in the immediate presence of her God, among "the spirits of the just made perfect." The services of that evening were closed with the following hymn from Dobell's collection, which is beautifully descriptive of her happy change:

> " 'Tis finish'd! the conflict is past,
> 　The heav'n-born spirit is fled;
> Her wish is accomplish'd at last,
> 　And now she's entomb'd with the dead.
>
> The months of affliction are o'er,
> 　The days and the nights of distress,
> We see her in anguish no more—
> 　She's gained her happy release.
>
> No sickness, or sorrow, or pain,
> 　Shall ever disquiet her now;
> For death to her spirit was gain,
> 　Since Christ was her life when below.
>
> Her soul has now taken its flight
> 　To mansions of glory above,
> To mingle with angels of light,
> 　And dwell in the kingdom of love.
>
> The victory now is obtain'd;
> 　She's gone her dear Savior to see;
> Her wishes she fully has gain'd—
> 　She's now where she longed to be.
>
> The coffin, the shroud, and the grave
> 　To her were no objects of dread;
> On Him who is mighty to save,
> 　Her soul was with confidence stay'd.

> Then let us forbear to complain,
>   That she is now gone from our sight;
> We soon shall behold her again,
>   With new and redoubled delight."

Mrs. Graham's death created a strong sensation in the public mind. Magistrates of the city were careful to express their sense of the public loss sustained, and many charitable institutions paid affectionate tributes to her memory. Several clergymen also made her death the subject of their discourses, among whom was her beloved pastor Dr. John M. Mason, who, on Sabbath evening, August 14th, delivered the well known powerful sermon, "Christian Mourning," from 1 Thess. 4 : 13, 14. "I would not have you to be ignorant, brethren, concerning them which are asleep; that ye sorrow not, even as others which have no hope. For if Jesus died and rose again, even so them also which sleep in Jesus will God bring with him."

Contrasting the consolations afforded to the christian with the darkness and doubt of the pagan or infidel; dwelling on the christian's death as "sleeping in Jesus;" his immediate entrance into bliss, and his glorious resurrection and reigning with Christ in the judgment, he thus proceeds :

"In this faith the apostles labored and the martyrs bled. Ages have elapsed and it is still the same. It is not a distant wonder; not a brilliant vision; but a solid and present reality under the power of which at this moment, while the words are on my lips, christians, in various parts of the world, are closing their eyes to sleep in Jesus. It has come home to our own *business and bosoms.* It has chosen our houses to be the scene of its miracles. But rarely does it fall to the lot of human eyes to witness so high a display of its value and virtue, as was witnessed in that blessed woman whose entrance into the joy of her Lord has occasioned our assembling this evening.

"As we are commanded to be *followers of them who through faith and patience inherit the promises*, we should have their example before us, that we may learn to imbibe their spirit, to imitate their graces, and be ready for their reward. With this view permit me to lay before you some brief recollections of our deceased friend.

"It is not my intention to relate the history of her life. That will be a proper task for biography. I design merely to state a few leading facts, and to sketch such outlines of character as may show to those who knew her not, *what manner of person she was in all holy conversation and godliness*. Those who knew her best require no such remembrancer, and will be able, from their own observation, to supply its defects.

"ISABELLA MARSHALL, known to us as Mrs. GRAHAM, received from nature qualities which, in circumstances favorable to their development, do not allow their possessor to pass through life unnoticed and inefficient.

"An intellect strong, prompt and inquisitive—a temper open, generous, cheerful, ardent—a heart replete with tenderness, and alive to every social affection and every benevolent impulse—a spirit at once enterprising and persevering—the whole crowned with that rare and inestimable endowment, good sense—were materials which required only skilful management to fit her for adorning and dignifying any female station. With that sort of cultivation which the world most admires, and those opportunities which attend upon rank and fortune, she might have shone in the circles of the great without forfeiting the esteem of the good. Or had her lot fallen among the literary unbelievers of the continent, she might have figured in the sphere of the Voltaires, the Duffauds, and the other *esprits forts* of Paris. She might have been as gay in public, as dismal in private, and as wretched in her end, as any of the most distinguished among them for their wit and their wo. But God had destined her for other scenes and services—scenes from which greatness turns away appalled; and services which all the cohorts of infidel wit are unable to perform. She was to be prepared by poverty, bereavement and grief, to pity and to succor the poor, the bereaved and the grieving. The sorrows of widowhood were to teach her the heart of the widow—her babes, deprived of their father, to open the springs of her compassion to the fatherless and orphan—and the consolations of God, her "refuge and strength, her very present help in trouble," to make her a daughter of consolation to them who were "walking in the valley of the shadow of death."

"To train her betimes for the future dispensations of his providence, the Lord touched the heart of this *chosen vessel* in her early youth. The spirit of prayer sanctified her infant lips, and taught her, as far back as her memory could go, to *pour out her heart* before God. She had not reached her eleventh year when she selected a bush in the retirement of the field, and there devoted herself to her God by faith in the Redeemer. The incidents of her education, thoughtless companions, the love of dress, and the dancing-school, as she has herself recorded, chilled for a while the warmth of her piety, and robbed her bosom of its peace. But her gracious Lord revisited her with his mercy, and bound her to himself in an everlasting covenant which she sealed at his own table about the 17th year of her age.

"Having married, a few years after, Dr. John Graham, surgeon to the 60th British regiment, she accompanied him first to Montreal, and shortly after to Fort Niagara. Here, during four years of temporal prosperity, she had no opportunity, even for once, of entering *the habitation of God's house,* or hearing the sound of his Gospel. Secluded from the waters of the sanctuary and all the public means of growth in grace, her religion began to languish and its leaf to droop. But the root was pe-rennial—it was of *the seed of God, which liveth and abideth for ever.* The Sabbath was still to her the sign of his covenant. On that day of rest, with her Bible in her hand, she used to wander through the woods, renew her self-dedication, and pour out her prayer for the salvation of her husband and her children. He who " dwelleth not in temples made with hands " heard her cry from the wilds of Niagara, and " strengthened her with strength in her soul."

" By one of those vicissitudes which checker military life, the regiment was ordered to the island of Antigua in the West Indies. Here she met with that exquisite enjoyment to which she had been long a stranger—the communion of kindred spirits in the love of Christ: and soon did she need all the soothing and support which it is fitted to administer ; for in a very short time the husband of her youth, the object of her most de-

voted affection, her sole earthly stay, was taken from
her by death. The stroke was, indeed, mitigated by the
sweet assurance that he slept in Jesus. But a heart
like hers, convulsed by a review of the past and anticipation of the future, would have burst with agony, had
she not known how to pour its sorrows into the bosom
of her heavenly Father. Trials which beat sense and
reason to the ground, raise up the faith of the christian, and draw her closer to her God. O how divine to
have him as the rock of our rest when every earthly
reliance is *a broken reed!*

"Bowing to his mysterious dispensation, and committing herself to his protection as the *Father of the
fatherless and the Husband of the widow,* she returns
with her charge to her native land, to contract alliance
with penury, and to live by faith for her daily bread.
That same grace under whose teaching she *knew how
to abound,* taught her also how *to suffer need.* With a
dignity which belongs only to them who have treasure
in heaven, she descended to her humble cot, employment and fare. But her humility, according to the
Scripture, was the forerunner of her advancement.
The light of her virtues shone brightest in her obscurity, and pointed her way to the confidential trust of
forming the minds and manners of young females of
different ranks in the metropolis of Scotland. Here,
respected by the great and beloved by the good; in
sacred intimacy with ' devout and honorable women,' and
the friendship of men who were in truth servants of
the most high God, she continued in the successful
discharge of her duties till Providence conducted her
to our shores.

"She long had a predilection for America, as a land in which, according to her favorite opinion, the church of Christ is signally to flourish. Here she wished to end her days and leave her children. And we shall remember with gratitude, that in granting her wish God cast her lot with ourselves. Twenty-five years ago she opened in this city a school for the education of young ladies, the benefits of which have been strongly felt, and will be long felt hereafter, in different and distant parts of our country. Evidently devoted to the welfare of her pupils—attentive to their peculiarities of character—happy in discovering the best avenue of approach to their minds—possessing in a high degree the talent of simplifying her instruction and varying its form, she succeeded in that most difficult part of a teacher's work, the inducing youth *to take an interest in their own improvement, and to educate themselves by exerting their own faculties.*

"In governing her little empire she acted upon those principles which are the basis of all good government on every scale and under every modification—to be *reasonable*, to be *firm*, and to be *uniform*. Her authority was both tempered and strengthened by condescension. It commanded respect while it conciliated affection. Her word was law, but it was the law of kindness. It spoke to the conscience, but it spoke to the heart; and obedience bowed with the knee of love. She did not, however, imagine her work to be perfected in fitting her *élèves* for duties and elegance of life. Never did she forget their immortal nature. Utterly devoid of sectarian narrowness, she labored to infuse into their minds those vital principles of evangelical piety which form the common distinction of the disciples of Christ, the peculiar glory of the female name, and the surest pledge of domestic bliss. Her voice, her example, her prayers concurred in recommending that pure and undefiled religion without which no human being shall see the Lord. Shall we wonder that her scholars should be tenderly attached to such a preceptress? that they should leave her with their tears and their blessing? that they should carry an indelible remembrance of her into the bosom of their families? that the reverence of pupils should ripen with their years into the affection of friends? and that there should be among them, at this day, many a wife who is "*a crown to her husband;*" and many a mother who is a blessing to her children; and who owes, in a great degree, the felicity of her character to the impressions, the principles and the habits which she received while under the maternal tuition of Mrs. GRAHAM?

"Admonished at length by the infirmities of age, and importuned by her friends, this venerable matron retired to private life. But it was impossible for her to be idle. Her leisure only gave a new direction to her activity. With no less alacrity than she had displayed in the education of youth, did she now embark in the relief of misery. Her benevolence was unbounded, but it was discreet. There are charities which increase the wretchedness they are designed to diminish; which, from some fatal defect in their application, bribe to iniquity while they are relieving want; and make food, and raiment, and clothing to warm into life the most poisonous seeds of vice. But the charities of our departed friend were of another order. They selected the fittest objects— the widow—the fatherless—the orphan—the untaught child—and the ignorant adult. They combined intellectual and moral benefit with the communication of physical comfort.

"In her house originated the *Society for the relief of poor widows with small children.* Large, indeed, is this branch of the family of affliction, and largely did it share in her sympathy and succor. When at the head of this noble association, she made it her business to see with her own eyes the objects of their care; and to give, by her personal presence and efforts, the strongest impulse to their humane system. From morning till night has she gone from abode to abode of these destitute, who are too commonly unpitied by the great, despised by the proud, and forgotten by the gay. She has gone to sit beside them on their humble seat, hearing their simple and sorrowful story—sharing their homely meal—ascertaining the condition of their children—stirring them up to diligence, to economy, to neatness, to order—putting them into the way of obtaining suitable employment for themselves and suitable places for their children—distributing among them the word of God, and Tracts calculated to familiarize its first principles to their understanding—cherishing them in sickness—admonishing them in health—instructing, reproving, exhorting, consoling—sanctifying the whole with fervent prayer. Many a sobbing heart and streaming eye is this evening embalming her memory in the house of the widow.

"Little, if any less is the debt due to her from that invaluable charity, the *Orphan Asylum.* It speaks its own praise, and that praise is hers. Scores of orphans redeemed from filth, from ignorance, from wretchedness, from crime—clothed, fed, instructed—trained in cleanliness to habits of industry—early imbued with the knowledge and fear of God—gradually preparing for respectability, usefulness and happiness—is a spectacle for angels. Their infantine gayety, their healthful sport, their cherub faces, mark the contrast between their present and former condition; and recall very tenderly the scenes in which they used to cluster round their patron-mother, hang on her gracious words, and receive her benediction.

"Brethren, I am not dealing in romance, but in sober fact. The night would be too short for a full enumeration of her worthy deeds. Suffice it to say that they ended but with her life. The Sabbath previous to her last sickness occupied her with a recent Institution—*a Sunday-school for ignorant adults;* and the evening preceding the touch of death found her at the side of a faithful domestic, administering consolation to his wounded spirit.

"Such active benevolence could hardly be detected in company with a niggardly temper. Wishes which cost nothing; pity which expires on the lips; *be ye warmed and be ye clothed,* from a cold heart and an unyielding gripe, never imprinted their disgraceful brand upon Isabella Graham. What she urged upon others she exemplified in herself. She kept a purse for God. Here, in obedience to his command, she deposited *the first fruits of all her increase;* and they were sacred to his service, as, in his providence, he should call for them. No shuffling pretences, no pitiful evasions, when a fair demand was made upon the hallowed store; and no frigid affectation in determining the quality of the demand. A sense of duty was the prompter, candor the interpreter, and good sense the judge. Her disbursements were proportioned to the value of the object, and were ready at a moment's warning, to the very last farthing.* How pungent a reproof to those ladies of opulence and fashion who sacrifice so largely to their dissipation or their vanity, that they have nothing left for mouths without food, and limbs without raiment! How far does it throw back into the shade those men of prosperous enterprise and gilded state who, in the hope of some additional lucre, have thousands and ten thousands at their beck; but who, when asked for decent contributions to what they themselves acknowledge to be all-important, turn away with this hollow excuse, 'I cannot afford it.' Above all, how should her example redden the faces of many who profess to belong to Christ; to have received gratuitously from him what he procured for them at the expense of his own blood, 'an inheritance incorruptible and undefiled, and that fadeth not away;' and yet, in the midst of abundance which *he* has lavished upon them, when the question is about relieving his suffering members, or promoting the glory of his kingdom, are sour, reluctant, mean. Are *these the christians?* Can it be that they have committed their bodies, their souls, their eternal hope, to a Savior whose thousand promises on this very point of '*honoring* HIM *with their substance,*' have less influence upon their hearts and their hands than the word of any honest man? Remember the deceased, and hang your

---

* "The author knew her, when in moderate circumstances, to give, unsolicited, *fifty pounds at once* out of that sacred purse to a single most worthy purpose."

heads—remember her and tremble—remember her, and *bring forth fruits meet for repentance.*

"In that charity, also, which far surpasses mere almsgiving, however liberal, the charity of the Gospel, our friend was conspicuous. '*The love of God shed abroad in her own heart by the Holy Ghost,*' drew forth her love to his people wherever she found them. Assuredly she had in herself this witness of her having '*passed from death unto life,*' that she *loved the brethren.* The epistle written not with ink, but with the Spirit of the living God; not in tables of stone, but in fleshly tables of the heart; yet read and known of all men: that is, the christian temper manifested by a christian conversation, was to her the best letter of recommendation. Unwavering in her own faith as to the peculiar doctrines of the Gospel, she could, nevertheless, extend love without dissimulation, and the very bowels of Christian fellowship to others, who, whatever might be their mistakes, their infirmities or their differences in smaller matters, agreed in the great christian essential of *acceptance in the Beloved.* Deeply did she deplore the conceit, the bigotry and the bitterness of sect. O that her spirit were more prevalent in the churches! that we could labor to abase our *crown of pride;* to offer up with one consent upon the altar of evangelical charity, those petty jealousies, animosities and strifes which are our common reproach; and walk together as children of the same Father, brethren of the same Redeemer, and heirs of the same salvation!

"To these admirable traits of character were added great tenderness of conscience and a spirit of prayer. Her religion, not contented to *justify her before men,* habitually aimed at pleasing *God, who looketh upon the heart.* It was not enough for her to persuade herself that a thing *might* be right. Before venturing upon it, she studied to reduce the question of right to a clear certainty. How cautious, and scrupulous, and jealous of herself she was in this matter, they best can tell who saw her in the shade of retirement as well as in the sunshine of public observation. Perhaps it is not going too far to say, that her least guarded moments would, in others, have been marked for circumspection. At the same time her vigilance had nothing austere, gloomy, constrained or censorious: nothing to repress the cheerfulness of social intercourse; or to excite in others, even the thoughtless, a dread of merciless criticism after they should retire. It was sanctified nature moving gracefully in its own element. And with respect to the character and feelings of her neighbors, she was too full of christian kindness not to ' *keep her tongue from evil and her lips from speaking guile.*'

" These virtues and graces were maintained and invigorated by her habit of prayer. With the ' new and living way into the holiest by the blood of Jesus ' she was intimately familiar. Thither the Spirit of grace and supplication daily conducted her; there taught her to *pray*, and in praying to *believe*, and in believing to have ' fellowship with the Father and with his Son Jesus Christ.' She knew her God as the God that heareth prayer; and could attest that ' *blessed is she that believeth, for there shall be a performance of those things which were told her from the Lord.*'

" Under such influence her course could not but be correct, and her steps well ordered. The ' secret of the

Lord is with them that fear him; and he will show them his covenant—he will guide them in judgment.' Thus he did with his handmaid whom he hath called home. Wherever she was, and in whatever circumstances, she remembered the guide of her youth, who, according to his promise, *never left her nor forsook her;* but continued his gracious presence with her when she was *old and gray-headed.*

"You may perhaps imagine, that with such direction and support it was impossible she should see trouble. Nay, but *waters of a full cup were wrung out to her.* She often ate the bread of sorrow steeped in wormwood and gall. Her heavenly Father ' showed her great and sore adversities; that he might try her as silver is tried, and bring her forth from the furnace purified seven times.' It was during these refining processes that she found the worth of being a christian. Though her way was planted with thorns and watered with her tears, yet the candle of the Lord shone upon her head; and from step to step she had reason to cry, ' *Hitherto hath Jehovah helped.*'

"In a word, like Enoch, she walked with God—like Abraham, she staggered not at his promise through unbelief—like Jacob, she wrestled with the angel and prevailed—like Moses, endured as seeing Him who is invisible—like Paul, finished her course with joy. Blessed were the eyes of the preacher, for they saw the victory of her faith; and his ears, for they heard her song of salvation. 'You can say with the apostle, *I know whom I have believed, and am persuaded that he is able to keep that which I have committed unto him?*' 'O yes! but I cannot say the other, *I have fought a good fight*—I must say, *I have fought a poor fight, I have run a poor race ;* but *Christ fought for me—Christ ran with me—and through Christ I hope to win.*' ' But you have no fear, no doubts, about your going to be with Christ?' ' O no! not a doubt; I am as sure of that as if I were already in my Savior's arms.' It was her final conversation with children of the dust. The next day, *when her flesh and her heart had so far failed* that she was incapable of uttering a sentence, she still proved her God to be the *strength of her heart,* and knew him to be *her portion for ever.* I said to her, *It is peace.* She opened her eyes, smiled, closed them again, bowed her dying head, and breathed out *Peace.* It was her last word on this side heaven. The attending spirits caught it from her lips, and brought to her the next day permission to sleep in Jesus

" From this review allow me to urge the *value of private exertions in promoting general good.*

" In pursuing his *gratifications,* man is apt to look upon himself as a being of great importance : in fulfilling his *duties,* to account himself as nothing. Both are extravagances which it will be his wisdom and happiness to correct. He is neither supreme in worth nor useless in action. Let him not say, 'I am but one ; my voice will be drowned in the universal din ; my weight is lighter than a feather in the public scale. It is better for me to mind my own affairs, and leave these higher attempts to more competent hands.' This is the language, not of reason and modesty, but of sloth, of selfishness and of pride. The amount of it is, 'I cannot do every thing, therefore I will do nothing.' But you can do much. Act well *your* part according to your faculties, your station and your means. The result will be honorable to yourself, delightful to your friends and beneficial to the world. I advise not to gigantic aims, to enormous enterprise. The world has seen but one Newton and one Howard. Nothing is required of you but to make the most of the opportunities within your reach.

"Recall the example of Mrs. Graham. Here was a woman—a widow—a stranger in a strange land—without fortune—with no friends but such as her letters of introduction and her worth should acquire—and with a family of daughters dependent upon her for their subsistence. Surely if any one has a clear title of immunity from the obligation to carry her cares beyond the domestic circle, it is this widow—it is this stranger. Yet within a few years this stranger, this widow, with no means but her excellent sense, her benevolent heart and her *persevering will* to do good, awakens the charities of a populous city, and gives to them an impulse, a direction and an efficacy unknown before.

"What might not be done by *men*—by men of talent, of standing, of wealth, of leisure? How speedily, under their well-directed beneficence, might a whole country change its physical, intellectual and moral aspect; and assume, comparatively speaking, the face of another Eden—a second garden of God? Why then do they not diffuse thus extensively the seeds of knowledge, of virtue and of bliss? I ask not for their pretences; they are as old as the lust of lucre, and are refuted by the example which we have been contemplating; I ask for the true reason, for the inspiring principle of their conduct. It is this—let them look to it when God shall call them to account for the abuse of their time, their talents, their station, their '*unrighteous mammon*,'—it is this: they believe not '*the words of the Lord Jesus, how he said, It is more blessed to give than to receive.*' They labor under no want but one—they want *the heart*. The bountiful God add this to the other gifts which he has bestowed upon them! I turn to the other sex.

"That venerable mother in Israel who has exchanged the service of God on earth for his service in heaven, has left a legacy to her sisters—she has left the example of her faith and patience; she has left her prayers; she has left the monument of her christian deeds; and by these she *being dead, yet speaketh*. Matrons! has she left her *mantle* also? Are there none among you to hear her voice from the tomb, *Go and do thou likewise?* None whom affluence permits, endowments qualify, and piety prompts, to aim at her distinction by treading in her steps? Maidens! Are there none among *you* who would wish to array yourselves hereafter in the honors of this *virtuous woman?* Your hearts have dismissed their wonted warmth and generosity, if they do not throb as the revered vision rises before you. Then prepare yourselves now, by seeking and serving the God of her youth. You cannot be too early 'adorned with the robes of righteousness and the garments of salvation' in which she was wedded, in her morning of life, to Jesus the King of glory. That same grace which threw its radiance around her shall make you also to shine in the *beauty of holiness;* and the fragrance of those virtues which it shall create, develope and ennoble, will be 'as the smell of a field which the Lord hath blessed.'

"Yea, let me press upon all the transcendent excellence of christian character, and the victorious power of christian hope. The former bears the image of God; the latter is as imperishable as his throne. We fasten our eyes with more real respect and more heart-felt approbation upon the moral majesty displayed in *walking as Christ also walked*, than upon all the pomps of the monarch or decorations of the military hero. More touching to the sense and more grateful to high heaven is the soft melancholy with which we look after our departed friend, and the tear which embalms her memory, than the thundering plaudits which rend the air with the name of a conqueror. She has obtained a triumph over that foe who shall break the arm of valor and strike off the crown of kings. 'The fashion of this world passeth away.' Old Time approaches toward his last hour. The proudest memorials of human grandeur shall be food for the conflagration to be kindled when 'the Lord Jesus shall be revealed from heaven in flaming fire. Then shall he be glorified in his saints, and admired in all them that believe.'

"There are those, perhaps in the present assembly, who repute godliness fanaticism, and the sobriety of christian peace the gloom of a joyless spirit; but who cannot forbear sighing out, with the prophet of mammon, 'Let me die the death of the righteous, and let my last end be like his.' If they proceed no further their wish will not be granted. None shall die the death of the righteous, unless by a rare dispensation of mercy, who do not live his life. They only are fit to be with God who love God and keep his commandments. In that day of transport and of terror which we shall all witness, how many of the thoughtless fair who now 'sport themselves with their own deceivings,' would give all the treasures of the east and thrones of the west to sit with Isabella Graham on the right hand of Jesus Christ! If ye be wise betimes, ye may. 'Now is the accepted time; to-day is the day of salvation.' The Gospel of the Son of God offers you, at this very moment, the forgiveness of your sins and an inheritance among them that are sanctified. The blessing comes to you as a free gift— accept it and live; accept it and be safe; accept it, and put away the shudderings of guilt and the fear of death. Then shall you too, like our friend, go, in due season, to be with Christ. Your happy spirit shall rejoin hers in the mansions of the saved. God shall bring you in soul and body with her when he makes up his jewels. Then shall he gather his elect from the four winds of heaven, shall perfect that which concerneth them, and make them fully and for ever blessed. Be our place among them in that day!"

Extract from Mrs. Graham's last Will and Testament.

"My children and my grand-children I leave to my covenant God; the God who hath fed me all my life with the bread that perisheth, and the bread that never perisheth; who has been a Father to my fatherless children, and a Husband to their widowed mother thus far. And now, receiving my Redeemer's testimony, John, 3 : 33, I set to my seal that God is true; and believing the record in John's Epistle, that God hath given to me eternal life, and this life is in his Son, who, through the eternal Spirit, offered himself without spot unto God, and being consecrated a priest for ever, hath, with his own blood, entered into the holy place, having ob-

tained eternal redemption for me! I also believe that he
will perfect what concerns me, support and carry me
safely through death, and present me to his Father, complete in his own righteousness, without spot or wrinkle.
Into the hands of this redeeming God—Father, Son, and
Holy Ghost, I commit my redeemed spirit."

———

Mrs. Graham's epitaph, on a tablet in the Pearl-street
Church, is associated with that of her son-in-law Mr.
Bethune, to whom before his connection with the family she was a spiritual mother; who prepared her memoir, wrote and printed Tracts for her widows, im-
ported Bibles for her to distribute, replenished her charity purse when exhausted; with whom she "took
sweet counsel and walked to the house of God in company;" and for whom she was pleased to leave the
written and honorable testimony: "He stands, in my
mind, in temper, conduct, and conversation, the nearest
to the Gospel standard of any man or woman I ever
knew as intimately. Devoted to his God, to his church,
to his family, to all to whom he may have opportunity
of doing good, duty is his governing principle; cast
upon his care, under God he nourishes me with kindness," &c. They have entered into rest. One sepulchre
contains their sleeping dust, and one monument bears
the following tribute to their memory:

SACRED

TO THE MEMORY OF

DIVIE BETHUNE,

MERCHANT OF THIS CITY,

Who died September 18, 1824, aged 53 Years;

AND OF

ISABELLA GRAHAM,

HIS MOTHER-IN-LAW,

Who died July 27, 1814, aged 72 Years.

THEY WERE BOTH NATIVES OF SCOTLAND.

THIS MONUMENT

IS REARED BY HIS BEREAVED WIDOW AND HER ORPHAN DAUGHTER,

AS A TESTIMONIAL OF TWO SERVANTS OF JESUS CHRIST;

THE ONE A RULING ELDER IN HIS CHURCH, THE OTHER A MOTHER IN ISRAEL;

WHO, LIKE ENOCH, WALKED WITH GOD,

LIKE ABRAHAM, OBTAINED THE RIGHTEOUSNESS OF FAITH,

AND, LIKE PAUL, FINISHED THEIR COURSE WITH JOY.

THEY WERE LOVELY AND PLEASANT IN THEIR LIVES,

AND THEY REST HERE TOGETHER IN THEIR GRAVES.

"The blessing of him that was ready to perish came upon them; and they caused the widow's heart to sing for joy."—*Job*, 30 : 13.

"Oh! how great is thy goodness, which thou hast laid up for them that fear thee; which thou hast wrought for them that trust in thee before the sons of men."—*Psalm* 31 : 19.

PROVISION

MY LAST JOURNEY THROUGH THE WILDERNESS,

PASSAGE OVER JORDAN.*

" Joshua, 1 : 11, and chapter 3. ' Prepare you victuals, for within three days ye shall pass over this Jordan, to go in to possess the land which the Lord your God giveth you to possess it. When ye see the ark of the covenant of the Lord your God, and the priests bearing it, then ye shall remove, and go after it : that ye may know the way by which ye must go, for ye have not passed this way heretofore.'

" ' Sanctify yourselves, for to-morrow the Lord will do wonders among you.'

" ' Behold, the ark of the covenant of the Lord of all the earth passeth over before you into Jordan : and it shall come to pass, that as soon as the soles of the feet of the priests that bear the ark of the Lord—the Lord of all the earth—shall rest in the waters, that the waters of Jordan shall be cut off from the waters that come down from above : and they shall stand upon a heap.'

" ' And it came to pass, that when the people removed from their tents to pass over Jordan, and the priests bearing the ark of the covenant before the people, that as they that bare the ark were come into Jordan ; and the feet of the priests were dipped in the brim of the

* Found in Mrs. Graham's pocket after her decease.

water, that the waters that came down from above stood and rose up upon a heap; and the priests that bare the ark of the covenant of the Lord stood firm on dry ground in the midst of Jordan, and all the Israelites passed over on dry ground.'

" ' And Joshua set up twelve stones in the midst of Jordan, in the place where the feet of the priests that bare the ark of the covenant of the Lord stood, and they are there unto this day.'

" ' When your children shall ask their fathers in time to come, saying, what mean these stones? ye shall let your children know, saying, Israel came over this Jordan on dry land: for the Lord your God dried up the waters from before you until ye were passed over, as the Lord your God did to the Red Sea, which he dried up until we were passed over. That all people of the earth might know the hand of the Lord, that it is mighty: that ye might fear the Lord your God for ever.' Amen.

" Oh! thou Jehovah! Israel's God, and by thy new covenant, my God! Thus far hast thou brought me through the wilderness: bearing, chastising, forgiving, restoring. Well hast thou made out thy wilderness name to me, ' The Lord, the Lord God, merciful and gracious, long-suffering, abundant in goodness and truth, keeping mercy for thousands, forgiving iniquity, transgression and sin.' Great have been my provocations, but greater still thy covenant mercy. I have not perished with them that believed not; sore bitten I am, but thou hast fixed mine eyes on the lifted-up Healer, and I am in his hand for further cure. My journey has been long, and my way devious; but my blessed Joshua is still in view. I must be near to Jordan's flood; I have been preparing victuals from thine own repository of truth. And now, my blessed High Priest and Ark of the Covenant, lead on my staggering steps the little further. I have not gone this way heretofore, but thou hast measured these waters while they overflowed all their banks. Thou hast passed through, and made the passage safe for thy people. At thy command the waters stand up upon a heap, and they pass through in thy presence on faith's firm ground. Keep then mine eye upon thee, and I shall fear no evil. And Oh, my blessed Leader! if it might please thee, I would ask a *boon*, yet with submission, that thy sensible presence might be with me all the way through; and that thou wouldst bring from my quivering lips a testimony to the glory of thy grace, that my children may know that thou hast pardoned, restored, perfected, dried up the waters of terror, carried triumphantly through, and put me in possession of the purchased inheritance. Amen.

" 1 Timothy, 1 : 15. 'This is a faithful saying, and worthy of all acceptation, that Christ Jesus came into the world to save sinners, of whom I am chief.'

" I have often inquired what is there within us, or without us, on which a sinner can rest in peace in a dying hour ? If it be a holy life, there can be no peace for me—taking the law of God for my standard; backslider is my name; yet I think in this sacred volume I find a hope even for me, the chief of sinners.

" John, 3 : 14. 'As Moses lifted up the serpent in the wilderness, even so must the Son of man be lifted up, that whosoever believeth on him should not perish, but have eternal life. For God so loved the world, that he gave his only begotten Son, that whosoever believeth on him should not perish, but have eternal life. For God sent not his Son into the world to condemn the world, but that the world through him might be saved.' Verse 31, 'He that cometh from heaven is above all, and what he hath seen and heard, that he testifieth.' Verse 33, 'He that receiveth his testimony has set to his seal that God is true.' Verse 35, 'The Father loveth the Son, and hath given all things into his hand; he that believeth on the Son hath everlasting life.' Here is a hope for me; the world is made up of sinners, I am one of them, and though the chief, am not excluded. Matthew, 18 : 11, 'The Son of man came to save that which was lost;' I am of that description. Matthew, 9 : 13, 'The Pharisees said, why eateth your master with publicans and sinners? Jesus said, the whole need not a physician, but they that are sick.' I am a sinner, and sick. 'I will have mercy and not sacrifice, for I am not come to call the righteous, but sinners to repentance.' I am a sinner, and need repentance. 'Him hath God exalted with his right hand, to be a Prince and a Savior, to give repentance and forgiveness of sins to Israel.' Acts, 3 : 31. 2 Peter, 3 : 9, 'The Lord is long-suffering, not willing that any should perish; but that all should come to repentance.'

" Christ said to the woman of Samaria, a notorious sinner, John, 4 : 10, 'If thou knewest the gift of God, and who it is that saith to thee, give me to drink, thou wouldest have asked of him, and he would have given thee living water. Whosoever drinketh of this water shall thirst again; but whosoever drinketh of the water that I shall give him, shall never thirst, but the water that I shall give him shall be in him a well of water springing

up into everlasting life.' Yes, my Redeemer! a draught
of this water, received in faith from the hand of the
Spirit, will give life in death. O pour it into my thirsty
soul in that searching hour!

"Jesus said to a mixed multitude of sinners like me,
John, 6 : 27, 'Labor not for the meat which perisheth,
but for that meat which endureth unto everlasting life,
which the Son of man shall give unto you; for him hath
God the Father sealed.' These sinners said unto him,
'what shall we do that we might work the works of
God?' 'That ye believe on him whom he hath sent.
My Father giveth you the true bread from heaven, for
the bread of God is he which cometh down from heaven, and giveth life unto the world: I am the bread of
life; he that cometh unto me shall never hunger, and
he that believeth on me shall never thirst. I am the
living bread which came down from heaven; if any man
eat of this bread, he shall live for ever. And the bread
which I shall give is my flesh, which I will give for the
life of the world. Jesus said unto them, except ye eat
the flesh, and drink the blood of the Son of man, ye
have no life in you: whoso eateth my flesh, and drinketh my blood, dwelleth in me, and I in him. As the
living Father hath sent me, and I live by the Father: so
he that eateth me, even he shall live by me.' The Father giveth this bread, the Son giveth this bread; whosoever will, may take of this bread, and the promise
with it. Father, I take this bread, I take and believe that
I have in thee eternal life, according to thy word. O
holy and blessed Comforter! Spirit of the Father and
of the Son, whose office it is to take of the things of
Christ and show them unto his redeemed; when the

bread and the water that perish can no longer refresh this dying body, apply this living bread and living water to my soul, that life may spring up in the midst of death; and in that trying hour, bear witness with my spirit that I dwell in Christ, and Christ in me, and that I shall never die.

"John, 7 : 37. 'In the last day, that great day of the feast, Jesus stood and cried, If any man thirst, let him come unto me and drink; he that believeth on me, as the Scripture hath said, out of his belly shall flow rivers of living water. This spake he of the Spirit, that they who believe on him should receive.' This he proclaimed to a mixt multitude of sinners like myself. Lord, I believe, and am sure that thou art that Christ, the Son of the living God. Be it unto me according to thy word. John, 11 : 25. 'I am the resurrection and the life; he that believeth on me, though he were dead, yet shall he live; and whosoever liveth and believeth on me, shall never die. Believest thou this?' I believe that thou art the Christ, the son of the living God, which should come into the world; the promised Messiah; the gift of the Father, the covenant given to the people; the anointed Prophet and King, and consecrated High Priest; who through the eternal Spirit offeredst thyself without spot unto God; who came to do that most perfect will of God, by which we are sanctified through the offering of the body of Christ once for all. Lamb of God, which takest away the sins of the world! on thee I lay my precious never-dying soul; wash me in thy blood, clothe me in thy righteousness; sanctify me, soul, spirit, and body, to thy service. I have no other foundation of hope, nothing within me, nothing without me; my entire dependence is on thy finished work; into thy hands I commit my spirit.

"Let me hear thy consoling voice, compassionate Savior! John, 14 : 1, 'Let not your heart be troubled; ye believe in God, believe also in me; in my Father's house are many mansions; if it were not so I would have told you; I go to prepare a place for you; I will come again and receive you unto myself, that where I am, there ye may be also.' Oh! seal this upon my heart, and it is enough. To be where thou art, is heaven enough to me. To be where thou art, to see thee as thou art, and to be made like thee, the last sinful motion for ever past: no more opposition, no more weariness, listlessness, dryness, deadness; but conformed to my blessed Head, every way capacitated to serve him, and to enjoy him. This is heaven.

"'Jesus said, I am the way, the truth, and the life; no man cometh to the Father, but by me.' Blessed Comforter! do thine office; take these things of Christ and show them unto me; lead me in this way, feed me with this truth, and animate me with this life: 'whatsoever ye shall ask of the Father in my name, that will I do, that the Father may be glorified in the Son. If ye ask any thing in my name, I will do it.' Blessed Comforter! here also do thine office; I know not what to ask for as I ought; help mine infirmities as thou hast said; suggest the prayer, be in me the spirit of prayer and supplication, and especially in that hour of need, when sickness saps the clay tabernacle, discomposing the spirit, and confusing perhaps the ideas: still, still, let my thoughts rise to my God. Oh! let no unhallowed subject get hold of me in that hour, but keep my Savior's name in my heart, and on my lips. Is not this according to thy will; watch over it then, and keep the avenues of my soul from every vain idea.

"'If ye love me, keep my commandments, and I will pray the Father, and he shall give you another Comforter, that he may abide with you for ever, even the Spirit of truth, whom the world cannot receive, because it seeth him not, neither knoweth him; but ye know him, for he dwelleth with you, and shall be in you. He that hath my commandments and keepeth them, he it is that loveth me, and he that loveth me shall be loved of my Father, and I will love him, and will manifest myself unto him; and we will come and make our abode with him. The Comforter, which is the Holy Ghost, whom the Father will send in my name, he shall teach you all things, and bring all things to your remembrance, whatsoever I have said unto you. Peace I leave with you; my peace I give unto you; not as the world giveth, give I unto you: let not your heart be troubled, neither let it be afraid.' In that last warfare, when nothing on earth can give peace; when the world recedes, and disappears; when friends must stand aloof and leave me to the combat alone; Oh! blessed and promised Comforter, bring to my remembrance, and impress on my weary spirit these sweet words of my Savior. But it has often occurred to me, and may in that hour, that though Jesus received sinners, they were ignorant sinners. The Jews understood not the Gospel contained in their types and sacrifices; they were unenlightened and unconverted; the Gentiles were totally blind, serving dumb idols; neither had known the Gospel; never had tasted the grace of God: neither were backsliders like me. I have known the truth, been enlightened, tasted of the heavenly gift, been made a partaker of the Holy Ghost, tasted of the good word of God, and of the power of the world to come.

"Fifty years ago the Lord convinced me of my sin, my misery, and my total helplessness. I was also, I think, enabled to lay hold on the hope set before me.

"I have, in numerous exercises and acts, accepted of God's gift of Jesus Christ to me a condemned sinner; taking hold of the Scripture words of invitation and promise held out for my acceptance. I have pleaded his own covenant provision, in the substitution of his own Son in my stead, 'making him to be sin, who knew no sin, that sinners might be made the righteousness of God in him.' I put in my claim as a sinner, among the ungodly for whom Christ died. I believed his testimony, and set to my seal that God is true. I rested on this foundation—I yet have no other —I know there is no other. The foundation standeth sure. But Oh! what am I to think of the fruits! I have again and again turned back into the world: grieved the Spirit, crucified the Son of God afresh, and put him to open shame. No wonder I stand alarmed at the Apostle's assertion: my conscience testifies that my character is nearly, if not altogether, such as the Apostle, by the Holy Spirit, says it is impossible to renew to repentance. Hebrews, 6:4, 5. But thou hast renewed to repentance! Thy name is 'the Lord, the Lord God, merciful and gracious, long-suffering, and abundant in goodness and truth, keeping mercy for thousands, forgiving iniquity, transgression, and sin.

Thou wilt by no means clear the guilty;' but thou hast provided a substitute, and laid my guilt and guilty person on thine own Son.

"By this gracious name thou wast known to thy backsliding Israel in the wilderness; whose heart, ike mine, was not right with God; neither were they steadfast in his covenant; but he, 'being full of compassion, forgave their iniquity, and destroyed them not.' Many a time turned he his anger away, and did not stir up all his wrath. They forgot God their Savior, who had done great things for them; they transgressed his commandment, and in their heart turned back again to Egypt; they brought upon themselves many afflictions, and many times did he deliver them; they provoked him with their counsel, and were brought low for their iniquity; *nevertheless*, he heard their cry, and repented according to the multitude of his mercies; while the blood of bulls and of goats typified the great propitiatory sacrifice, by which 'God can be just and justify the ungodly.' By this name was the Lord God merciful and gracious known in the pleasant land, and by the same sacrifice, the blood of Christ, which cleanseth from all sin, was typified. Psalms 103 and 51.

"The prophets prophesied in his name. 'All we, like sheep, have gone astray, and the Lord hath laid on him the iniquity of us all. He was wounded for our transgressions, and bruised for our iniquities; the chastisement of our peace was laid on him, and by his stripes we are healed.' 'Deliver from going down to the pit; I have found a ransom.' Even backsliders, among whom I stand chief, have been recalled. Jeremiah, 2. 'My people have committed two great evils: they

have forsaken the fountain of living waters, and have
hewn out to themselves cisterns, broken cisterns,
that can hold no water. Is Israel a servant; is he a
home-born slave; wherefore is he spoiled? Hast thou
not procured this to thyself, in that thou hast forsaken
the Lord thy God, when he led thee by the way? and
now what hast thou to do in the way of Egypt, to
drink the waters of Sihor? what hast thou to do in
the way of Syria, to drink the waters of the river?
Thy own wickedness shall correct thee, and thy backslidings shall reprove thee. Know therefore, and see
that it is an evil and bitter thing that thou hast forsaken the Lord thy God; and that my fear is not in
thee, saith the Lord God of hosts. For of old I have
broken thy yoke and burst thy bands: and thou saidst,
I will not transgress; when upon every high hill and
under every green tree thou wanderest, playing the
harlot. Yet I had planted thee a noble vine, wholly a
right seed: how art thou turned into the degenerate
plant of a strange vine unto me? Why gaddest thou
about so much to change thy way? thou also shalt be
ashamed of Egypt, as thou wast ashamed of Assyria.
Have I been a barren wilderness or a land of darkness
unto thee? Wherefore say my people, we are lords,
and will come no more unto thee? Can a maid forget
her ornaments, or a bride her attire? yet my people
have forgotten me, days without number.' Jeremiah, 3.
' They say if a man put away his wife, and she go from
him, and become another man's, shall he return to her
again? shall not that land be greatly polluted? But thou
hast played the harlot with many lovers; yet return
again unto me, saith the Lord; wilt thou not from this

time cry unto me, my Father, thou art the guide of my youth?' What can I say to such grace? Thou art infinite in thy mercy to pardon, and in thy power to save! Such has been my character, and such the amazing mercy of my offended God! Often, often has he pardoned, restored, blessed and made me happy. But, Oh! just is the renewed charge against me! 'For the house of Israel and the house of Judah have dealt very treacherously with me, saith the Lord. They have belied the Lord, and said, it is not he, neither shall evil come upon us.' Verse 12. 'Go and proclaim these words, and say, Return, thou backsliding Israel, saith the Lord, and I will not cause mine anger to fall upon you: for I am merciful, saith the Lord, I will not keep anger for ever! Only acknowledge thine iniquity, that thou hast transgressed against the Lord thy God; and ye have not obeyed my voice, saith the Lord. Turn, O backsliding children, for I am married unto you.' What! O what can I say to such grace? Truly, 'thy ways are not as our ways, nor thy thoughts as our thoughts! For as the heavens are higher than the earth, so are thy ways higher than our ways, and thy thoughts than our thoughts!' Oh! how is my guilt aggravated by all this grace! and yet thou callest, *Return!* and thou thyself turnest me. I do, O Lord God, merciful and gracious! I do acknowledge my iniquity; every time I turn back my eyes upon my past life my sins rise in magnitude, heightened by more enlarged views of thy goodness. It is of the Lord's mercies that I am not consumed, because his compassions fail not.

"'A voice was heard upon the high places, weeping and supplication of the children of Israel, for they have perverted their ways, and they have forgotten the Lord their God.' Yes, thou hast, my gracious God, granted repentance! Thine eye has seen the tears I have shed; thou hast given me a contrite heart. I have looked upon him whom I have pierced, and been in bitterness as for a first-born. I feel it now, and must feel it while the body of sin exists. But Oh! Lord God, merciful and gracious! the cause is in thyself, that I hear thy voice, and that I answer. 'Return, ye backsliding children, and I will heal your backslidings! Behold, I come unto thee, for thou art the Lord our God! Truly in vain is salvation hoped for from the hills and the multitude of mountains. Truly, in the Lord God is the salvation of Israel: we lie down in our shame, our confusion covereth us: for we have sinned against the Lord our God; we and our fathers, even from our youth; and have not obeyed the voice of the Lord God. Thus, saith the Lord God, I will even deal with thee as thou hast done, who hast despised the oath in breaking the covenant. Nevertheless, I will remember my covenant with thee in the days of thy youth; and I will establish unto thee an everlasting covenant, and thou shalt know that I am the Lord. That thou mayest remember and be confounded, and never open thy mouth any more because of thy shame, when I am pacified towards thee, saith the Lord God.' Amen, Lord God, merciful and gracious! Be it so.—It is so *now*,—it *must*, it will be so, until death shall open mine eyes on that mystery. The glory of God arising out of the abounding of sin, through the superabounding of grace, and grace reigning through righteousness unto eternal life, by Jesus Christ our Lord!

"Till then, while sin dwelleth in me, let me enjoy the blessedness of a contrite heart; yea, even *shame and confusion*, since it is the sign that thou art pacified with me. Thou hast dealt with me, thou hast chastened, and in some instances taken vengeance on my inventions. But thou art pacified with me, and I dare look again to thy holy temple, to the temple not made with hands, to the minister of the sanctuary, and the 'true tabernacle which the Lord pitched, and not man; to the blessed High Priest, who through the eternal Spirit offered himself a sacrifice without spot unto God, and by his own blood entered in once into the holy place, having obtained eternal redemption for us, and when he had purged our sins, sat down on the right hand of the Majesty on high; to the blessed Mediator of the new and better covenant, established on better promises; to the surety of the new testament, and sealed with his own blood.' O I will look unto Jesus! the Object, the Author, and the Finisher of that faith which interests in himself and the whole of his purchase! He bids me look unto him and be saved! I do look unto him, and I am saved! Who dares condemn the sinner whom Christ acquits? Who shall lay any thing to his charge? 'It is Christ that died; yea, rather, who is risen again; who is even at the right hand of God; who also maketh intercession for us!'"

ISAIAH, 44:22. RETURN UNTO ME, &c.

(A Scripture paraphrase by D. B——.)

Return to thee, my God! dost thou
The invitation yet renew?
Return to thee! my chiefest joy,
Till sin did all my peace destroy!

And yet, to hear thy pardoning voice
Must make my trembling heart rejoice;
Though sin is there, thou well dost know
It is my burden and my foe.

O let me hear those gracious words!
Be still, my soul, they are the Lord's;
That God, who once on thee did shine,
And fill'd thee with a hope divine.

"Thy black transgressions, trembling soul,
"Thy sin so heinous and so foul,
"Which like a cloud obscure thy day,
"I've blotted out, I've wash'd away.

"Return to me, thou'rt mine; I own
"Thee for my servant, and my son;
"I have redeem'd thy precious soul,
"And none my purchase shall control."

I hear, I come, my Cov'nant God!
Thy love's my life, my raiment, food;
Thy favor, through my Jesus given,
Is to my soul the bliss of heaven.

I come, my Jesus! hold me fast,
Till, life and Jordan's journey past,
My faith to vision yield her place,
And I shall see thy unveil'd face.

Then, with the loudest of the throng,
Of sins forgiv'n I'll raise the song
Of pardon bought with Jesus' blood,
Sinners made kings and priests to God.

Psalm 103. Fifty years ago.

Oh! thou, my soul, bless God the Lord,
  And all that in me is
Be stirred up his holy name
  To magnify and bless. &c.

"John 14. 'I will not leave you comfortless; I will come unto you; yet a little while and the world seeth me no more; but ye see me: because I live, ye shall live also. At that day ye shall know that I am in the Father, and you in me, and I in you! Believest thou not that I am in the Father and the Father in me? He that hath seen me, hath seen the Father. Howbeit, when the Spirit of truth is come, he will guide you into all truth. He shall glorify me, for he shall receive of mine, and shall show it unto you. All things that the Father hath are mine; therefore said I, he shall take of mine, and shall show it unto you.' John, 17. 'Neither pray I for these alone, but for them also which shall believe on me through their word: that they all may be one, as thou, Father, art in me and I in thee, that they may be one in us: that the world may believe that thou hast sent me; and the glory which thou gavest me I have given them, that they may be one, even as we are one. I in them and thou in me, that they may be made perfect in one: that the world may know that thou hast sent me; and hast loved them as thou hast loved me. Father, I will that they also whom thou hast given me be with me where I am, that they may behold my glory, which thou hast given me; for thou lovedst me before the foundation of the world.' 1 Cor. 3 : 22. 'All are yours, and ye are Christ's, and Christ is God's.' Col. 3:3. 'Ye are dead, and your life is hid with Christ in God. When Christ, who is our life, shall appear, then shall we appear with him in glory.' Col. 2:9. 'For in him dwelleth all the fulness of the Godhead bodily, and ye are complete in him, who is the head of all principality and power.'

Eph. 4:4. 'There is one body and one spirit, even as ye are called in one hope of your calling: one Lord, one faith, one baptism, one God and Father of all, who is above all, and through all, and in you all: and unto every one of us is given grace according to the measure of the gift of Christ.'

" Gal. 2 : 20. 'I am crucified with Christ: nevertheless I live; yet not I, but Christ liveth in me; and the life which I now live in the flesh, I live by the faith of the Son of God, who loved me, and gave himself for me.'

" John, 1 : 29. 'Behold the Lamb of God, which taketh away the sins of the world. And looking upon Jesus as he walked, John saith, Behold the Lamb of God.'

" 1 Cor. 3 : 21. 'Therefore, let no man glory in men, for all things are yours; whether Paul, or Apollos, or Cephas, or the world, or life, or death, or things present, or things to come: all are yours, and ye are Christ's, and Christ is God's ! ! !'

"Lam. 3 : 27. 'It is good for a man that he bear the yoke in his youth: he sitteth alone and keepeth silence; he putteth his mouth in the dust, if so be there may be hope; he giveth his cheek to him that smiteth him; he is filled with reproach.'

"Ezek. 16 : 63. 'That thou mayest remember, and be confounded, and never open thy mouth any more, because of thy shame, when I am pacified toward thee for all that thou hast done, saith the Lord.' *Amen.*

" Joel, 2 : 2. 'A day of darkness and of gloominess, a day of clouds and of thick darkness, as the morning spread upon the mountains. Therefore, also now, saith the Lord, turn ye unto me with all your heart, with fasting, with weeping, and with mourning. Rend your heart and not your garments, and turn unto the Lord your God: for he is gracious and merciful, slow to anger, and of great kindness, and repenteth him of the evil.'

" Hosea 2. 'I will visit upon her the days of Baalim: she went after her lovers, and forgat me, saith the Lord. I will allure her, and bring her into the wilderness, and speak comfortably unto her. And I will betroth thee unto me for ever: yea, I will betroth thee unto me in righteousness, and in judgment, and in loving-kindness, and in mercies. I will even betroth thee unto me in faithfulness: and thou shalt know the Lord.'

" Hosea, 13. 'O Israel, thou hast destroyed thyself, but in me is thine help.' Chapter 14. 'Return unto the Lord thy God, for thou hast fallen by thy iniquities. Take with you words, and return to the Lord; say unto him, take away all iniquity, and receive us graciously: so will we render the calves of our lips. Ashur shall not save us, we will not ride upon horses, neither will we say any more to the works of our hands, ye are our gods: for in thee the fatherless findeth mercy.'

" 'I will heal their backsliding; I will love them freely, for mine anger is turned away from him. I will be as the dew unto Israel; he shall grow as the lily, and cast forth his roots as Lebanon. Ephraim shall say, what have I to do any more with idols? I have heard him, and observed him. I am like a green fir-tree: from me is thy fruit found.'

" Daniel, 9. 'O Lord, to us belongeth confusion of face, because we have sinned against thee. To the Lord our God belong mercies and forgiveness, though we have rebelled against him.'

" Isaiah, 40 : 11. 'He shall feed his flock like a shepherd, he shall gather the lambs in his arms, and carry them in his bosom; and shall gently lead those that are with young. Why sayest thou, O Jacob, and speakest, O Israel; my way is hid from the Lord, and my judgment passed over from my God. Hast thou not known, hast thou not heard, that the everlasting God fainteth not, neither is weary; there is no searching of his understanding. He giveth power to the faint; and to him that hath no might he increaseth strength. Even the youths shall faint and be weary, and the young men shall utterly fall: but they that wait on the Lord shall renew their strength, they shall mount up with wings as eagles; they shall run and not be weary; they shall walk and not faint.'

"Isaiah, 42 : 24. 'Who gave Jacob for a spoil, and Israel to the robbers? Did not the Lord, he against whom we have sinned? For they would not walk in his way, neither were they obedient to his law. Therefore he hath poured upon him the fury of his anger, and the strength of battle: and it hath set him on fire round about, and he knew not; and it burned him, yet he laid it not to heart. But now thus saith the Lord that created thee, O Jacob, and that formed thee, O Israel, fear not: for I have redeemed thee, I have called thee by thy name; thou art mine. When thou passest through the waters I will be with thee; and through the rivers, they shall not overflow thee: when thou walkest through the fire, thou shalt not be burnt; neither shall the flame kindle upon thee. For I am the Lord thy God, the Holy One of Israel, thy Savior. Since thou wast precious in my sight thou hast been honorable, and I have loved thee.'

"Yes, my God! I remember and am confounded! amazed at my ingratitude, amazed at thy grace!' I am thy witness, just so has been thy way with me. What can I say? Thou hast wrought with me for thy name's sake. I am dumb before thee, O I am vile—and yet I am thine! Thou hast redeemed me! it is thy good pleasure to save me. Glorify thy name. 'I have blotted out, as a thick cloud, thy transgressions, and as a cloud, thy sins: return unto me; for I have redeemed thee. Sing, O ye heavens; for the Lord hath done it: shout, ye lower parts of the earth: break forth into singing, ye mountains, O forest, and every green tree therein: for the Lord hath redeemed Jacob, and glorified himself in Israel.'

"'For if by one man's offence, death reigned by one; much more they which receive abundance of grace, and of the gift of righteousness, shall reign in life by one, Christ Jesus. Where sin abounded, grace did much more abound: that as sin hath reigned unto death, so might grace reign through righteousness unto eternal life, by Jesus Christ our Lord.'

"Isaiah, 45 : 22. 'Look unto me, and be ye saved, all the ends of the earth: for I am God, and there is none else. I have sworn by myself, the word is gone out of my mouth in righteousness, and shall not return, that unto me every knee shall bow, every tongue shall swear. Surely shall one say, in the Lord have I righteousness and strength: even to him shall men come; and all that are incensed against him shall be ashamed. In the Lord shall all the seed of Israel be justified, and shall glory.' chapter 46 : 3. 'Hearken unto me, O house of Jacob, and all the remnant of the house of Israel: even to your old age, I am he; and even to hoar hairs will I carry you: I have made, and I will bear; even I will carry, and I will deliver you.'

" Ezek. 34 : 11. ' Thus saith the Lord; I, even I, will both search my sheep, and seek them out. As a shepherd seeketh out his flock in the day that he is among his sheep that are scattered; so will I seek out my sheep, and will deliver them out of all places where they have been scattered in the cloudy and dark day. And I will bring them out from the people, and gather them to their own land, and feed them upon the mountains of Israel by the rivers, and in all the inhabited places of the country. And I will feed them in a good pasture, and upon the high mountains of Israel shall their fold be: there shall they lie in a good fold, and in a fat pasture shall they feed upon the mountains of Israel. I will feed my flock, and I will cause them to lie down, saith the Lord God. I will seek that which was lost, and bring again that which was driven away, and will bind up that which was broken, and will strengthen that which was sick.' He hath done it, I am his witness: I, the poor wanderer, the happy subject of this grace. ' And I will raise up for them a plant of renown, (my Jesus,) and they shall be no more consumed with hunger in the land, neither bear the shame of the heathen any more. Thus shall they know that I the Lord their God am with them, and that they, even the house of Israel, are my people, saith the Lord God. And ye my flock, the flock of my pasture, are men, and I am your God, saith the Lord God.' ' As the mountains are round about Jerusalem, so the Lord is round about his people from henceforth and for ever.' Psalm 125.

"Ezek. 36. 'When the house of Israel dwelt in their own land, they defiled it by their own way and by their doings. And I scattered them among the heathen, and they were dispersed through the countries: according to their ways and according to their doings I judged them. And when they entered unto the heathen, whither they went, they profaned my holy name, when they said to them, these are the people of the Lord, and are gone forth out of his land. But I had pity for mine holy name, which the house of Israel had profaned among the heathen whither they went. Therefore, say unto the house of Israel, thus saith the Lord God; I do not this for your sakes, O house of Israel, but for mine holy name's sake, which ye have profaned among the heathen, whither ye went. And I will sanctify my great name, which was profaned among the heathen, which ye have profaned in the midst of them; and the heathen shall know that I am the Lord, saith the Lord God, when I shall be sanctified in you before their eyes. For I will take you from among the heathen, and gather you out of all countries, and will bring you into your own land. Then will I sprinkle clean water upon you, and ye shall be clean: from all your filthiness, and from all your idols, will I cleanse you. A new heart also will I give you, and a new spirit will I put within you: and I will take away the stony heart out of your flesh, and I will give you a heart of flesh. And I will put my Spirit within you, and cause you to walk in my statutes, and ye shall keep my judgments, and do them. I will also save you from all your uncleannesses: and I will call for the corn, and will increase it, and lay no famine upon you. And I will multiply the fruit of the tree, and the increase of the field, that ye shall receive no more reproach of famine among the heathen. Then shall ye remember your own evil ways, and your doings that were not good, and shall loathe yourselves in your own sight for your iniquities, and for your abominations. *Not for your sakes* do I this, saith the Lord God, be it known unto you: be ashamed and confounded for your own ways, O house of Israel.'

EZEKIEL, 16 : 63, AND 36 : 32.

(A Scripture paraphrase, by D. B——.

Not for your sakes; for born unclean,
The slaves of Satan and of sin :
I saw no comeliness in you,
To bid my grace such wonders do.

Not for your sakes; for when my love
And grace should your affections move,
The working of an evil heart
Still makes you from my truth depart.

Not for your sakes; for bold and blind,
To lust and avarice inclin'd,
Each shado vy idol you obey,
Disowning my paternal sway.

Not for your sakes; with heav'n in view,
For sin you sell your souls anew ;
You barter, for a gilded bait,
The joys of an eternal state.

Not for your sakes; for though you ey'd
The cross of Christ, on which he died ;
You scorn his love for worldly ends,
And wound him in the house of friends.

Not for your sakes; with Jesus' name,
You put him to an open shame ;
And by your sins, consent again
To have the dear Redeemer slain.

Not for your sakes; 'tis my free grace
That grants you pardon, life, and peace;
And works a change on all your frame,
And binds you to adore my name.

Nor for my sake !—I hail the sound !
Let pow'r of grace my pride confound ;
Salvation is a work divine ;
Confusion and the shame be mine.

Not for my sake !—did I but trust
To weakness, vanity, and dust ;
I ne'er could reach the heav'nly prize,
Nor hope a mansion in the skies.

Not for my sake !—yet save and call ;
Let Jesus be my all in all :
When glory comes I'll self disown,
And grace, free grace shall wear the crown.

" Psalm 104. ' Praise ye the Lord. O give thanks unto the Lord, for he is good, for his mercy endureth for ever.'

" Psalm 106. ' Remember me, O Lord, with the favor that thou bearest unto thy people: O visit me with thy salvation, that I may see the good of thy chosen, that I may rejoice in the gladness of thy nation, that I may glory with thine inheritance.'

" Eph. 2. ' At that time ye were without Christ, be-ing aliens from the commonwealth of Israel, and stran-gers from the covenants of promise, having no hope, and without God in the world: but now, in Christ Jesus, ye, who sometime were far off, are made nigh by the blood of Christ.' '

" Psalm 10 : 17. ' Lord, thou hast heard the desire of the humble: thou wilt prepare their heart, thou wilt cause thine ear to hear: to judge the fatherless and the oppressed, that the men of the earth may no more oppress.'

"Deut. 8. 'Thou shalt remember all the way that the Lord thy God led thee these forty years in the wilderness, to humble thee, to prove thee, to know what was in thy heart, whether thou wouldest keep his commandments or no. And he humbled thee, and suffered thee to hunger, and fed thee with manna, which thou knewest not, neither did thy fathers know; that he might make thee know that man doth not live by bread alone, but by every word that proceedeth out of the mouth of the Lord doth man live. Thy raiment waxed not old upon thee, neither did thy foot swell these forty years.'

"'Thou shalt also consider in thine heart, that as a man chasteneth his son, so the Lord thy God chasteneth thee. Therefore thou shalt keep the commandments of the Lord thy God, to walk in his ways and to fear him.'

"'Thou, God, seest me.'

"Eph. 1. 'Blessed be the God and Father of our Lord Jesus Christ, who hath blessed us with all spiritual blessings in heavenly places in Christ; according as he hath chosen us in him before the foundation of the world, that we should be holy and without blame before him in love: having predestinated us to the adoption of sons by Jesus Christ to himself, according to the good pleasure of his will, to the praise of the glory of his grace, wherein he hath made us accepted in the Beloved; in whom we have redemption through his blood, the forgiveness of sins, according to the riches of his grace; wherein he hath abounded towards us in all wisdom and prudence; having made known unto us the mystery of his will, according to his good pleasure which he purposed in himself, that in the dispensation of the fulness of time he might gather together in one all things in Christ, both which are in heaven, and which are on earth, even in him, in whom also we have obtained an inheritance, being predestinated according to the purpose of him who worketh all things after the counsel of his own will, that we should be to the praise of his glory, who first trusted in Christ.'

"Chapter 2 and 4. 'God, who is rich in mercy, for his great love wherewith he loved us, even when we were dead in sins, hath quickened us together with Christ, (by grace ye are saved,) and hath raised us up together, and made us sit together in heavenly places in Christ Jesus; that in the ages to come he might show the exceeding riches of his grace, in his kindness towards us through Christ Jesus: for by grace are ye saved, through faith, and that not of yourselves, it is the gift of God: not of works, lest any man should boast; for we are his workmanship, created in Christ Jesus unto good works, which God hath before ordained that we should walk in them. Now therefore, ye Gentiles are no more strangers and foreigners, but fellow-citizens with the Saints, and of the household of God, and are built upon the foundation of the apostles and prophets, Jesus Christ himself being the chief corner stone; in whom all the building, fitly framed together, groweth into an holy temple in the Lord: in whom ye also are builded together for an habitation of God through the Spirit.' Chapter 3. 'I Paul bow my knees unto the Father of our Lord Jesus Christ, of whom the whole family in heaven and earth is named, that he would grant you according to the riches of his glory, to be strengthened with might by his Spirit in the inner man: that Christ may dwell in your hearts by faith; that ye being rooted and grounded in love, may be able to comprehend with all saints, what is the breadth, and length, and height, and depth, and to know the love of Christ, which passeth knowledge, that ye might be filled with all the fulness of God. Now unto him that is able to do exceeding abundantly above all that we can ask or think, according to the power that worketh in us: unto him be glory in the church by Jesus Christ, throughout all ages, world without end.' Amen.

"Chapter 4. 'I therefore, the prisoner of the Lord, beseech you, that ye walk worthy of the vocation wherewith ye are called; with all lowliness and meekness, with long-suffering, forbearing one another in love, endeavoring to keep the unity of the Spirit in the bond of peace. There is one body and one Spirit, even as ye are called in one hope of your calling: one Lord, one faith, one baptism, one God and Father of all, who is above all, and through all, and in you all. But unto every one of us is given grace according to the measure of the gift of Christ. That we may grow up into him in all things which is the head, even Christ: from whom the whole body fitly joined together and compacted by that which every joint supplieth,—(ministers and people in the use of all appointed means,)—according to the effectual working in the measure of every part, maketh increase of the body to the edifying of itself in love.'

"John, 15. 'I am the vine, ye are the branches; he

that abideth in me and I in him, the same bringeth forth much fruit; for without me ye can do nothing.'

"Exodus, 16. 'And Moses said, The Lord heareth your murmurings that ye murmur against him; and what are we? your murmurings are not against us, but against the Lord. And Moses said, This is the bread which the Lord giveth you to eat. And the children of Israel did eat manna until they came unto the borders of the land of Canaan.'

"John, 6. 'I am the living bread which came down from heaven: if any man eat of this bread, he shall live for ever: and the bread that I shall give is my flesh, which I will give for the life of the world. He that eateth my flesh, and drinketh my blood, dwelleth in me, and I in him. The words which I speak unto you, they are spirit, and they are life.'

"1 Cor. 1. 'For of him are ye in Christ Jesus, who of God is made unto us wisdom, and righteousness, and sanctification, and redemption.'

"Heb. 4. 'Seeing then that we have a great High Priest who is passed into the heavens, Jesus the Son of God, let us hold fast our profession. For we have not a High Priest who cannot be touched with the feeling of our infirmities; but was in all points tempted like as we are, yet without sin. Let us, therefore, come boldly to the throne of grace, that we may obtain mercy, and find grace to help in time of need.' Chapter 8. 'For this is the covenant that I will make with the house of Israel after those days, saith the Lord. I will put my laws into their mind, and write them on their hearts, and I will be to them a God, and they shall be to me a people; and they shall not teach every man his neighbor, and every man his brother, saying, Know the Lord, for all shall know me, from the least to the greatest; for I will be merciful to their unrighteousness, and their sins and their iniquities will I remember no more. In that he saith, a new covenant, he hath made the first old: now that which decayeth, and waxeth old, is ready to vanish away.'

"1 John, 5. 'This is the record, that God hath given to us eternal life, and this life is in his Son. He that hath the Son hath life, and he that hath not the Son, hath not life. Thanks be to God for his unspeakable gift.'

"Psalm 62. 'Truly my soul waiteth upon God; from him cometh my salvation; he is my defence, I shall not be greatly moved. My soul, wait thou only upon God, my expectation is from him; he only is my rock and my salvation; he is my defence, I shall not be moved. In God is my salvation and my glory: the rock of my strength, and my refuge is in God.'"

REST.

"Genesis, 2. 'Thus the heavens and the earth were finished, and on the seventh day God ended his work which he had made, and he rested the seventh day from all his work which he had made; and God blessed the seventh day, and sanctified it, because that in it he had rested from all his work that he had created and made.'

" Exodus, 16. ' And Moses said, To-morrow is the rest of the holy Sabbath unto the Lord. So the people rested on the seventh day.'

" Luke, 23. ' And the women followed after, and beheld the sepulchre, and how his body was laid ; and they returned, and prepared spices and ointments; and rested the Sabbath day according to the commandment.'

" Christ rested in the tomb of Joseph the last Sabbath under the law: but the evening and the morning were the first day. On that morning he closed his work of humiliation, manifested his victory over death, the curse denounced, by rising from the tomb, and rested on the first day of the week from all his humiliation work ; his death, burial, and rest in the grave on the seventh day, being the last part of that work."

" My God, thy service well demands
   The remnant of my days:
Why is this feeble life preserved,
   But to repeat thy praise.

" Thine arms of everlasting love
   Do this weak frame sustain,
While life is hov'ring o'er the grave
   And nature sinks with pain.

" Thou, when the pains of death assail,
   Wilt chase the fears of hell,
And teach my pale and quivering lips
   Thy matchless grace to tell.

" Calmly I'll lay my fainting head
   On thy dear faithful breast ;
Pleas'd to obey my Father's call
   To his eternal rest.

" Into thy hands, my Savior God,
   Do I my soul resign,
In firm dependence on that truth
   That made salvation mine."

The inward Warfare.

" Strange and mysterious is my life !
   What opposites I feel within:
A stable peace, a constant strife,
   The rule of grace, the power of sin!
      Too often I am captive led,
      Yet daily triumph in my Head.

" I prize the privilege of prayer :
   But oh! what backwardness to pray !
Though on the Lord I cast my care,
   I feel its burden every day.
      I seek his will in all I do,
      Yet find my own is working too.

" I call the promises mine own,
   And prize them more than mines of gold:
Yet, though their sweetness I have known,
   They leave me unimpress'd and cold
      One hour upon the truth I feed ;
      The next, I know not what I read.

" I love the holy day of rest,
　When Jesus meets his gather'd saints :
Sweet day, of all the week the best,
　For its return my spirit pants :
　　Yet often, through my unbelief,
　　It proves a day of guilt and grief.

" While on my Savior I rely,
　I know my foes shall lose their aim ;
And therefore dare their power defy,
　Assur'd of conquest through his name ;
　　But soon my confidence is slain,
　　And all my fears return again.

" Thus diff'rent powers within me strive,
　And death, and sin, by turns, prevail
I grieve, rejoice, decline, revive,
　And vict'ry hangs in doubtful scale :
　　But Jesus has his promise passed,
　　That grace shall overcome at last."

Flesh and Spirit.

" What diff'rent powers of grace and sin
　Attend our mortal state !
I hate the thoughts that work within,
　Yet do the works I hate.

" Now I complain, and groan, and die ?
　While sin and Satan reign ;
Now raise my songs of triumph high,
　For grace prevails again.

" So darkness struggles with the light,
　Till perfect day arise ;
Water and fire maintain the fight,
　Until the weaker dies.

" Thus will the flesh and spirit strive,
　And vex and break my peace ;
But I shall quit this mortal life,
　And sin for ever cease."

" Join all the names of love and pow'r
That ever men or angels bore ;
All are too mean to speak his worth,
Or set Emmanuel's glory forth.

" But, oh ! what condescending ways
He takes to teach his heavenly grace !
Mine eyes, with joy and wonder, see
What forms of love he bears for me.

" The Angel of the covenant stands
With his commission in his hands ;
Sent from his Father's milder throne,
To make his great salvation known.

" Great Prophet ! let me bless thy name !
By thee the joyful tidings came,
Of wrath appeas'd and sins forgiv'n,
Of hell subdu'd, and peace with heav'n.

" My bright Example, and my Guide,
I would be walking by thy side ;
Oh ! let me never run astray,
Nor follow the forbidden way.

Mrs. Graham.　　　18

" I love my Shepherd, he shall keep
My wand'ring soul among his sheep;
He feeds his flock, he tells their names,
And in his bosom bears the lambs.

" My Surety undertakes my cause,
Answ'ring his Father's broken laws;
Behold my soul at freedom set;
My Surety paid the dreadful debt.

" Jesus, my great High Priest, has died,
I seek no sacrifice beside;
His blood did once for all atone,
And now it pleads before the throne.

" My Advocate appears on high;
The Father lays his thunders by;
Not all that earth or hell can say,
Shall turn my Father's heart away.

" My Lord, my Conq'ror, and my King,
Thy sceptre and thy sword I sing;
Thine is the vict'ry, and I sit
A joyful subject at thy feet.

" Aspire, my soul, to glorious deeds:
The Captain of salvation leads;
March on, nor fear to win the day,
Though death and hell obstruct thy way.

" Though death, and hell, and powers unknown,
Put all their forms of mischief on;
I shall be safe, for Christ displays
Salvation in more sov'reign ways."

" Be this my one great business here,
With holy trembling, holy fear,
  To make my calling sure ;
Thine utmost counsel to fulfil,
And suffer all thy righteous will,
  And to the end endure.

" Then, Savior, then my soul receive,
Transported from this vale, to live
  And reign with thee above :
Where faith is sweetly lost in sight,
And hope in full supreme delight,
  And everlasting love."

" Hush, my distrustful heart,
  And cease to flow, my tears ;
For greater, Lord, thou art
  Than all my doubts and fears.
    Did Jesus once upon me shine ?
    Then Jesus is for ever mine.

" Unchangeable his will,
  Whatever be my frame :
My Savior's heart is still
  Eternally the same.
    My soul through many changes goes,
    His love no variation knows.

" Thou, Lord, wilt carry on,
  And perfectly perform,
The work thou hast begun
  In me, vile sinful worm.
    Mine own self-will brings grief and wo
    But Jesus will not let me go.

" The bowels of thy grace
 At first did freely move ;
And still I see thy face,
 And feel that God is Love.
  Into thine arms my soul I cast ;
  By sov'reign mercy sav'd at last."

" The Priest and Ark now move
 To Jordan's gulfy strand ;
Come now thy cov'nant love,
 Take firm thy promis'd stand :
  Only to me thy count'nance show,
  I ask no more the Jordan through."

" Come, let us join our cheerful songs
 With angels round the throne ;
Ten thousand thousand are their tongues,
 But all their joys are one.

" Worthy the Lamb that died, they cry,
 To be exalted thus ;
Worthy the Lamb, our souls reply,
 For he was slain for us.

" Jesus is worthy to receive
 Honor and power divine ;
And blessings, more than we can give
 Be, Lord, for ever thine.

" The whole creation join in one ;
 To bless the sacred name
Of Him that sits upon the throne,
 And to adore the Lamb."

" Give me the wings of faith, to rise
　　Within the veil, and see
The saints above, how great their joys,
　　How bright their glories be.

" Once they were mourners here below,
　　And wet their couch with tears;
They wrestled hard, as we do now,
　　With sins, and doubts, and fears.

" I ask them, whence their vict'ry came:
　　They, with united breath,
Ascribe their conquest to the Lamb,
　　Their triumph to his death.

" They mark'd the footsteps that he trod:
　　His zeal inspir'd their breast;
And, following the incarnate God,
　　Possess'd the promis'd rest.

" Our glorious Leader claims our praise,
　　For his own pattern given;
While the long cloud of witnesses
　　Show the same path to heaven."

With heart and hands, and lifted eyes,
　　I'll praise thee while I've life and breath;
And, while my loosen'd spirit flies,
　　I'll gasp thy praise in very death.

Faith fain would say, in cheerful mood,
　　Thy name be glorified:
By leading through the swelling flood,
　　Or through the channel dried.

If grace in time of need I have,
  And strength as is my day,
I'll triumph through the foaming wave,
  As through the side-wall'd way

" I'll praise my Maker while I've breath;
And, when my voice is lost in death,
  Praise shall employ my noblest powers;
My days of praise shall ne'er be past,
While life and thought and being last,
  And immortality endures."

" My God, indulge my humble claim;
  Thou art my Hope, my Joy, my Rest;
The glories that compose thy name
  Stand all engag'd to make me blest.

" Thou Great and Good, thou Just and Wise,
  Thou art my Father and my God;
And I am thine by sacred ties,
  Thy child, thy servant, bought with blood.

" With heart, and eyes, and lifted hands,
  For thee I long, to thee I look;
As travellers in thirsty lands
  Pant for the cooling water brook."

" Jesus, the weary wanderer's rest,
  Give grace thy sov'reign will to bear ;
With steadfast patience arm my breast,
  With holy love and lowly fear.

" Thankful, I take the cup from thee,
  Prepar'd and mingled by thy skill ;
Though bitter to the taste it be,
  It has a sov'reign power to heal.

" Be thou a Rock of ages nigh ;
  My saved soul on thee alone
Shall safely rest, and fears shall fly,
  As clouds before the mid-day sun.

" Speak to my troubled conscience peace—
  Say to my trembling heart, Be still:
My power thy strength and fortress is:
  Amen : to all thy sov'reign will.

" O Death, where is thy sting, where now
  Thy boasted victory, O grave ?
Who shall contend with God, or who
  Condemn whom he delights to save."

" How sweet the name of Jesus sounds
  In a believer's ear !
It sooths his sorrows, heals his wounds,
  And drives away his fear.

" It makes the wounded spirit whole,
  And calms the troubled breast ;
'Tis manna to the hungry soul,
  And to the weary rest.

" Dear Name! the Rock on which I build,
   My Shield and Hiding-Place;
My never failing Treas'ry, fill'd
   With boundless stores of grace.

" Jesus, my Shepherd, Husband, Friend,
   My Prophet, Priest, and King,
My Lord, my Life, my Way, my End,
   Accept the praise I bring.

" Weak is the effort of my heart,
   And cold my warmest thought;
But, when I see thee as thou art,
   I'll praise thee as I ought.

" Till then I would thy love proclaim
   With ev'ry fleeting breath;
And may the music of thy name
   Refresh my soul in death "

" Amazing grace, how sweet the sound
   That sav'd a wretch like me!
I once was lost, but now am found;
   Was blind, but now I see.

" 'Twas grace that taught my heart to fear,
   And grace my fears reliev'd:
How precious did that grace appear
   The hour I first believ'd!

" Through many dangers, toils, and snares
   Already I have come:
'Twas grace that brought me safe thus far,
   And grace will lead me home.

" Yes, when this heart and flesh shall fail,
   And mortal life shall cease,
I shall possess, within the vail,
   A life of joy and peace."

A swelling Jordan rolls between—
   A timid pilgrim, I ;
But grace shall order all the scene,
   And Christ himself be nigh.

He shall roll back the foaming wave,
   Command the channel dry ;
No sting has death, no vict'ry grave,
   With Jesus in my eye.

" Come, thou Fount of ev'ry blessing
   Tune my heart to sing thy grace ;
Streams of mercy, never ceasing,
   Call for songs of endless praise.

" Teach me some melodious sonnet
   Sung by flaming tongues above ;
Praise the mount, I'm fix'd upon it,
   Mount of God's unchanging love.

" Here I raise my Ebenezer,
   Hither by thy help I'm come,
And I hope, by thy good pleasure,
   Safely to arrive at home.

" Jesus sought me when a stranger,
   Wand'ring from the fold of God ;
He, to save my soul from danger,
   Interpos'd with precious blood.

" Oh, to grace how great a debtor
    Daily I'm constrain'd to be !
Let that grace, Lord, like a fetter,
    Bind my wand'ring heart to thee.

" Prone to wander, Lord, I feel it,
    Prone to leave the God I love;
Here's my heart, O take and seal it,
    Seal it from thy courts above."

" Eternal God, I bless thy name,
The same thy power, thy grace the same;
The tokens of thy friendly care
Open, and crown, and close the year.

" I 'midst ten thousand dangers stand,
Supported by thy gracious hand;
And see, when I survey thy ways,
Ten thousand monuments of grace.

" Thus far thine arm has led me on;
Thus far I make thy mercy known;
And while I tread this desert land,
New mercies shall new songs demand.

" My grateful soul on Jordan's shore
Shall raise one sacred pillar more :
Then bear, in thy bright courts above,
Inscriptions of immortal love."

" No works to rest upon have I,
No boast of moral dignity ;
If e'er I lisp a song of praise,
Grace is the note my soul shall raise.

" 'Twas grace that quicken'd me when dead;
'Twas grace my soul to Jesus led,
Grace brings me pardon for my sin,
And grace subdues my lusts within.

" 'Tis grace that sweetens every cross,
'Tis grace supports in ev'ry loss:
In Jesus' grace my soul is strong,
Grace is my hope, and Christ my song.

" Thus, 'tis alone of grace I boast,
And 'tis alone in grace I trust :
For all that's past, grace is my theme,
For what's to come 'tis still the same."

And when I come to Jordan's shore,
I'll raise one Ebenezer more:
Th' Ark of the Cov'nant in my view,
I'll sing of grace the Jordan through.

" Is this the kind return ?
   And these the thanks we owe ?
Thus to abuse eternal love,
   Whence all our blessings flow ?

" To what a stubborn frame
   Has sin reduc'd our mind!
What strange rebellious wretches we,
   And God as strangely kind !

" Turn us again, O God!
    And mould our souls afresh ;
Break, sov'reign grace, these hearts of stone,
    And give us hearts of flesh.

" Let past ingratitude
    Provoke our weeping eyes :
And hourly, as new mercies fall,
    Let hourly thanks arise."

" O the sweet wonders of that cross,
    Where Christ my Savior lov'd and died ;
Her noblest life my spirit draws
    From his dear wounds and bleeding side."

I would for ever speak his name
    In sounds to mortal ears unknown ;
With Angels join to praise the Lamb,
    And worship at his Father's throne.

" Jesus, the vision of thy face
    Hath overpowering charms ;
Scarce shall I feel death's cold embrace,
    If Christ be in my arms."

" O glorious hour ! O blest abode !
    I shall be near and like my God ;
And flesh and sin no more control
    The sacred pleasures of my soul."

" When in death's gloomy vale I tread,
With joy e'en there I'll lift my head ;
From fear and dread he'll keep me free,
His rod and staff shall comfort me."

" Jesus, to thy dear faithful hand
  My naked soul I trust ;
My flesh but waits for thy command,
  To drop into the dust."

" Before we quite forsake our clay,
  Or leave this dark abode,
The wings of love bear us away
  To see our smiling God."

O make it true, my Savior God ;
  Raise me all fears above ;
And, when I think on Jesus' blood,
  Let my last pulse beat love.

" O for an overcoming faith,
  To cheer my dying hours ;
To triumph o'er the monster death,
  And all his frightful powers !

" Joyful, with all the strength I have,
  My quivering lips should sing :
Where is thy boasted vict'ry, Grave,
  And where the monster's sting ?

"If sin be pardon'd, I'm secure;
  Death has no sting beside;
The law gives sin its damning power,
  But Christ, my Ransom, died.

" Now to the God of victory
  Immortal thanks be paid;
Who makes us conqu'rors while we die,
  Through Christ, our living Head."

All mortal vanities be gone,
  Nor tempt mine eyes, nor tire mine ears;
Behold! amidst th' eternal throne,
  A vision of the Lamb appears.

All the assembling saints around,
  Fall worshipping before the Lamb;
And, in new songs of Gospel sound,
  Address their honors to his name

Our voices join the heavenly strain,
  And with transporting pleasure sing,
Worthy the Lamb that once was slain,
  Our blessed Prophet, Priest, and King.

Thou hast redeem'd our souls from hell,
  With thine invaluable blood;
And wretches, that did once rebel,
  Are now made fav'rites of their God.

Worthy, for ever, is the Lord,
  That died for treasons not his own,
By every tongue to be ador'd,
  And dwell upon his Father's throne.

The New Testament in the Blood of Christ

" The promise of my Father's love
  Shall stand for ever good ;
He said, and gave his soul to death,
  And seal'd it with his blood.

" To this dear cov'nant of thy word
  I set my worthless name ;
I seal th' engagement of the Lord,
  And make my humble claim.

" The light, and strength, and pard'ning grace,
  And glory, shall be mine :
My life and soul, my heart and flesh,
  And all my powers are thine.

" I call that legacy mine own,
  Which Jesus did bequeath :
'Twas purchas'd with a dying groan,
  And ratified in death.

" Sweet is the mem'ry of his name,
  Who bless'd us in his will ;
And, to his testament of love,
  Made his own life the seal.

" To him that wash'd me in his blood,
  Be everlasting praise ;
Salvation, honor, glory, power,
  Eternal as his days."

" Blest be the Father, and his love,
  To which celestial source we owe
Rivers of endless joys above,
  And rills of comfort here below.

" Glory to the great Son of God;
  From his dear wounded body rolls
A precious stream of vital blood,
  Pardon and life for dying souls.

" We give thee, sacred Spirit, praise,
  Who, in our hearts of sin and wo,
Mak'st living springs of grace arise,
  And into boundless glory flow.

" Thus God the Father, God the Son,
  And God the Spirit, we adore;
The Sea of life and love unknown,
  Without a bottom or a shore."

" Let me but hear my Savior say,
Strength shall be equal to thy day;
Then I rejoice in deep distress,
Leaning on all-sufficient grace.

" I glory in infirmity,
That Christ's own power may rest on me;
When I am weak, then am I strong;
Grace is my shield, and Christ my song

" I can do all things, or can bear
All sufferings, if my Lord be there;
Sweet pleasures mingle with the pains,
While his strong hand my head sustains.

" Faith has an overcoming power,
Can triumph in the dying hour ;
Christ is my Life, my Joy, my Hope ;
I cannot sink with such a prop."

" Jesus, I love thy charming name,
  'Tis music to mine ear ;
Fain would I sound it out so loud
  That heaven and earth should hear.

" Yes, thou art precious to my soul,
  My Transport and my Trust ;
My Savior, Shepherd, Husband, Friend,
  No other good I boast.

" All my capacious powers can wish,
  In thee doth richly meet ;
Not to mine eye is light so dear,
  Nor friendship half so sweet.

" Thy grace still dwells upon my heart,
  And sheds its fragrance there :
The noblest balm of all my wounds,
  The cordial of my care.

" I'll speak the honors of thy name
  With my last falt'ring breath ;
Then, speechless, clasp thee in my arms,
  The antidote of death."

" Grace, 'tis a charming sound,
   Harmonious to my ear;
Heaven with the echo shall resound,
   And all the earth shall hear.

" Grace first contriv'd the way
   To save rebellious man;
And all the steps *that* grace display,
   Which drew the wondrous plan

" Grace taught my wand'ring feet
   To tread the heav'nly road;
And new supplies each hour I meet,
   While pressing on to God.

" Grace all the work shall crown,
   Through everlasting days:
It lays in heaven the topmost stone,
   And well deserves the praise."

" My God, the Spring of all my joys,
   The Life of my delights,
The Glory of my brightest days,
   And Comfort of my nights:

" In darkest shades, if thou appear,
   My dawning is begun;
Thou art my soul's sweet Morning Star,
   And thou, my Rising Sun.

" The op'ning heavens around me shine
   With beams of sacred bliss;
While Jesus shows his heart is mine,
   And whispers, I am his.

' My soul would leave this heavy clay,
   At that transporting word ;
Run up with joy the shining way,
   T' embrace my dearest Lord.

" Fearless of hell and ghastly death,
   I'd break through ev'ry foe ;
The wings of love, and arms of faith,
   Should bear me conqueror through."

" Backward, with humble shame, I look
   On my original—
How is my nature dash'd and broke,
   In our first father's fall !

" To all that's good averse and blind,
   But prone to all that's ill ;
What dreadful darkness veils my mind !
   How obstinate my will !

" Conceiv'd in sin : O wretched state !
   Before I drew my breath
My first young pulse began to beat
   Iniquity and death.

" How strong in my degen'rate blood
   The old corruption reigns !
And, mingling with the crooked flood,
   Wanders through all my veins.

" Yet, mighty God, thy wondrous love
   Can make my nature clean ;
While Christ and grace prevail above
   The tempter, death, and sin.

" The second Adam shall restore
　　The ruins of the first ;
Hosanna to that sov'reign power
　　That new-creates our dust."

Jordan.[*]

Joshua, chap. 1 : 11, and chap. 3 ; Psalm 23 : 4 ; 73 : 24.

The solemn hour, my soul, draws near,
The holy Ark and Priests appear;
They forward move to Jordan's flood,
The type, thou knowest, thy cov'nant God.

The signal too to thee is known,
Obey, remove, and follow on;
The Ark appears, thy hallow'd guide ;
Shrink not, but face the rolling tide.

The waves toss high their foaming heads,
But can'st thou perish ? Jesus leads.
This way before I ne'er did pass,
But Jesus, thy Forerunner, has.

* The three following effusions by Mrs. Graham, constituting a part of her " Provision," were found in a separate paper after her funeral sermon was preached. The hymn of Newton which she had annexed to the first, was selected by Dr. Mason and sung on that occasion ; and the circumstances described at the beginning of the third, (p. 435,) occurred at her death, as narrated in the memoir, though the existence of this paper was then unknown.

When all its banks it overflow'd,
All nature wrapt in midnight cloud;
While darkness held its awful power,
And all God's billows pass'd him o'er.

The waves for him must not divide,
Deep calls to deep on every side;
Around his head the surges roll,
And rush into his inmost soul.

HE was the suff'rer in my stead,
The curse for sin lay on his head;
The law's demands came like a flood,
My Surety met them with his blood!

'Till every tittle had been paid,
'Till due atonement had been made,
No beam appear'd of heavenly grace,
A cloud conceal'd his Father's face.

From brim to bottom he drank up,
Of wrath, the deep mysterious cup;
This Jordan pass'd, then rose on high,
And captive led captivity.

Justice now fully satisfied,
The law now honored, magnified,
At God's right hand he takes his place,
Executor of cov'nant grace

Crown'd, by Jehovah's firm decree,
With universal sov'reignty;
All nature owns his powerful sway,
He speaks, the elements obey.

The emblem, then thou may'st pursue,
And safely pass this Jordan through;
The priests but touch the watery space,
When, lo! the floods desert their place.

They gather up upon a heap,
Leave dry the channel of the deep;
The ark and priests there take their stand,
And beckon thee to leave the land.

I come, my best Belov'd, I come;
Now lead me to our Father's home;
On thy dear person fix mine eye,
And faith firm footing shall supply

I fear no ill while thou art near,
But let thy voice salute my ear,
(Should spirits faint, and 'scape the sigh,)
With these sweet words, "Fear not, 'tis I."

With courage fresh my soul shall tread
On faith's firm ground where thou dost lead;
While still upon thy gracious face
My steady eye maintains its place.

And now, my Joshua, choose, and lay
The stones in Jordan's middle way;
Let them o'ertop the flowing wave,
Memorial of thy power to save.

For, once a suit I did prefer,
With feeble hope, and trembling fear;
That I might have a Pisgah view,
In Jordan's swells, of Canaan new.

Thy soft'n'd glory let me see,
Then cause thy face to shine on me ;
And tune my heart, and tune my voice,
And language furnish to rejoice.

That all around may lend their tongue,
And sweetly join my dying song ;
Then, NEWTON, sav'd by grace, like me,
We'll sing of sov'reign grace with thee—

———

*" Let us love, and sing, and wonder,
Let us praise the Savior's name :
He has hush'd the law's loud thunder,
He has quench'd Mount Sinai's flame.
He has wash'd us in his blood,
He has brought us nigh to God.

" Let us love the Lord who bought us,
Pitied us when enemies ;
Call'd us by his grace, and taught us ;
Gave us ears, and gave us eyes :
He has wash'd us in his blood,
He presents our souls to God.

" Let us sing, though strong temptation
Threaten hard to bear us down :
For, the Lord, our strong Salvation,
Holds in view the conqu'ror's crown.
He who wash'd us in his blood,
Soon shall bring us home to God.

* Olney Hymns, 82, Book 3.

" Let us wonder, grace and justice
  Join and point to mercy's store;
When, through grace, in Christ our trust is,
  Justice smiles, and asks no more.
    He who wash'd us in his blood
    Has secur'd our way to God.

" Let us praise, and join the chorus
  Of the saints enthron'd on high
Here they trusted him before us,
  Now their praises fill the sky.
    Thou hast wash'd us in thy blood,
    Thou art worthy, Lamb of God.

" Hark, the name of JESUS sounded
  Loud from golden harps above;
On that Rock our hopes are founded:
  Sov'reign grace, and sov'reign love.
    We shall conquer through his blood,
    Kings and priests be made to God."

Heaven.

To be where thou, my Savior, art,
  To see, and be conform'd to thee—
Perfect in holiness this heart—
  This, this is heaven itself to me.

To see thee in thy glory, Lord,
  Thy Father's glory and thy own;
Th' eternal, the incarnate Word,
  Ador'd upon his Father's throne.

To see as seen, to know as known,
  My Savior in my flesh and blood;
To be made like him, with him one,
  I in him, and he in God.

The holy, holy, holy One,
  Who was, and is, and is to come,
The earth his footstool, heaven his throne,
  The Church his Bride, he her Bridegroom.

Angels and Elders, earth and heaven,
  Are summon'd to unseal the book;
But silent all, no answer giv'n,
  None worthy found therein to look.

But Judah's Lion, David's Son,
  And David's Root, the great I AM,
Appears upon his Father's throne,
  As slain for sacrifice, the Lamb.

He takes the book, he can unseal;
  He worthy is, and he has power
God's secret counsels to reveal,
  And to fulfil each in its hour.

Th heav'nly host united fall,
  In humble worship at his feet,
One glorious theme inspires them all,
  The joy is full, the concert sweet.

New odors to the throne ascend,
  In accents new their praises soar;
Each finds in each a glowing friend,
  And all the God of all adore.

Mrs. Graham.   19

And shall I join that prostrate throng,
  In love's extatic heaven-taught lays,
With pow'rs expanded, that new song,
  Hymn to the Lamb's exalted praise!

" Worthy art thou to take the book,
  And loose the seals, and read therein,
God's holy myst'ries to unlock;
  Worthy art thou, for thou wast slain.

" Thou hast redeem'd us with thy blood,
  From ev'ry nation of the earth ;
And made us kings and priests to God,
  And sharers of a heavenly birth."

Myriads of angels stand around,
  Uniting in the loud acclaim ;
And fill the temple with the sound
  Of our Redeemer's gentle name.

" Worthy the Lamb that once was slain,
  A sacrifice for ev'ry sin,
All pow'r and glory to obtain,
  And universal empire win."

Heav'n, earth, and sea shall swell the tone
  Of fervent universal praise ;
And grateful joy around the throne,
  Its voice from age to age shall raise.

In all these myriads is there one
  Who had on earth so much forgiven ?
And shall I reach their highest tone
  Of love to Jesus? THIS IS HEAVEN!!!

And when this breast to heave shall cease,
And heart and lungs are hush'd to peace,
Some friendly hand the eye-lids close,
And leave the clay to short repose.

Still on your knees be thanks exprest,
According as the Lord has blest;
This tongue, then mute, can now foretell,
Jesus shall have done all things well.

Should the great Sov'reign will it so,
That I in secret with him go,
'Twill be enough that He stands by,
He all my wants will well supply.

Upon his dear, his faithful breast,
My heart and head shall safely rest;
The flutt'ring pulse and bursting sigh
He'll soothe with " Fear not, it is I."

Into his hands my spirit I'll breathe,
Inhaling life from him, in death:
Though none should see, faith can foretell,
My Jesus shall do all things well.

Though he deny my half-form'd pray'r,
Well may I cast on Him my care;
All things are mine, or life or death,
In praise of Him I'll spend my breath.

Be this my only wish beside,
That God's great name be glorified,
What me concerns faith can foretell,
My Jesus shall do all things well.

Widowhood.

Written in the Island of Antigua shortly after
Dr. Graham's death.

PART I.

Hail! thou state of widowhood,
State of those that mourn to God;
Who from earthly comforts torn,
Only live to pray and mourn.

Meanest of the number, I
For my dear companion sigh;
Patiently my loss deplore,
Mourn for one that mourns no more.

Me my consort hath outrun,
Out of sight he quite has gone;
He his course has finish'd here,
First come to the sepulchre.

Following on with earnest haste,
Till my mourning days are past,
I my partner's steps pursue,
I shall soon be happy too;

Find the ease for which I pant,
Gain the only good I want;
Quietly lay down my head,
Sink into my earthy bed.

There my flesh shall rest in hope,
Till the quicken'd dust mount up;
When to glorious life I'll rise
To meet my husband in the skies.

PART II.

Happy they who trust in Jesus,
  Jesus turns our loss to gain;
Still his balmy mercies ease us,
  Sweeten all our grief and pain.

When he calls our friends t' inherit
  All the glories of the blest,
He assures the widow'd spirit,
  " Thou shalt quickly be at rest."

Though my flesh and spirit languish,
  Let me not too much complain;
Sure at last t' outlive my anguish,
  Sure to find my friend again.

Ransom'd from a world of sorrow,
  He to-day is taken home;
I shall be releas'd to-morrow;
  Come, my dear Redeemer, come.

From my sanctified distresses,
  Now, or when thou wilt, receive,
Grant with him in thine embraces,
  After all my deaths, to live.

PART III.

Hail holy, holy, holy Lord!
  Mysterious Three in One;
For ever be thy name ador'd,
  Thy will for ever done

For this alone on earth I wait,
  To glorify my God ;
And suffer, since thou will'st, the state
  Of sacred widowhood.

And may I, in thy strength fulfil
  My awful character ;
And prove thine acceptable will,
  And do thy pleasure here :

The children to thyself restore,
  Whom thou to me hast given ;
And rule my house with all my pow'r,
  And train them up for heav'n.

Be this my hospitable care,
  The stranger to receive,
The burthen of thy church to bear,
  And all their wants relieve.

My labor of unwearied love
  With pleasure to repeat ;
My faith unto thy saints to prove,
  And gladly wash their feet.

The servant of thy servants bless
  With active earnest zeal ;
And ev'ry work of righteousness
  I shall with joy fulfil.

Lines

Occasioned by viewing the portrait of Mrs. GRAHAM, prefixed to the first edition of her Memoir. By the late Mrs. Margaret Brown daughter of Rev. Dr. John Mason.

Whilst in this faded form I trace
   The features which I lov'd so well,
Remembrance brings each mental grace
   Within its hallow'd shrine to dwell.

For I have seen that darken'd eye
   In all the fire of genius roll,
With eagle-gaze explore the sky,
Or with a keener glance descry
   The secret workings of the soul.

And I have seen this pallid cheek
   Suffus'd with feeling's richest glow;
And virtue's brightest halo deck
   With sacred charms these locks of snow.

And on these lips in silence clos'd,
   With rapt attention oft I hung,
And heard those wondrous truths disclos'd
   Which sages taught or seraphs sung.

And I have known this wither'd hand
   Extended wide the poor to bless—
And this contracted breast expand
   With gen'rous schemes to aid distress.

And now, though far remov'd from earth,
  And every scene of mortal pain,
This dear memorial of her worth
  Shall many a drooping heart sustain.

Still shall it dry the widow's tear,
  The hapless orphan's want supply,
Guide to a blest asylum here,
  And point to happier realms on high.

My Father's friend !—How poor the praise,
  By his unworthy offspring given,
Who thus records, in humble lays,
  What angels register'd in heav'n.

Frankfort, Kentucky August, 1816.

THE END.

Titles in this Series

1. *The American Deaconess Movement in the Early Twentieth Century*
   Edited with an Introduction by Carolyn De Swarte Gifford

   a. Horton, Isabelle. *The Burden of the City*, New York: 1904

   b. "The Early History of Deaconess Work and Training Schools for Women in American Methodism, 1883–1885." Detroit c. 1912.

2. *The American Ideal of the "True Woman" as Reflected in Advice Books to Young Women*
   Edited with an Introduction by Carolyn De Swarte Gifford

   a. Wise, Daniel. *Bridal Greetings, A Mariage Gift in Which the Mutual Duties of Husband and Wife Are Familiarly Illustrated and Enforced*. New York: 1854.

   b. Wise, Daniel. *The Young Lady's Counsellor; Or, Outlines and Illustrations of the Sphere, the Duties, and the Dangers of Young Women*. New York: 1855.

3. *The Debate in the Methodist Episcopal Church Over Laity Rights for Women*

Edited with an Introduction by Carolyn De Swarte Gifford

    a. Buckley, James Monroe. "Because They Are Women, and Other Editorials From the Christian Advocate on the Admission of Women to the General Conference." New York: 1891.

    b. Hughey, George W. *The Admission of Women to the General Conference: A Reply to Dr. Buckley's Pamphlet "Because They Are women."* Chicago: 1891

    c. Kynett, Alpha J. "Our Laity and Their Equal Rights Without Distinction of Sex in the Methodist Episcopal Church." Cincinnati: 1896

    d. Palmer, Willis. "Are Women Eligible as Lay Delegates to the General Conference?" New Richmond, Ohio: 1888.

4. *The Defense of Women's Rights to Ordination in the Methodist Episcopal Church*
Edited with an Introduction by Carolyn De Swarte Gifford

    a. Willard, Francis E. *Woman in the Pulpit.* Chicago: 1889.

    b. Warren, William Fairfield. "The Dual Human Unit: The Relations of Men and Women According to the Sociological Teachings of Holy Scripture" in *Constitutional Law Questions Now Pending in the*

Methodist Episcopal Church. Cincinnati: 1894.

5. *The Ideal of "The New Woman" According to the Woman's Christian Temperance Union*
Edited with an Introduction by Carolyn De Swarte Gifford

   a. Willard, Francis E. *How to Win: A Book for Girls*. New York: 1886.

   b. Willard, Francis E. *Do Everything: A Handbook for the World's White Ribboners*. Chicago: c. 1895.

   c. Willard, Francis E. *Home Protection Manual: Containing an Argument for the Temperance Ballot for Women and How to Obtain It as a Means of Home Protection*. New York: 1879.

6. *The Nineteenth-Century American Preacher's Wife*
Edited with an Introduction by Carolyn De Swarte Gifford

   a. Eaton, Herrick M. *The Itinerant's Wife: Her Qualifications, Duties, Trials, and Rewards*. New York: 1851

   b. Tucker, Mary Orne. *Itinerant Preaching in the Early Days of Methodism*. Boston: 1872.

7. John Holmes Acornley. *The Colored Lady Evangelist, Being the Life, Labors and Experiences of Mrs. Harriet A. Baker*. Brooklyn: 1892

8. C. W. Andrews. *Memoir of Mrs. Ann R. Page.* New York: 1856.

9. Francis J. Baker. *The Story of the Woman's Foreign Missionary Society of the Methodist Episcopal Church, 1869–1895.* Cincinnati: 1896.

10. Joanna Bethune. *The Power of Faith, Exemplified in the Life and Writings of the Late Mrs. Isabella Graham.* New York: 1843.

11. George Brown. *The Lady Preacher: Or, the Life and Labors of Mrs. Hannah Reeves, Late the Wife of the Rev. William Reeves of the Methodist Church.* Springfield, Ohio: 1870.

12. Oswald E. Brown and Anna M. Brown. *Life and Letters of Laura Askew Haygood.* Nashville: 1904.

13. Fanny Jackson–Coppin. *Reminiscences of School Life, and Hints on Teaching.* Philadelphia: 1913.

14. John O. Foster. *Life and Labors of Mrs. Maggie Newton Van Cott, the First Lady Licensed to Preach in the Methodist Episcopal Church in the United States.* Cincinnati: 1872.

15. Marietta Holley. *Samantha Among the Brethren, By Josiah Allen's Wife.* New York: 1890.

16. Isabelle Horton. *High Adventure: Life of Lucy Rider Meyer.* New York: 1928.

17. Sarah R. Ingraham. *Walks of Usefulness. Or, Reminiscences of Mrs. Margaret Prior*. New York: 1843.

18. James D. Knowles. *Memoir of Mrs. Ann H. Judson, Late Missionary to Burmah. Including a History of the American Baptist Mission in the Burman Empire*. Boston: 1831.

19. Mrs. Robert W. MacDonell. *Belle Harris Bennett, Her Life Work*. Nashville: 1928.

20. Helen Barrett Montgomery. *Western Women in Eastern Lands. An Outline Study of Fifty Years of Woman's Work in Foreign Missions*. New York: 1910.

21. Elizabeth Mason North. *Consecrated Talents: Or, the Life of Mrs. Mary W. Mason*. New York: 1870.

22. George L. Prentiss. *The Life and Letters of Elizabeth Prentiss*. New York: 1882.

23. Lydia Sexton. *Autobiography of Lydia Sexton. The Story of Her Life Through a Period of Over Seventy-Two Years from 1799–1872. Her Early Privations, Adventures, and Reminiscences*. Dayton, Ohio: 1882.

24. Sarah Sleeper. *Memoir of the Late Martha Hazeltine Smith*. Boston: 1843.

25. Amanda Berry Smith. *An Autobiography. The Story of the Lord's Dealings with Mrs. Amanda Smith, the Colored Evangelist, Containing an Account of Her Life Work of Faith, and Her Travels in America, England, Ireland, Scotland, India and Africa, as an Independent Missionary*. Chicago: 1893.

26. Lee Anna Starr. *The Bible Status of Woman*. New York: 1926.

27. Abel Stevens. *The Women of Methodism: Its Three Foundresses, Susanna Wesley, The Countess of Huntingdon, and Barbara Heck; with Sketches of Their Female Associates and Successors in the Early History of the Denomination*. New York: 1869.

28. Clara A. Swain. *A Glimpse of India, Being a Collection of Extracts from the Letters of Dr. Clara A. Swain, First Medical Missionary to India of the Woman's Foreign Missionary Society of the Methodist Episcopal Church in America*. New York: 1909.

29. James Mills Thoburn. *Life of Isabella Thoburn*. New York: 1903.

30. Alexander Harrison Tuttle, ed. *Mary Porter Gamewell and Her Story of the Siege in Peking*. New York: 1907.

31. Uldine Utley. *Why I Am a Preacher: A Plain Answer to an Oft-Repeated Question*. New York: 1931.

32. Alma White. *Looking Back from Beulah*. Zarephath, New Jersey: 1902.

33. Mary Culler White. *The Portal of Wonderland; The Life–Story of Alice Culler Cobb*. New York: c. 1925.

34. Elizabeth Wilson. *Fifty Years of Association Work Among Young Women, 1866–1916*. New York: 1916.

35. Miron Winslow. *Memoir of Mrs. Harriet L. Winslow, Thirteen Years a Member of the American Mission in Ceylon*. New York: 1840.

36. Annie Turner Wittenmeyer. *Women's Work for Jesus*. New York: 1873.